Spokesman For Our Time

Here is the eloquent wisdom of Winston Churchill—a dynamic collection of memorable utterances on the conflicts, personalities, and events of our century by the famous world statesman, Nobel Prize author, and consummate master of the English language.

This volume reveals Sir Winston's brilliance in outstanding moments of his career—in thundering defiance of tyranny, in the cut and thrust of debate, in witty asides on his contemporaries. It contains thought-provoking opinions on history, politics, writing, and human behavior, voiced by the versatile genius who has held virtually every major British post during over forty years of public office, and whose lifetime of authorship was crowned with the Nobel Prize for Literature. In these pages, too, are the soul-stirring phrases from his wartime speeches—the majestic, impassioned words that Lewis Gannett says "seem destined to go ringing down the years."

These are the profound thoughts and history-making opinions of a distinguished and beloved international leader, offering inspiring commentaries on the challenges of modern mankind.

SIGNET KEY and MENTOR Books
of Special Interest

The Eloquence of
WINSTON CHURCHILL

Edited by F. B. CZARNOMSKI

A SIGNET KEY BOOK

Published by THE NEW AMERICAN LIBRARY

Published as a SIGNET KEY BOOK

FIRST PRINTING, APRIL, 1957

Library of Congress Catalog Card No. 57-9178

SIGNET KEY BOOKS are published by
The New American Library of World Literature, Inc.
501 Madison Avenue, New York 22, New York

CONTENTS

Introduction

Winston Churchill was not always right.

As he sailed to join the 4th Hussars in India, in 1896, he said: "The Churchills peg out early. So I'm going to make sure of my innings." Three years later he remarked to a friend: "The worst of it is that I am not a good life. My father died too young. I must try to accomplish whatever I can by the time I am forty."

It was fortunate for the world that he proved to be wrong. His story is an amazing medley of tragedy and triumph, of frustration and achievement. He has provoked all responses from anger to veneration, and has exhibited many of the frailties of human nature with the highest capacity for service and leadership.

He has shown a burning faith in the issues which have moved him, an amazing vitality, a mastery of English, a gift of scientific invention—such an array of talent as to rouse a feeling of awe. Moreover, coupled with his brilliance has been a remarkable wisdom. His outstanding feature has certainly been a tremendous courage. Yet when a friend remarked during the war that he was giving courage to the people, he said: "You are mistaken. They already have the courage. I only focus it."

But what a focus, scintillating in its sharp brilliance! A commonplace politician after the Battle of Britain would have plunged into cliché and verbiage [at great length]. Churchill said: "Never in the field of human conflict was so much owed by so many to so few."

Any student of English—and any would-be orator—would do well to study this sentence: not only its concentration and drama, but its perfect balance. "Never was so much owed by so many to so few" is not nearly as telling: the insertion of "in the field of human conflict" makes the sentence perfect to read or to hear.

This book reveals many examples of Churchill's concentration of wisdom. One of the most remarkable phrases in literary history occurs in his *World Crisis*. Referring to the naval situation in the first World War, a casual sentence appears in a paragraph: "Jellicoe was the only man on either side who could lose the war in an afternoon." Whole volumes were written by "experts" to say no more.

(When Churchill uses words excessively, it is usually to aid his impish humour. One of the earliest instances was the use of "terminological inexactitude" for "lie"—eleven syllables instead of one. More recently he had reversed his decision on the roles of British and American admirals. In Parliament he began: "My views—" A Labour Member promptly interjected "change"—which was probably the word which Churchill was about to use. Instead he continued: "My views are subject to a harmonious process which keeps them in relation to the current movements of events."

(He had the courage to change his opinions when events or reason proved them wrong. Loyalty to a Party is admirable, but blind loyalty is foolish or even dangerous. Politics are generally founded not on principles but upon opinions.)

While he could roll out distinguished phrases with emphatic sonority, for dramatic effect he preferred the short and simple word. In his thrilling defiance to Hitler: "We shall go on to the end; we shall fight in France, we shall fight on the seas and oceans . . ." through a rising series of affirmations to the final and passionate "we shall never surrender"—in all the long paragraph there is no big word—indeed, there are only two of three syllables!

When he was made Prime Minister in 1940 he could offer to Parliament and people nothing but "blood, toil, tears and sweat," but the incisive concentration was a hundred times more compelling than a demagogic spate of oratory. Churchill never forgot the example of Lincoln. At the cemetery of Gettysburg the leading American orator of the day, Everett, spoke for nearly two hours. Lincoln uttered only ten sentences —but his speech remains a classic inspiration while Everett's has long been forgotten.

Churchill would have been outstanding had it been only for his mastery of the English language [which enabled him to clothe his ideas in noble words] but oratory only enhanced his genius: it did not create it.

His wisdom was not omniscience. His failures usually concerned the simple things of the day: he was at his greatest when surveying the broad scene of world history in the making. He made a sad error of judgment in his "Gestapo" broadcast, which may have lost him the 1945 election. In marked contrast was his Fulton speech of 1946—a vivid picture of the world situation painted years before any of his contemporaries realized its accuracy. Even more startling was his speech of October, 1939, on the Nazi threat to Russian interests. It was bitterly derided by Stalin and his associates—but was adopted as Russian policy in June, 1941. Or his comment on the appeasement surrender at Munich, when people were rejoicing at Chamberlain's boast of "peace in our time"—but Churchill de-

clared, "We have sustained a defeat without a war." Not less
forceful was his comment on the hesitant neutrals, in January,
1940: "Each one of them hopes that if he feeds the crocodile
enough, the crocodile will eat him last."

The words of Churchill's speeches are important, but so are
the dates on which they were uttered. Many smaller politicians
have been very wise after the events; the role of the real statesman is to foresee them.

With Churchill's dramatic life it is not unnatural that he
is best remembered for his achievements in times of peril. His
prescience had the British fleet mobilized in August, 1914.
His viewpoint was always more far-sighted and realistic than
that of his worthy colleagues, experts in liberal social changes
but novices in world war. It was Churchill who first perceived
the weakness of Russia and promoted the Dardanelles expedi-
tion which, had it succeeded, could have shortened the war
by two years—and would have fantastically changed the subsequent course of history.

Nor were his interventions confined to strategic ideas. He
soon perceived the character of the trench deadlock, and while
politicians and professional soldiers dallied helplessly he, then
First Lord of the Admiralty, developed the tank as a *naval*
weapon! His scientific outlook was practical and always advanced. In 1917 an attack on the Frisian Islands of Borkum
and Sylt was projected. Churchill outlined a scheme for concrete caissons to be towed to the area and sunk "to create a
weather-proof harbour in the open sea."

Here was the origin of the Mulberry harbours which made
possible the Normandy invasion. "It was just one of those brilliant ideas that Winston has," said President Roosevelt. "He
has a hundred a day, and about four of them are good." How
many people can claim four good ideas a day?

"All wisdom is not new wisdom." Churchill, himself steeped
in history, quoted freely from classical sources—his "blood,
toil, tears and sweat" was echoed from Garibaldi. Churchill's
genius often lay in his historic sense, in the application of the
wisdom of the past to the problems of the present.

Although normally his language was that of Macaulay or
Gibbon, he did not hesitate to descend to the commonplace or
even to slang. There was his famous speech to the Canadian
Parliament in 1941. "When I warned them [the French Gov-
ernment] that Britain would fight on alone whatever they did,
their generals told their Prime Minister and his divided Cabinet: 'In three weeks England will have her neck wrung like
a chicken.' Some chicken! Some neck!" This was scarcely the
pompous diplomatic language expected of a Prime Minister,
but the four words—with Churchill's tongue, bulk and per-

sonality behind them—were more expressive than any long argument. Their crudity covered and expressed a vital policy, firmly and irrevocably decided. This is important. Many people have been misled by Churchill's brilliant oratory; they imagine that it consists only of words magnificently chosen and no less magnificently delivered; yet its real value is that it expresses vital and sincere ideas.

An even better example comes from a broadcast, intended for American hearers, in 1941, at a time when many of them thought that Britain's prospects were hopeless. "We shall not fail or falter: we shall not weaken or tire," the voice boomed. "Neither the sudden shock of battle nor the long-drawn trials of vigilance and exertion will wear us down." This was typical Churchill, an expression of the infectious courage by now so well known. Then suddenly he snapped: "Give us the tools, and we will finish the job." The effects of this homely phrase were so vast as to be incalculable.

His judgment of people was admirable. (Consider his comment on Baldwin: "It is a fine thing to be honest, but it is also very important to be right.") Unlike some who attain the highest office, he was not afraid to gather brilliant men about him, and to learn from them. But in his own sphere he was the leader, and held his place with determined confidence. When he was appointed Prime Minister on May 10, 1940—at a moment when frightful disaster impended, he wrote: "I felt as if I were walking with Destiny, and that all my past life had been but a preparation for this hour and for this trial."

This superlative confidence sustained him in the darkest moments. In a distracted world he had no doubts. He had studied his famous ancestor Marlborough, and had written brilliantly about him—pointing out that Marlborough knew that military prowess was not enough: the best army is helpless without the home organization behind it. Marlborough ensured the efficient support of this by infiltrating his friends into its control. Churchill reversed the process. He, the politician, also controlled the war strategy—and his mental resources, experience and insight were so powerful that his professional advisers could not deny his right to do so. His direction of the war was unchallenged: it was always intelligent and often inspired. He had to shoulder the responsibility for failures and defeats: he is legitimately entitled to the glory of victory.

His very eminence during the war led to his downfall: retaining command of the war effort, he delegated domestic issues to others—many of them Labour colleagues. They were thus more in touch with the popular mood: while Churchill was thinking forward about the dangers still inherent in the world, and apprehensive of the vast price still to be paid for the recovery of economic stability, the ordinary man was blissfully assuming that victory would automatically bring a new and better life, and of course voted for the people who agreed with him.

Churchill was deeply humiliated by his defeat at the 1945 elections. Yet his courage defied despair; and though planning ahead for domestic victory, he never lost sight of the world's complicated problems. In this he was surely right: politicians may preen themselves over the blessings of welfare states—admirable objectives, but which could disappear in an hour because of world chaos promoted by some blunder or lassitude in a distant part of the world.

The present generation esteems Churchill most highly as an incomparable war leader. The historian of the future may turn rather to his post-war schemes—so far-sighted, and the product of his vast experience and authority: his advocacy of a United States of Europe—a great nationalist, he preached internationalism: his work for peace—even while he was absurdly dubbed a "warmonger." (A close friend has related that after Churchill utters the loyal toast, "The Queen!" he adds in a whisper: "and no war!") Think of his uncompromising denunciation of Germany in two world wars, and consider the following: "I am now going to say something that will astonish you. The first step in the re-creation of the European family must be a partnership between France and Germany. In this way only can France recover the moral and cultural leadership of Europe. There can be no revival of Europe without a spiritually great France and a spiritually great Germany." Thus spoke Churchill at Zürich on September 19, 1946.

He never spoke in a minor key: he was a believer. He always saw things in black and white, never in indeterminate shades. He was a man of great loyalties, but would dismiss his best friend should he fail to act his part. From his youth ambitious and of admitted brilliance, he took forty years to attain his objective; a master of foreign affairs, he was never Foreign Secretary; a great orator, he lost more elections than any other politician. He has suffered disaster and achieved triumph; derided and booed, then cheered and admired by the same public: his versatility was amazing and maybe served to detract him, since many believed that one man could not possibly be so brilliant in so many spheres. For many years he was isolated: it was for long the fashion to deride him even when he was successful.

His genius needed a broad canvas, and not until 1940 was this afforded. Then he painted in his picture of the world in firm and glowing colours.

Wit is not necessarily wisdom: nor is great oratory: nor,

indeed, is vast experience. But the three are powerful allies. Readers of this book, even though they knew Churchill well, may be surprised at the amazing range of knowledge, understanding and foresight which it displays.

It was indeed happy that he was utterly wrong in his forecast of a short life, but emphatically he had his innings. The world has been immeasurably benefited by his presence—the world of to-morrow at least as much as the world of to-day.

I. THE MAN OF REFLECTION

Personal Philosophy

Authority. It was quite impossible to determine any exact relation between the penalties at the command of authority and the respect in which the authority was held.

Commons, February 11, 1902.

Nature of Man. I believe that, generally speaking, given free institutions on a fair basis, the best side of men's nature will in the end surely come uppermost. But this doctrine has its limits.

Commons, February 22, 1906.

The Individual and the Mass. It is in the nice adjustment of the respective ideas of collectivism and individualism that the problem of the world and the solution of that problem lies in the years to come.

Kinnaird Hall, Dundee, October 14, 1908.

Purpose of Life. What is the use of living, if it be not to strive for noble causes and to make this muddled world a better place for those who will live in it after we are gone? How else can we put ourselves in harmonious relation with the great verities and consolations of the infinite and the eternal? And I avow my faith that we are marching towards better days. Humanity will not be cast down. We are going on—swinging bravely forward along the grand high road— and already behind the distant mountains is the promise of the sun.

Kinnaird Hall, Dundee, October 10, 1908.

Action. Where every step is fraught with grave consequences and with real peril to the cause, deliberate and measured action is not merely prudent, but decent.

Commons, February 22, 1910.

Personal Criticism. I have derived continued benefit from criticism at all periods of my life, and I do not remember any time when I was ever short of it.

November 27, 1914.

Agreements. When an agreement has been reached, everyone who is a party to it is bound by it, and previous misgivings and differences of opinion are blotted out and ought not to be referred to. In every walk of life, in every sphere of human activity, this is the invariable rule and it is the only safe and honest rule. *Commons, March 5, 1917.*

Power and Mercy. The finest combination in the world is power and mercy. The worst combination in the world is weakness and strife. *Commons, March 3, 1919.*

Staff. There is no excuse for superior authority not choosing the most suitable agents for particular duties, and not removing unsuitable agents from particular duties.
Commons, July 8, 1920.

Facts. You must look at facts because they look at you.
Commons, May 7, 1925.

Bias. You cannot ask us to take sides against arithmetic. You cannot ask us to take sides against the obvious facts of the situation. *Commons, August 31, 1926.*

Public Conduct. When you embark on a course of restriction or oppression, caution and hesitancy should rightly impose themselves upon you; but when you are embarked upon a course of relief and liberation, advance with courage.
Commons, June 7, 1928.

Panic. It is very much better sometimes to have a panic feeling beforehand, and then be quite calm when things happen, than to be extremely calm beforehand and to get into a panic when things happen. *Commons, May 22, 1935.*

Two Ideals. The second question I have asked myself is much more personal. Am I by temperament and conviction able sincerely to identify myself with the main historical conceptions of Toryism, and can I do justice to them and give expression to them spontaneously in speech and action? My life, such as it has been, has been lived for forty years in the public eye, and very varying opinions are entertained about it—and about particular phases in it. I shall attempt no justification, but this I will venture most humbly to submit and also to declare, because it springs most deeply from the convictions of my heart, that at all times according to my lights and throughout the changing scenes through which we are all hurried, I have always faithfully served two public causes which I think stand supreme—the maintenance of the enduring greatness of Britain and her Empire and the historical continuity of our island life.
Caxton Hall, London, October 9, 1940.

Democracy. I am a child of the House of Commons. I was brought up in my father's house to believe in democracy. "Trust the people"—that was his message. I used to see him cheered at meetings and in the streets by crowds of working men way back in those aristocratic Victorian days when, as Disraeli said, the world was for the few, and for very few. Therefore I have been in full harmony all my life with the tides which have flowed on both sides of the Atlantic against privilege and monopoly, and I have steered confidently towards the Gettysburg ideal of "government of the people, by the people, for the people."

U. S. Congress, Washington, D. C., December 26, 1941.

Courage. However tempting it might be to some when much trouble lies ahead to step aside adroitly and put someone else up to take the blows, I do not intend to take that cowardly course, but, on the contrary, to stand to my post and persevere in accordance with my duty as I see it.

Commons, February 25, 1942.

Apologies. I have no intention of passing my remaining years in explaining or withdrawing anything I have said in the past, still less in apologizing for it.

Commons, April 21, 1944.

Conviction. So long as I am acting from duty and conviction, I am indifferent to taunts and jeers. I think they will probably do me more good than harm.

Barbs. I am not at all worried about anything that may be said about me. Nobody would attempt to take part in controversial politics and not expect to be attacked.

Commons, December 6, 1945.

Opportunities. With opportunities comes responsibility. Strength is granted to us all when we are needed to serve great causes.

New York, March 15, 1946.

War. Great wars come when both sides believe they are more or less equal, when each thinks it has a good chance of victory.

New York, October 14, 1947.

Agreement. It is a sort of British idea that when you reach agreement you take the rough with the smooth.

Commons, February 16, 1948.

Conscience. Conscience and muddle cannot be reconciled; conscience apart from truth is mere stupidity, regrettable but by no means respectable.

Commons, July 15, 1948.

Authorship. Writing a book was an adventure. To begin with it was a toy, and amusement; then it became a mistress, and then a master, and then a tyrant.

London, November 2, 1949.

Hate. Hate is not a good guide in public or in private life. I am sure that class hatred and class warfare, like national revenge, are the most costly luxuries in which anyone can indulge.

Commons, April 24, 1950.

The Right. It is better to be both right and consistent. But if you have to choose—you must choose to be right.

Scarborough, October 11, 1952.

Tradition and Innovation. The function of the Royal Academy is, I think, to hold a middle course between tradition and innovation. Without tradition art is a flock of sheep without shepherds, and with innovation it is a corpse. It is not the function of the Royal Academy to run wildly after every curious novelty.

Royal Academy Banquet, London, April 30, 1953.

Socialism and Communism

Socialists. A good many of those gentlemen who have delightful rosy views of a noble and brilliant future for the world are so remote from hard facts of daily life and of ordinary politics that I am not very sure that they will bring any useful or effective influence to bear upon the immediate course of events.

Liberalism and Socialism. Liberalism has its own history and its own tradition. Socialism has its own formulas and aims. Socialism seeks to pull down wealth; Liberalism seeks to raise up poverty. Socialism would destroy private interests; Liberalism would preserve private interests in the only way in which they can be safely and justly preserved, namely, by reconciling them with public right. Socialism would kill enterprise; Liberalism would rescue enterprise from the trammels of privilege and preference. Socialism assails the pre-eminence of the individual; Liberalism seeks, and shall seek more in the future, to build up a minimum standard for the mass. Socialism exalts the rule; Liberalism exalts the man. Socialism attacks capital; Liberalism attacks monopoly.

Kinnaird Hall, Dundee, May 14, 1908.

Bolshevism. Bolshevism is not a policy; it is a disease. It is not a creed; it is a pestilence. It presents all the characteristics of a pestilence. It breaks out with great suddenness; it is violently contagious; it throws people into a frenzy of excitement; it spreads with extraordinary rapidity; the mortality is terrible; so that after a while, like other pestilences, the disease tends to wear itself out. The population of the regions devastated by its first fury are left in a sort of stupor. Then gradually and painfully they begin to recover their sanity; they are feeble; they are shattered; and the light of human reason once again comes back to their eyes. Those regions which have been most afflicted by the fury of this storm are the first to recover, and once having recovered, they are specially immune from all subsequent attacks. . . .

Bolshevism is a great evil, but it has arisen out of great social evils.   *Commons, May 29, 1919.*

Totalitarianism. Socialism is inseparably interwoven with Totalitarianism and the abject worship of the State. . . . This State is to be the arch-employer, the arch-planner, the arch-administrator and ruler, and the arch-caucus-boss.
London, June 4, 1945.

State Socialism. Although it is now put forward in the main by people who have a good grounding in the Liberalism and Radicalism of the early part of this century, there can be no doubt that Socialism is inseparably interwoven with Totalitarianism and the abject worship of the State. It is not alone that property, in all its forms, is struck at, but that liberty, in all its forms, is challenged by the fundamental conceptions of Socialism.   *B. B. C., June 4, 1945.*

Capitalism and Socialism. The inherent vice of Capitalism is the unequal sharing of blessings. The inherent virtue of Socialism is the equal sharing of miseries.
Commons, October 22, 1945.

Socialism in Britain. For my part, I believe profoundly that the attempt to turn Great Britain into a Socialist State will, as it develops, produce widespread political strife, misery and ruin at home; and that, if this attempt involves nationalization of all the means of production, distribution and exchange —to quote the orthodox phrase which I understand was re-affirmed at the Labour Party meeting in May—then this island will not be able to support above three quarters of the population which now inhabits it.

Commons, December 6, 1945.

Socialism. Socialism is the philosophy of failure, the creed of ignorance, and the gospel of envy.
Perth, May 28, 1948.

Socialism is based on the idea of an all-powerful State which owns everything, which plans everything, which distributes everything, and thus through its politicians and officials decides the daily life of the individual citizen.

London, January 21, 1950.

The All-powerful State. The concentration of all power over the daily lives of ordinary men and women in what is called "the State," exercised by what is virtually single-chamber government, is a reactionary step contrary to the whole trend of British history and to the message we have given to the world.   *Huddersfield, October 15, 1951.*

Socialism and Communism. Hitherto, British Socialist policy has been to nationalize what industries they thought fit and to pay reasonable compensation to the owners and shareholders. This is a matter of principle in which they differ from the Communist Party. That and the maintenance of political liberty are the two main points of difference.

Commons, May 21, 1952.

Domestic Economy and Social Legislation

Cause of Economy. I stand here to plead the cause of economy. I think it is about time that a voice was heard from this side of the House pleading that unpopular cause; that someone not on the bench opposite, but a conservative by tradition, whose fortunes are linked indissolubly to the Tory Party, who knows something of the majesty and power of Britain beyond the seas, upon whom rests no taint of cosmopolitanism should stand forward and say what he can to protest against the policy of daily increasing the public burden. If such a one is to stand forward in such a cause, then I say it humbly but with, I hope, becoming pride, no one has a better right than I have, for this is a cause for which the late Lord Randolph Churchill made the greatest sacrifice of any Minister of modern times.   *Commons, May 13, 1901.*

Human Rights. I lay down this principle in this democratic Parliament, that no man should be imported into a country as a labourer unless you also accept him as a human being.

Commons, February 22, 1906.

Public Funds. The great principle which this House ought to guard and cherish is that, when the tax collector comes to the private citizen and takes from him of his wealth for the service of the public, the whole of that money taken shall go for the purposes for which it is intended, and that no private interests, however powerfully they may be organized and however eloquently advocated, shall thrust their dirty fingers into the pie and take the profit for themselves.

Commons, June 2, 1908.

Old Age Pensions. It marks the assertion in our social system of an entirely new principle in regard to poverty, and that principle, once asserted, cannot possibly be confined within its existing limits. Old age pensions will carry us all a very long way. They have opened a door which will not soon or easily be closed. The Members of both Houses of Parliament have been led to the verge of the cruel abyss of poverty, and have been in solemn session assembled to contemplate its depths and its gloom. All alike have come to gaze; none have remained unmoved. There are some distinguished and eminent men, men whose power and experience I cannot impugn, who have started back appalled by what they have seen, and whose only idea is to slam the door on the grim and painful prospect which has been revealed to their eyes.

But that is not the only spirit which has been awakened in our country; there are others, not less powerful, and a greater number, who will never allow that door to be closed; they have got their feet in it, they are resolved that it shall be kept open. Nay, more, they are prepared to descend into the abyss, and grapple with its evils—as sometimes you see after an explosion at a coal mine a rescue party advancing undaunted into the smoke and steam.

Kinnaird Hall, Dundee, October 10, 1908.

Without a hitch, perfectly smoothly, punctual to the minute, regular as clockwork, nearly 600,000 aged persons are being paid their pensions every week. That is a wonderful and beneficent achievement, a good job well worth some risk and sweat to finish. Nearly eight millions of money are being sent circulating through unusual channels, long frozen by poverty, circulating in the homes of the poor, flowing through the little shops which cater for their needs, cementing again family unions which harsh fate was tearing asunder, uniting the wife to the husband, and the parent to the children.

Social Progress. The social field lies open. There is no great country where the organization of industrial conditions more urgently demands attention. Wherever the reformer casts his eyes he is confronted with a mass of largely preventable and even curable suffering. The fortunate people of Britain are more happy than any other equally numerous class have been in the whole history of the world. I believe the left-out millions are more miserable. Our vanguard enjoys all the delights of all the ages. Our rearguard straggles out into conditions which are crueller than barbarism. The unemployed artisan, the casual labourer and the casual labourer's wife and children, the sweated worker, the infirm worker, the worker's widow, the underfed child, the untrained, undisciplined and exploited boy labourer—it is upon these subjects that our minds should dwell in the early days of 1909.

Birmingham, January 13, 1909.

Reformers. I do not at all quarrel with him [Keir Hardie] for having expressed impatience, because reformers should always be impatient. If they don't provide the driving power from day to day and month to month the coach will move forward more slowly. *Commons, February 17, 1909.*

Social Organization. We are not going to measure the strength of great countries only by their material resources. We think that the supremacy and predominance of our country depend upon the maintenance of the vigour and health of its population, just as its true glory must always be found in the happiness of its cottage homes. We believe that if Great Britain is to remain great and famous in the world, we cannot allow the present social and industrial disorders, with their profound physical and moral reactions, to continue unchecked. We propose to you a financial scheme, but we also advance a policy of social organization. It will demand sacrifices from all classes; it will give security to all classes. By its means we shall be able definitely to control some of the most wasteful processes in our social life, and without it our country will remain exposed to vital dangers, against which fleets and armies are of no avail. *Commons, May 19, 1909.*

Unemployment. I think it is our duty to use the strength and resources of the State to arrest the ghastly waste, not merely of human happiness but of national health and strength, which follows when a working man's home, which has taken him years to get together, is broken up and scattered through a long spell of unemployment, or when, through the death, the sickness or the invalidity of the bread-winner, the frail boat in which the fortunes of the family are embarked founders, and the women and children are left to struggle helplessly on the dark waters of a friendless world.

Old Age Pensions. There is no inconsistency or contradiction between a non-contributory system of old age pensions and a contributory system of insurance against unemployment, sickness, invalidity and widowhood. The circumstances and conditions are entirely different. The prospect of attaining extreme old age, of living beyond threescore years and ten, which is the allotted span of human life, seems so doubtful and remote to the ordinary man when in the full strength of manhood that it has been found in practice almost impossible to secure from any very great number of people the regular sacrifices which are necessary to guard against old age.

Insure. If I had my way, I would write the word "insure" over the door of every cottage, and upon the blotting book of every public man, because I am convinced that by sacrifices which are conceivably small, which are all within the power of the very poorest man in regular work, families can be secured against catastrophes which otherwise would smash them up for ever.

Free Trade Hall, Manchester, May 23, 1909.

Security of Property. The vital processes of civilization require, and the combined interests of millions guarantee, the security of property. A society in which property was insecure would speedily degenerate into barbarism; a society in which property was absolutely secure, irrespective of all conceptions of justice in regard to the manner of its acquisition, would degenerate, not into barbarism, but death.

Abernethy, July 7, 1909.

Private Property. The best way to make private property secure and respected is to bring the processes by which it is gained into harmony with the general interests of the public. When and where property is associated with the idea of reward for services rendered, with the idea of recompense for high gifts and special aptitudes displayed or for faithful labour done, then property will be honoured. When it is associated with processes which are beneficial, or which at the worst are not actually injurious to the commonwealth, then property will be unmolested; but when it is associated with ideas of wrong and of unfairness, with processes of restriction and monopoly, and other forms of injury to the community, then I think that you will find that property will be assailed and will be endangered.

Edinburgh, July 17, 1909.

The Rich. It is very easy for rich people to preach the virtues of self-reliance to the poor. It is also very foolish, because, as a matter of fact, the wealthy, so far from being self-reliant, are dependent on the constant attention of scores, and sometimes even hundreds, of persons who are employed in waiting upon them and ministering to their wants.

Norwich, July 26, 1909.

Pensions. I have always understood that the theory upon which a pension is granted is that it has been earned, and is to be regarded as deferred pay.

Commons, April 9, 1913.

Triumphs of Liberalism. The great triumphs and successes of Liberalism in the nineteenth century came from the fact that they were consistently, over several generations, advocating the striking off of shackles on enterprise, trade and the social life of the country.   *Commons, June 7, 1928.*

Social Progress. I have always been a bit shy of defining war aims, but if these great communities, now struggling not only for their own lives but for the freedom and progress of the world, emerge victorious, there will be an electric atmosphere in the world which may render possible an advance towards a greater and broader social unity and justice than could otherwise have been achieved in peacetime in a score of years. We are no theorists or doctrinaires. Trade unionists are practical men aiming at practical results. I might say that our aim will be to build a society in which there will be wealth and culture, but where wealth shall not prey on commonwealth nor culture degenerate into class and pride.

Speech at a luncheon in London, March 27, 1941.

Compulsory Insurance. The time is now ripe for another great advance, and anyone can see what large savings there will be in the administration once the whole process of insurance had become unified, compulsory, and national. Here is a real opportunity for what I once called "bringing the magic of averages to the rescue of the millions." Therefore you must rank me and my colleagues as strong partisans of national compulsory insurance for all classes for all purposes from the cradle to the grave.   *London, March 21, 1943.*

Nationalization. We must also be careful that a pretext is not made of war needs to introduce far-reaching social or political changes by a side wind. Take the question of nationalizing the coal mines. Those words do not terrify me at all. I advocated nationalization of the railways after the last war, but I am bound to say that I was a bit affected by the experience of the national control of the railways after the war, which led to the public getting a very bad service, to the shareholders having very unsatisfactory returns, and to one of the most vicious and hazardous strikes with which I have ever been concerned. However, as I say, the principle of nationalization is accepted by all, provided proper compensation is paid. The argument proceeds not on moral grounds but on whether in fact we could make a better business of the whole thing for ourselves, a more fertile business for the nation as a whole, by nationalization than by relying on private enterprise and competition.   *Commons, October 13, 1943.*

Bread Rationing. The German U-boats in their worst endeavour never made bread rationing necessary in war. It took a Socialist Government and Socialist planners to fasten it on us in time of peace when the seas are open and the world harvests good. At no time in the two world wars have our people had so little bread, meat, butter, cheese and fruit to eat.
Conservative Party Conference, Blackpool, October 5, 1946.

Wealth and Poverty. You may try to destroy wealth, and find that all you have done is to increase poverty.
Commons, March 12, 1947.

Incentives. We shall not allow the advance of society and economic well-being of the nation to be regulated and curtailed by the pace of the weakest brethren among us. Proper incentives must be offered and full freedom given to the strong to use their strength in the commonweal. Initiative, enterprise, thrift, domestic foresight, contrivance, good housekeeping and natural ability must reap their just reward. On any other plan the population of this island will sink by disastrous and agonizing stages to a far lower standard of life and to two-thirds of its present numbers.   *Blenheim Palace, August 4, 1947.*

Regimentation. I warn you solemnly, if you submit yourselves to the totalitarian compulsion and regimentation of our national life and labour, there lies before you an almost measureless prospect of misery and tribulation of which a lower standard of living will be the first result, hunger the second, and a dispersal or death of a large proportion of our population the third.   *Blenheim Palace, August 16, 1947.*

State Management. State Management has proved, in every case where it is applied, to be cumbrous, wasteful, and incompotent. Moreover, the wage earners in all these nationalized industries are rapidly finding out how far more flexible and comprehending compared to the all-powerful, remote and sullen control of the State was the private employer.
Woodford Green, July 10, 1948.

Rich Men. Rich men, although valuable to the revenue, are not vital to a healthy state of society, but a society in which rich men are got rid of, from motives of jealousy, is not a healthy state.   *Commons, April 24, 1950.*

Nationalization. The complete nationalization of all means of production, distribution and exchange would make it impossible for this small island to support a large part of its population.   *Huddersfield, October 15, 1951.*

Labour

Miners. We must not only regard the financial interests of these prosperous companies, but we must remember the human interest of the miner at the bottom of the mine.
                              Commons, May 5, 1904.

Cheap Labour. There is no greater delusion than that low wages mean high profits. No labour is so dear as cheap labour, and the labour which costs nothing is the dearest of all.
                         Commons, Fabruary 22, 1906.

Labour. Labour! It is a great word. It moves the world, it comprises the millions, it combines many men in many lands in the sympathy of a common burden.

State as Employer. I am of the opinion that the State should increasingly assume the position of the reserve employer of labour.

Free Competition. We want to draw a line below which we will not allow persons to live and labour, yet above which they may compete with all the strength of their manhood. We want to have free competition upwards; we decline to allow free competition to run downwards.
               St. Andrew's Hall, Glasgow, October 11, 1906.

Miners' Demands. I do not wonder at the miners' demand. I cannot find it in my heart to feel the slightest surprise, or indignation, or mental disturbance at it. My capacity for wonder is entirely absorbed, not by the miners' demand, but by the gentleman in the silk hat and white waistcoat who has the composure and the complacency to deny that demand and dispute it with him.

Leisure. The general march of industrial democracy is not towards inadequate hours of work, but towards sufficient hours of leisure. That is the movement among the working people all over the country. They are not content that their lives should remain mere alternations between bed and the factory; they demand time to look about them, time to see their homes by

daylight, to see their children, time to think and read and cultivate their garden—time, in short, to live.
Commons, July 6, 1908.

Casual Labour. The casual unskilled labourer who is habitually under-employed, who is lucky to get three, or at the outside four days' work in the week, who may often be out of a job three or four weeks at a time, who in bad times goes under altogether, and who in good times has no hope of security and no incentive to thrift, whose whole life and the lives of his wife and children are embarked in a sort of blind, desperate, fatalistic gamble with circumstances beyond his comprehension or control, this poor man, this terrible and pathetic figure, is not as a class the result of accident or chance, is not casual because he wishes to be casual, is not casual as the consequence of some temporary disturbance soon put right. No; the casual labourer is here because he is wanted here. He is here in answer to a perfectly well-defined demand. He is here as the result of economic causes which have been too long unregulated. He is not the natural product, he is an article manufactured, called into being, to suit the requirements, in the Prime Minister's telling phrase, of all industries at particular times and of particular industries at all times.
Kinnaird Hall, Dundee, October 10, 1908.

Labour Exchanges. Labour Exchanges are the gateway to industrial security. *Commons, February 17, 1909.*

Living Wage. It is a serious national evil that any class of His Majesty's subjects should receive in return for their utmost exertions less than a living wage.

Sweated Labour. We have seen from the investigations of the last twenty years, that there is no power of self-cure within the area of the evil. *Commons, April 28, 1909.*

Labour Exchanges and Unemployment Insurance. The two systems are complementary; they are man and wife; they mutually support and sustain each other.
Commons, May 19, 1909.

Human Labour. What we propose to do for human labour, for the services which one man has to render to another, which is the only thing the majority of human beings have to sell, is to give it the same facilities and advantages which every other trader and merchant in the world has secured for his less important and less sensitive commodity.
Commons, June 16, 1909.

General Strike. We now know with accuracy the injury which has been done, at any rate to our finances. We meet this afternoon under the shadow of last year. It is not the time to bewail the past; it is the time to pay the bill. It is not for me to apportion the blame; my task is only to apportion the burden. I cannot present myself before the Committee in the guise of an impartial judge; I am only the public executioner.

Commons, April 11, 1927.

Miners at War. I am very sorry that we have had to debar so many miners from going to the war in the armed forces. I respect their feelings, but we cannot afford it; we cannot allow it. Besides the need for their services in the pits, there is danger in the pits too, and where there is danger there is honour. "Act well thy part, there all the honor lies," and that is the motto I want to give out to all those who in an infinite variety of ways are playing an equally worthy part in the consummation of our high purpose.

Westminster Central Hall, London, October 31, 1942.

Power of Employers. It might well be in the interest of the factory workers, or indeed of the wage-earners generally, not to have too strong an employer over them. I should like to feel that he would be strong in the sense of being capable and efficient as a producer or competitor in the world markets. But it is abhorrent to our idea of freedom that the employer should have undue power over his employees.

London, June 21, 1945.

Freedom of Labour. It is in the interest of the wage-earner to have many other alternatives open to him than service under one all-powerful employer called the State. He will be in a better position to bargain collectively and production will be more abundant; there will be more for all and more freedom for all when the wage-earner is able, in the large majority of cases, to choose and change his work, and to deal with a private employer who, like himself, is subject to the ordinary pressures of life and, like himself, is dependent upon his personal thrift, ingenuity and good-housekeeping.

Blackpool, October 5, 1946.

Officialdom. Will not the daily toil of the actual producing worker have a heavier burden thrust upon it by the enormous hordes of disinterested and largely uninterested officials than would be the case under private management? And will not these officials be less efficient, more costly, and far more dictatorial than the private employers?

Ayr, May 16, 1947.

Bricklayer. I have always been a firm supporter of British trade unionism. I believe it to be the only foundation upon which the relations of employers and employed can be harmoniously adjusted. I have always advised Conservatives and Liberals to join the trade unions. I tried to join the Bricklayers' Trade Union and it is a complicated legal point whether I have in fact succeeded in doing so.

Woodford Green, July 10, 1948.

Nationalization. Nationalization of industry is the doom of trade unionism.   *Blackpool, October 14, 1950.*

This Is England

British Influence. It is known, alike by peoples and rulers that, upon the whole—and it is upon the whole that we must judge these things—British influence is a kindly and healthy influence and makes for the general happiness and welfare of mankind.   *Commons, May 17, 1901.*

The British Constitution. The British Constitution is mainly British common sense.

Class-Struggle. I will tell those wealthy and powerful people what the secret of the security of life and property in Britain is. The security arises from the continuation of that very class-struggle which they lament and of which they complain, which goes on ceaselessly in our country, which goes on tirelessly, with perpetual friction, a struggle between class and class which never sinks into lethargy, and never breaks into violence, but which from year to year makes possible a steady and constant advance. It is on the nature of that class-struggle in Britain that the security of life and property is fundamentally reposed. We are always changing; like nature, we change a great deal, although we change very slowly. We are always reaching a higher level after each change, but yet with the harmony of our life unbroken and unimpaired.

Class Hatred. There have always been men of power and position, who have sacrificed and exerted themselves in the popular cause; and that is why there is so little class hatred here, in spite of all the squalor and misery which we see around us.   *Kinnaird Hall, Dundee, May 14, 1908.*

New Age. The wonderful century which followed the Battle of Waterloo and the downfall of the Napoleonic domination, which secured to this small island so long and so resplendent a reign, has come to an end. We have arrived at a new time. Let us realize it. And with that new time strange methods, huge forces, larger combinations—a Titanic world—

have sprung up around us. The foundations of our power are changing. To stand still would be to fall; to fall would be to perish. We must go forward. We will go forward. We will go forward into a way of life more earnestly viewed, more scientifically organized, more consciously national than any we have known. Thus alone shall we be able to sustain and to renew, through the generations which are to come, the fame and the power of the British race.

Free Trade Hall, Manchester, May 23, 1909.

Destiny of Britain. What is the destiny of our country to be? Nothing is settled either for or against us. We have no reason to despair; still less have we any reason to be self-satisfied. All is still in our hands for good or for ill. We have the power to-day to choose our fortune, and I believe there is no nation in the world, perhaps there never has been in history, any nation which at one and the same moment was confronted with such opposite possibilities, was threatened on the one hand by more melancholy disaster, and cheered on the other by more bright, yet not unreasonable hopes. The two roads are open. We are at the crossways. If we stand on in the old happy-go-lucky way, the richer classes ever growing in wealth and in number, and ever declining in responsibility, the very poor remaining plunged or plunging ever deeper into helpless, hopeless misery, then I think there is nothing before us but savage strife between class and class, with an increasing disorganization, with an increasing destruction of human strength and human virtue—nothing, in fact, but that dual degeneration which comes from the simultaneous waste of extreme wealth and of extreme want.

Norwich, July 26, 1909.

Territorial Acquisitions. We have got all we want in territory, but our claim to be left in undisputed enjoyment of vast and splendid possessions, largely acquired by war and largely maintained by force, is one which often seems less reasonable to others than to us.

Commons, March 17, 1914.

Jurisprudence. The first maxim of English jurisprudence is that complainers should come into Court with clean hands.

Commons, April 28, 1914.

Conscription. There are many countries where a national army on a compulsory basis is the main foundation of the State and is regarded as one of the most important safeguards of democratic freedom. It is not so here. On the contrary, the civil character of our Government institutions is one of the most deeply cherished convictions of our island life, a conviction which our island position alone has enabled us to enjoy.

Commons, February 23, 1920.

British Empire. Governments who have seized upon power by violence and by usurpation have often resorted to terrorism in their desperate efforts to keep what they have stolen; but the august and venerable structure of the British Empire, where lawful authority descends from hand to hand and generation after generation, does not need such aid. Such ideas are absolutely foreign to the British way of doing things.

Commons, July 8, 1920.

Britain's Part in Europe. Our country has a very important part to play in Europe, but it is not so large a part as we have been attempting to play, and I advocate for us in future a more modest rôle than any of our peace-preservers and peace-lovers have sought to impose upon us.

Commons, April 13, 1933.

England. There are a few things I will venture to mention about England. They are spoken in no invidious sense. Here it would hardly occur to anyone that the banks would close their doors against their depositors. Here no one questions the fairness of the courts of law and justice. Here no one thinks of persecuting a man on account of his religion or his race. Here everyone, except the criminal, looks on the policeman as a friend and servant of the public. Here we provide for poverty and misfortune with more compassion, in spite of all our burdens, than any other country. Here we can assert the rights of the citizen against the State, or criticize the Government of the day, without failing in our duty to the Crown or in our loyalty to the King. This ancient, mighty London in which we are gathered is still the financial centre of the world. From the Admiralty building, half a mile away, orders can be sent to a fleet which, though much smaller than it used to be, or than it ought to be, is still unsurpassed on the seas. More than 80 per cent of the British casualties of the Great War were English. More than 80 per cent of the taxation is paid by the English taxpayers. We are entitled to mention these facts, and to draw authority and courage from them.

England, without Europe. Stripped of her Empire in the Orient, deprived of the sovereignty of the seas, loaded with debt and taxation, her commerce and carrying trade shut out by foreign tariffs and quotas, England would sink to the level of a fifth-rate power, and nothing would remain of all her glories except a population much larger than this island can support.

Intellectuals. Historians have noticed all down the centuries one peculiarity of the English people which has cost them dear. We have always thrown away after a victory the greater part of the advantages we gained in the struggle. The worst difficulties from which we suffer do not come from without. They come from within. They do not come from the cottages of the wage-earners. They come from a peculiar type of brainy people always found in our country, who, if they add something to its culture, take much from its strength.

Royal Society of St. George, London, April 24, 1933.

British Interests. The fortunes and the glory of the British Empire are inseparably interwoven with the fortunes of the world. We rise or we fall together. Indeed, if we survive to-day it is because even in bygone times our ancestors so managed that in the main the special interests of Britain conformed to the general interests of the world.

Commons, October 24, 1935.

Blessings of Civilization. In this island we have to-day achieved in a high degree the blessings of civilization. There is freedom; there is law; there is love of country; there is prosperity. There are unmeasured opportunities of correcting abuses and making further progress.

University of Bristol, July 2, 1938.

Circle of the Crown. In the British Empire we not only look out across the seas towards each other, but backwards to our own history, to Magna Charta, to Habeas Corpus, to the Petition of Right, to Trial by Jury, to the English Common Law and to Parliamentary democracy. These are the milestones and monuments that mark the path along which the British race has marched to leadership and freedom. And over all this, uniting each Dominion with the other and uniting us all with our majestic past, is the golden circle of the Crown. What is within the circle? Not only the glory of an ancient unconquered people, but the hope, the sure hope, of a broadening life for hundreds of millions of men.

Canada Club, London, April 20, 1939.

British Character. A few critical or scathing speeches, a stream of articles in the newspapers, showing how badly the war is managed and how incompetent are those who bear the responsibility—these obtain the fullest publicity; but the marvellous services of seamanship and devotion, and the organization behind them, which prove at every stage and step the soundness of our national life, the inconquerable, the inexhaustible adaptiveness and ingenuity of the British mind, the iron, unyielding, unwearying tenacity of the British character, by which we live, by which alone we can be saved, and by which we shall certainly be saved—and save the world—these, though fully realized by our foes abroad, are sometimes over-looked by our friends at home.   *Commons, June 25, 1941.*

Bureaucracy Rejected. Of all races in the world our people would be the last to consent to be governed by a bureaucracy. Freedom is their lifeblood.   *London, March 21, 1943.*

Cohesion of the British Empire. Among the various forces that hold the British Empire together is—and I certainly do not object to the expression which my hon. Friend and Member for Seaham used—"enlightened self-interest." That has a valuable and important part to play, but I am sure he would not make the mistake of placing it in front of those deeper and more mysterious influences which cause human beings to do the most incalculable, improvident, and, from the narrow point of view, profitless things. It is our union in freedom and for the sake of our way of living which is the great fact, reinforced by tradition and sentiment, and it does not depend upon anything that could ever be written down in any account kept in some large volume.   *Commons, April 21, 1944.*

Economic Structure of Britain. The attempt to socialize Great Britain is fraught with mortal danger. There has never been a community in the world like ours. Here in this small island we maintain forty-six millions of people, who played a greater part per head in winning the world war than any other people, and who, before the war, had developed a standard of living and social services above that of any country in Europe and in many respects above that of the United States. These forty-six millions differ from every other community that has ever existed in the world by the fact that they are perched upon the completely artificial foundation of not providing even one half of their food, and being dependent for the purchase of the bulk of their food and raw materials on persuading foreign customers to accept the wares and the services they offer. Vast, intricate, delicate, innumerable are the methods of acquiring external wealth which the British nation has developed in recent generations, and the population has grown step by step upon the livelihood produced.

    Friends House, London, November 28, 1945.

Instinctive Urge. The British race is not actuated mainly by the hope of material gain. Otherwise we should long ago have sunk in the ocean of the past. It is stirred on almost all occasions by sentiment and instinct, rather than by programmes or worldly calculations.   *Blackpool, October 5, 1946.*

Fair Play. Britain, like any other country, is always changing, but like nature never draws a line without smudging it. We have not the sharp logic of Continental countries. We seek to benefit private enterprise with the knowledge and guiding power of modern Governments, without sacrificing the initiative and drive of individual effort under free, competitive conditions. Our policy is based on the two main principles of fair play and adequate opportunity. We seek to establish a minimum standard of life and labour below which no one who is prepared to meet the obligations of good citizenship should be allowed to fall. Above that minimum standard, we wish to give the fullest possible play for competitive individual enterprise and every chance for the native genius of our island race, springing perennially from every class, to win its full and fair reward.

Ayr, May 16, 1947.

British Moods. In a long and varied life I have constantly watched and tried to measure the moods and inspirations of the British people. There is no foe they will not face. There is no hardship they cannot endure. Whether the test be sharp and short or long and wearisome, they can take it. What they do not forgive is false promises and vain boastings.

Brighton, October 4, 1947.

Rule of the People. Many forms of government have been tried, and will be tried in this world of sin and woe. No one pretends that democracy is perfect or all-wise. Indeed, it has been said that democracy is the worst form of government except all those other forms that have been tried from time to time; but there is the broad feeling in our country that the people should rule, continuously rule, and that public opinion, expressed by all constitutional means, should shape, guide and control the actions of ministers who are their servants and not their masters.

Commons, November 11, 1947.

Rule, Britannia. The tasks which the navy has performed in peacetime are hardly less magnificent than those they have achieved in war. From Trafalgar onwards, for more than 100 years, Britannia ruled the waves. There was a great measure of peace, the freedom of the seas was maintained, the slave trade was extirpated, the Monroe Doctrine of the United States found its sanction in British naval power—and that has been pretty well recognized on the other side of the Atlantic—and in those happy days the cost was about £10 million a year.

Commons, March 8, 1948.

British Climate. The British people have always been superior to the British climate. They have shown themselves capable of rising above it, and certainly they have derived from it many of those strong enduring principles and ways of life which make their existence in our island home different from any other community in the world.

Woodford Green, July 10, 1948.

Trial by Jury. The ancient Anglo-Saxon foundation of all our system of criminal justice is trial by jury. . . . We regard it as a fundamental safeguard of our democratic liberties and life and a principle which has been woven into the whole history of our judicial system that the supreme question, "Guilty or Not Guilty?" shall be decided by ordinary folk.

Commons, July 15, 1948.

Victorian Statesman. The statesman whom I saw in those days seemed to tower above the general level in a most impressive way. The tests were keener, the standards were higher, and those who surmounted them were men it was a treat and honour to meet. They were the representatives of an age of ordered but unceasing movement. Liberalism had stricken the shackles off the slave and broken down the barriers of privilege. The road was open to those of the highest natural quality and ability who chose to tread it.

Commons, December 6, 1950.

The British Judiciary. The British judiciary, with its traditions and record, was one of the greatest living assets of our race and people, and its independence was part of our message to the ever-growing world that was rising so swiftly around us.

Commons, March 23, 1954.

The Nature of Government

Elections. All these balancings, limitations, and half pledges, these little devices by which an embarrassed Government staved off ruin from day to day would, after the next election, be swept as smooth as the sands of the shore after a flood tide.

Duty of Government. There were some things which a government must do, not because the government will do them well, but because nobody else would do them at all.

Commons, February 10, 1904.

Position of a Minister. The position of a minister is one of considerable difficulty. He often has to defend rather an awkward case. When favourable facts are wanting, he has to depend upon the nimbleness of his wits, and when these fail him, he has to fall back upon the loyalty of his supporters.

Politics and War. It is the same in politics as it is in war. When one crest has been left, it is necessary to go to the next. To halt half-way in the valley between is to court swift and certain destruction.   *Commons, April 5, 1906.*

Liberalism. Liberalism supplies at once the higher impulse and the practicable path; it appeals to persons by sentiments of generosity and humanity; it proceeds by courses of moderation; by gradual steps, by steady effort from day to day, from year to year. Liberalism enlists hundreds of thousands upon the side of progress and popular democratic reform whom militant Socialism would drive into violent Tory reaction.

Liberalism and Peace. The first indispensable condition of democratic progress must be the maintenance of European peace. War is fatal to Liberalism. Liberalism is the worldwide antagonist of war.

St. Andrew's Hall, Glasgow, October 11, 1906.

Representative Government. The system of representative government without responsible ministers, without responsible powers, has led to endless friction and inconvenience wherever and whenever it has been employed. It has failed in Canada, it has failed in Natal and Cape Colony.

Faction. I suppose we are all in this House admirers of the Party system of government, but do not think that we should any of us carry our admiration of that system so far as to say that the nation is unfit to enjoy the privilege of managing its own affairs unless it can find someone to quarrel with and plenty of things to quarrel about.

Commons, December 17, 1906.

Finance. The whole procedure of our Parliament arises primarily from the consideration of finance, and finance is the peg on which nearly all our discussions are hung, and from which many of them arise. That is the historic origin of a great portion of the House of Commons procedure, and there is no more deeply rooted maxim than the maxim of "grievances before supply."

Imperial Conference, Downing Street, May 7, 1907.

Two-Party System. Much might be said for and against the two-Party system. But no one can doubt that it adds to the stability and cohesion of the State. The alternation of Parties in power, like the rotation of crops, has beneficial results. Each of the two Parties has services to render in the development of the national life; and the succession of new and different points of view is a real benefit to the country.

The Peers' Veto. It is quite true that there are rich members of the Liberal Party, and there are poor men who are supporters of the Conservative Party; but in the main the lines of difference between the two Parties are social and economic —in the main the lines of difference are increasingly becoming the lines of cleavage between the rich and the poor. Let that reflection be with us in the struggle which we are now undertaking, and in which we shall without pause press forward, confident of this, that, if we persevere, we shall wrest from the hands of privilege and wealth the evil, ugly and sinister weapon of the Peers' veto, which they have used so ill so long.

English Parties. There are two great characteristics about the Party institutions of this country; the equipoise between them, and their almost incredible durability.

Lords and Legislation. I proceed to inquire on what principle the House of Lords deals with liberal measures. The right hon. Member for Dover by an imaginative effort assures us that they occupy the position of the Empire. Are they ever a sieve, a strainer, to stop legislation if it should reveal an undue or undesirable degree of Radicalism or Socialism?

House of Lords. The House of Lords, as it at present exists and acts, is not a national institution, but a Party dodge, an apparatus and instrument at the disposal of one political faction; and it is used in the most unscrupulous manner to injure and humiliate the opposite faction.

Commons, June 29, 1907.

Political Controversy. It is a deplorable thing that, when persons are engaged in acute political controversy, they sometimes allow their language to be rather the means of giving relief to their feelings than an actual description of the facts. That is, no doubt, a very melancholy fact for us to reflect upon, but it has gone on in the past in English politics and it may sometimes recur in the future—I tremble to think that something of this nature may even at this moment be going on in this very city.

Commons, March 23, 1909.

Powers of the House of Lords. The powers of the House of Lords to impede, and by impeding to discredit, the House of Commons are strangely bestowed, strangely limited, and still more strangely exercised. There are little things which they can maul; there are big things they cannot touch; there are Bills which they pass, although they believe them to be wrong; there are Bills which they reject, although they know them to be right. The House of Lords can prevent the trams running over Westminster Bridge; but it cannot prevent a declaration of war.   *Birmingham, January 13, 1909.*

Feudal Assembly. It is not perhaps surprising in a country so fond of tradition, so proud of continuity, as ourselves that a feudal assembly of titled persons, with so long a history and so many famous names, should have survived to exert an influence upon public affairs at the present time. We see how often in England the old forms are reverently preserved after the forces by which they are sustained, and the uses to which they were put, and the dangers against which they were designed, have passed away.   *Norwich, July 26, 1909.*

Politics. Politics is not a game. It is an earnest business.
National Liberal Club, London, October 9, 1909.

Party Government. Party government is an outstanding feature of our political systems of all branches of the English-speaking race all over the world. I know of no equal force which assumes the stability of democratic institutions. I know of no other method by which the enfranchised millions can be continuously attracted to practical things. I know of no other method by which small intrigues, small combinations and petty personal rivalries can be prevented from swaying unevenly the course of public affairs.
Commons, March 31, 1910.

Cabinet. The Cabinet is the creature of the House of Commons. It springs from the House of Commons and dwells in the House of Commons. It is checked and corrected by the House of Commons, and by the shrug of the shoulder of the Private Members of the House the Cabinet can be scattered.
Commons, February 16, 1911.

House of Commons. The House of Commons is not an absolute power, its power is not unchecked. There never was a more sensitive body in the whole history of the world. I can understand it being criticized for being too sensitive sometimes. There are 670 members in touch with many constituencies, differing one from another in character and complexion, sitting here month after month in touch with their constituencies, in touch with public opinion, in touch with the criticism of the Press, in touch with each other, in touch with reason, in touch with reality.

Referendum. We believe that the system of a referendum is a vicious system in itself, that it is bad as the basis of the system of government in any country, but especially unsuited for this country. The mass of the people under the referendum are forced to take a decisive part in a continuous process of law-making.　　　　　　　*Commons, February 22, 1911.*

Change of Government. Nothing is so expensive as general elections and new governments. Every new administration, not excluding ourselves, arrives in power with bright and benevolent ideas of using public money to do good. The more frequent the changes of government, the more numerous are the bright ideas, and the more frequent the elections, the more benevolent they become.

Commons, April 11, 1927.

Gap. In my experience and interior knowledge of the working of governments which extends over nearly a quarter century, I cannot recall any time when the gap between the kind of words which statesmen used and what was actually happening in many countries was as great as it is now. The habit of saying smooth things and uttering pious platitudes and sentiments to gain applause, without relation to the underlying facts, is more pronounced now than it has ever been in my experience.

Commons, November 23, 1932.

Debate. One incident has certainly filled me with surprise. Some few weeks ago Sir Austen Chamberlain made a most serious speech of criticism, and even of censure, addressed to the Prime Minister [Stanley Baldwin] in his own presence. It astonished me that the Prime Minister did not rise at once and say whatever occurred to him to say. After all, this is a forum of debate, and an indictment preferred by a Member of high responsibility, especially a Member who has long been the buttress, and on one occasion at least the saviour, of the Prime Minister's Government, ought not to be left unanswered. There ought to be the cut and thrust of debate, and I am surprised that the right hon. Gentleman, if not at that moment, at any rate at the earliest opportunity, did not take up the points of argument which were addressed to him. If issues of this kind are pushed aside, and ignored, and an attempt is made to carry the business of Parliament forward with the influence of the Whips, of the Central Office and of an indulgent Press—if that is to become the process, there is bound to be a weakening in the ties which unite the House to the Government and which preserve the vitality of our Parliamentary institutions.

The King Can Do No Wrong. There is an old constitutional doctrine that the King can do no wrong, and if the King does what is thought to be wrong it is his bad advisers who are blamed; but to apply that doctrine to the controversial head of a political government would be an altogether undue extension of the principle.   *Commons, April 6, 1936.*

Stanley Baldwin. It has been my fortune to have ups and downs in my political relations with him, the downs on the whole predominating perhaps, but at any rate we have always preserved agreeable personal relations, which, so far as I am concerned, are greatly valued. I am sure he would not wish in his conduct of public affairs that there should be any shrinking from putting the real issues of criticism which arise, and I shall certainly proceed in that sense.

Commons, November 12, 1936.

Members of Parliament. In the palmy days of Queen Victoria, great respect was paid to the position of a Member of Parliament. His status and authority were everywhere considered. He was much looked up to. Then came an interlude. As the franchise became more democratic, it grew to be the fashion in certain social circles to speak with contempt about Members of Parliament as a class and as a type. They were represented as mere spouters and chatterboxes, the putters of awkward questions and the raisers of small points of procedure. Kipling wrote his poem:

"Paget, M.P., was a liar, and a fluent liar herewith."

Commons, February 27, 1941.

Vote of Confidence. I ask the House for a Vote of Confidence. I hope that those, if such there be, who sincerely in their hearts believe that we are not doing our best and that they could do much better, I hope that they will carry their opinion to its logical and ultimate conclusion in the Lobby. Here I must point out, only for the benefit of foreign countries, that they would run no risk in doing so. They are answerable only to their consciences and to their constituents. It is a free Parliament in a free country. We have succeeded in maintaining, under difficulties which are unprecedented, and in dangers which, in some cases, might well be mortal, the whole process and reality of Parliamentary institutions. I am proud of this. It is one of the things for which we are fighting.

Commons, May 7, 1941.

Generalities. We are often told that "The House of Commons thinks this" or "feels that." Newspapers write: "The general feeling was of grave uneasiness," "There was much disquiet in the Lobby," etc. All this is telegraphed all over the world and produces evil effects. No one has a right to say what is the opinion of the House of Commons. We suffer now from not having divisions. We have debates, to which a very small minority of Members are able to contribute, because of the time available. They express their anxiety and grievances and make our affairs out as bad as they possibly can, and these views bulk unduly in the reports which reach the public or are heard abroad. These Members do not represent the opinion of the House of Commons or of the nation, nor do their statements give a true picture of the prodigious war efforts of the British people. Parilament should be an arena in which grievances and complaints became vocal. The Press also should be a prompt and vigilant alarm bell, ringing when things are not going right. But it is a heavy burden added to the others we have to bear if, without a vote being cast, the idea should be spread at home and abroad that it is the opinion of the House of Commons that our affairs are being conducted in an incompetent and futile manner and that the whole gigantic drive of British industry is just one great muddle and flop.   *Commons, July 29, 1941.*

Public Men. I owe advancement entirely to the House of Commons, whose servant I am. In my country, as in yours, public men are proud to be the servants of the State and would be ashamed to be its masters. On any day, if they thought the people wanted it, the House of Commons could by a simple vote remove me from my office. But I am not worrying about it at all.

U.S. Congress, Washington, D.C., December 26, 1941.

Parliament, the Master. The House is absolutely master. If its confidence is not extended to the Government, if it does not believe that the war is being well managed, if it thinks it can make arrangements which would lead to the war being better managed, it is the duty and the right of the House to express its opinion, as it can do in a proper and a constitutional manner.   *Commons, February 17, 1942.*

Code of Parliament. The vitality and the authority of the House of Commons, and its hold upon an electorate based upon universal suffrage, depend to no small extent upon its episodes and great moments, even upon its scenes and rows, which, as everyone will agree, are better conducted at close quarters. Destroy that hold which Parliament has upon the public mind and has preserved through all these changing, turbulent times, and the living organism of the House of Commons would be greatly impaired. You may have a machine, but the House of Commons is much more than a machine; it has earned and captured and held through long generations the imagination and respect of the British nation. It is not free from shortcomings; they mark all human institutions. Nevertheless, I submit to what is probably not an unfriendly audience on that subject that our House has proved itself capable of adapting itself to every change which the swift pace of modern life has brought upon us. It has a collective personality which enjoys the regard of the public, and which imposes itself upon the conduct, not only of individual Members, but of Parties. It has a code of its own which everyone knows, and it has means of its own of enforcing those manners and habits which have grown up and have been found to be an essential part of our Parliamentary life.

Shape of Assembly. There are two main characteristics of the House of Commons which will command the approval and the support of reflective and experienced Members. They will, I have no doubt, sound odd to foreign ears. The first is that its shape should be oblong and not semi-circular. Here is a very potent factor in our political life. The semi-circular assembly, which appeals to political theorists, enables every individual of every group to move round the centre, adopting various shades of pink according as the weather changes.

Crossing the Floor. I am a convinced supporter of the Party system in preference to the group system. I have seen many earnest and ardent Parliaments destroyed by the group system. The Party system is much favoured by the oblong form of Chamber. It is easy for an individual to move through those insensible gradations from Left to Right, but the act of crossing the floor is one which requires serious consideration. I am well informed on this matter, for I have accomplished that difficult process, not only once but twice.

Rebuilding Commons. On the night of May 10, 1941, with one of the last bombs of the last serious raid, our House of Commons was destroyed by the violence of the enemy, and we have now to consider whether we should build it up again, and how, and when. We shape our buildings, and afterwards our buildings shape us. Having dwelt and served for more than forty years in the late Chamber, and having derived very great pleasure and advantage therefrom, I, naturally, should like to see it restored in all essentials to its old form, convenience and dignity.

Size of Parliamentary Chamber. The second characteristic of a Chamber formed on the lines of the House of Commons is that it should not be big enough to contain all its Members at once without overcrowding, and that there should be no question of every Member having a separate seat reserved for him. The reason for this has long been a puzzle to uninstructed outsiders, and has frequently excited the curiosity and even the criticism of new Members. Yet it is not so difficult to understand if you look at it from a practical point of view. If the House is big enough to contain all its Members, nine-tenths of its debates will be conducted in the depressing atmosphere of an almost empty or half-empty Chamber. The essence of good House of Commons speaking is the conversational style, the facility for quick, informal interruptions and interchanges. Harangues from a rostrum would be a bad substitute for the conversational style in which so much of our business is done. But the conversational style requires a fairly small space, and there should be a sense of the importance of much that is said, and a sense that great matters are being decided, there and then, by the House.

Commons, October 28, 1943.

Understanding Politics. It is hard enough to understand the politics of one's own country; it is almost impossible to understand those of foreign countries.

Commons, February 22, 1944.

Function of Parliament. It must be remembered that the function of Parliament is not only to pass good laws, but to stop bad laws.   *Commons, April 4, 1944.*

Change of Mind. It is always bad for a government to change its mind, yet it ought to do so from time to time, out of respect to the House of Commons and out of the influence made upon its collective mind by the debates. But what is still worse is to change your mind and then have to change it again. That is a double disadvantage, and we must certainly avoid that.   *Commons, October 6, 1944.*

Parliamentary Recess. In the high and far-off times when I first entered this building, there was usually a six months' or five months' recess, between the grouse on the 12th August and the latter part of January or the beginning of February, when the House reassembled. I do not consider those days were without their wisdom. Do not—and this has a bearing on some of the remarks which have recently been made—ever suppose that you can strengthen Parliament by wearying it, and by keeping it in almost continuous session. If you want to reduce the power of Parliament, let it sit every day in the year, one-fifth part filled, and then you will find it will be the laughing-stock of the nation, instead of being, as it continues to be, in spite of all the strains of modern life, the citadel as well as the cradle of Parliamentary institutions throughout the world; almost the only successful instance of a legislative body with plenary powers, elected on universal suffrage, which is capable of discharging, with restraint and with resolution, all the functions of peace and of war.

Commons, November 29, 1944.

Constitutional Monarchy. If it be true, as has been said, that every country gets the form of government it deserves, we may certainly flatter ourselves. The wisdom of our ancestors has led us to an envied and enviable situation. We have the strongest Parliament in the world. We have the oldest, the most famous, the most honoured, the most secure and the most serviceable monarchy in the world. King and Parliament both rest safely and solidly upon the will of the people expressed by free and fair election on the basis of universal suffrage.

Commons, May 15, 1945.

Rule of the People. It is not Parliament that should rule; it is the people who should rule through Parliament.

Commons, November 11, 1947.

Changing Opinions. It is curious that, while in the days of my youth I was much reproached with inconsistency and being changeable, I am now scolded for adhering to the same views I had in early life and even for repeating passages from speeches which I made long before most of you were born. Of course the world moves on and we dwell in a constantly changing climate of opinion. But the broad principles and truths of wise and sane political actions do not necessarily alter with the changing moods of a democratic electorate. Not everything changes. Two and two still make four, and I could give you many other instances which go to prove that all wisdom is not new wisdom.

Belle Vue, Manchester, December 6, 1947.

Compulsory Voting. I have the strong view that voting should be compulsory as it is in Australia and in Holland and that there should be a small fine for people who do not choose to exercise their civic duty.

Commons, June 23, 1948.

Function of Second Chamber. The attitude and function of a Second Chamber in any land is essentially one of safeguarding and delaying violent or subversive measures which may endanger the long-gathered heritage of the whole people, without the gravity and significance of the issues involved being fairly and intelligibly placed before them.

Commons, October 18, 1948.

Principles of Liberalism. The Liberal Government of 1906 was built around and upon those great principles of Liberalism which have since passed into the possession of every

Party except the Communists, and are still spreading with irresistible appeal throughout the world.

Commons, September 28, 1949.

Function of the House of Lords. It is not the function of the House of Lords to govern the people but to make sure that the people have the right to govern themselves.

Commons, November 16, 1949.

Check on Maladministration. Control over taxation and the revenues of the state has always been the foundation on which Parliamentary Government has rested, and indeed there is no other foundation upon which it can rest. Once the state acquires sources of revenue independent of Parliament, then the power of Parliament to curb and check maladministration is seriously diminished.

Usher Hall, Edinburgh, May 18, 1950.

Votes. We must not forget what votes are. Votes are the means by which the poorest people in the country, and all people in the country, can make sure that they get their vital needs attended to. *Commons, November 6, 1950.*

Object of Parliament. The object of Parliament is to substitute arguments for fisticuffs. *Commons, June 6, 1951.*

Re-elections. It was a very important provision that Members, on appointment to high office, should submit themselves to re-election; it was a very important provision because it prevented a government different from that which the electors had in mind at the time of the election from taking and holding office for a time, and filling up all its posts, without the country having a chance to challenge the matter, with different persons, of perhaps quite different policies from those the electorate had been led to contemplate, and from those that the country might wish. A government so formed, even without a majority in the House—such a government might take executive action which would have irrevocable consequences either in the direction of war or peace. It was a safeguard of immense consequence, but the House parted with it. It has been totally discarded by the House in my lifetime.

Commons, February 27, 1952.

Arguing. No constitutional or democratic principle with which I am acquainted compels a Minister of the Crown to argue. He may be tempted to do so; but he cannot be compelled. *Commons, July 30, 1952.*

The Parliamentary Thrust

Sir Charles Dilke. I think that the right hon. Baronet is also a remarkable instance of a very peculiar phenomenon. I have always noticed that whenever a radical takes to Imperialism he catches it in a very acute form.

W. St. J. Brodrick. If the capacity of a War Minister may be measured in any way by the amount of money he can obtain from his colleagues for military purposes, the right hon. Gentleman will most certainly go down to history as the greatest War Minister this country has ever had.
Commons, May 13, 1901.

I had ever noticed that the right hon. Gentleman always made a very good speech when he was in a very difficult position: the more there was to be said against the cause he was defending the better the speech he made.
Commons, February 24, 1903.

All-night Sittings. Many objections could be urged against all-night sittings, but the ancestors of present Members had not been afraid to subject themselves to considerable strain and exertion in the interests of public and free discussion.
Commons, March 16, 1905.

Economy of Nature. In looking at the views of these two hon. Members [the brothers Sir Edgar Vincent and Col. Sir C. E. H. Vincent], I have always marvelled at the economy of nature which had contrived to grow from a single stock the nettle and the dock.
Commons, July 24, 1905.

Aliens Bill. How was the Aliens Bill passed? It was introduced to the House of Commons in a tumbril. They began debating it on the steps of the scaffold, and before two days had passed in Committee they were hurried to the framework of the guillotine.
Commons, July 31, 1905.

Irresponsibility of Opposition. I will only venture to congratulate the great Imperial statesmen who sit upon that bench upon the ease and celerity with which they have exchanged the responsibilities of office for the irresponsibilities of opposition.
Commons, February 22, 1906.

The Wincing Marquis. Lord Landsdowne has explained, to the amusement of the nation, that he claimed no right on behalf of the House of Lords to "mince" the Budget. All,

44

he tells us, he has asked for, so far as he is concerned, is the right to "wince" when swallowing it. Well, that is a much more modest claim. It is for the Conservative Party to judge whether it is a very heroic claim for one of their leaders to make. If they are satisfied with the wincing Marquis, we have no reason to protest.

Norwich, July 16, 1909.

Gullets. I have heard of people straining at a gnat and swallowing a camel, but I have never before heard of people who, having already swallowed a camel, come forward and plead that their gullets are not sufficiently expansive to accommodate a gnat.

Commons, April 12, 1910.

Lord Charles Beresford, M.P. He is one of those orators of whom it was well said, "Before they get up, they do not know what they are going to say; when they are speaking, they do not know what they are saying; and when they sit down, they do not know what they have said."

Commons, December 20, 1912.

Anger. If I valued the hon. Gentleman's [Sir J. Lonsdale, M.P.] opinion I might get angry.

Commons, January 1, 1913.

Philip Snowden. A perverse destiny has seemed to brood over the right hon. Gentleman's career; all his life has been one long struggle to overcome the natural amiability of his character.

Commons, May 25, 1925.

Strong Language. I have no objection to a proper use of strong language, but a certain amount of art and a certain amount of selective power is needed, if the effect is to be produced.

Commons, December 9, 1925.

Ramsay MacDonald. The Government are defeated by thirty votes and then the Prime Minister rises in his place, utterly unabashed, the greatest living master of falling without hurting himself, and airily assures us that nothing has happened.

Commons, January 21, 1931.

I remember, when I was a child, being taken to the celebrated Barnum's Circus, which contained an exhibition of freaks and monstrosities, but the exhibit on the programme which I most desired to see was the one described as "The Boneless Wonder." My parents judged that that spectacle would be too revolting and demoralizing for my youthful eyes, and I have waited fifty years to see the Boneless Wonder sitting on the Treasury Bench.

Commons, January 28, 1931.

Here I say very little of the Prime Minister's oratorical style. We are familiar with it here. We know that he has, more than any other man, the gift of compressing the largest number of words into the smallest amount of thought. We have heard him on so many topics, from India to unemployment, providing us, apparently, with an inexhaustible flow of vague, well-sounding exhortations, the precise purpose of which is largely wrapped in mystery, and which, as far as it can be discerned, can be understood differently in different quarters, according to taste. *Commons, March 23, 1933.*

Lord Baldwin. In those days Mr. Baldwin was wiser than he is now; he used frequently to take my advice.

Commons, May 22, 1935.

Neville Chamberlain. I will avail myself of the avuncular relationship which I hope I may still possess in respect of the Government to put it to the Prime Minister personally and even intimately. Has he ever heard of Saint Anthony the Hermit? Saint Anthony the Hermit was much condemned by the Fathers of the Church because he refused to do right when the Devil told him to. My right hon. Friend should free himself from this irrational inhibition, for we are only at the beginning of our anxieties. *Commons, May 25, 1938.*

Guilty Conscience. My right hon. Friend the Air Minister [Sir Kingsley Wood] has not been long enough in the office to grow a guilty conscience.

Commons, November 17, 1938.

Strong Language. I do not think any expression of scorn or severity which I have heard used by our critics has come anywhere near the language which I have been myself accustomed to use, not only orally, but in a stream of written minutes. In fact, I wonder that a great many of my colleagues are on speaking terms with me.

Commons, June 25, 1941.

Criticizing the Government. There was a custom in ancient China that everyone who wished to criticize the Government had the right to memorialize the Emperor, and provided he followed that up by committing suicide, very great respect was paid to his words, and no ulterior motive was assigned. That seems to me to have been, from many points of view, a wise custom, but I certainly would be the last to suggest that it should be made retrospective.

Commons, November 12, 1941.

Laval. I am afraid I have rather exhausted the possibilities of the English language. *Commons, September 29, 1942.*

Mistakes. I am sure that the mistakes of that time [concerning German Reparations] will not be repeated; we shall make another set of mistakes.

Commons, June 8, 1944.

Aneurin Bevan. I should think it was hardly possible to state the opposite of the truth with more precision. I back up those who seek to establish democracy and civilization. The hon. Member must learn to take as well as to give. There is no one more free with interruptions, taunts, and jibes than he is. I saw him—I heard him, not saw him—almost assailing some of the venerable figures on the bench immediately below him. He need not get so angry because the House laughs at him: he ought to be pleased when they only laugh at him.

Commons, December 8, 1944.

Lord Winterton. He is a comparatively young Father of the House; he has many years of life before him. We still hope they may be years of useful life in this House, but unless in the future his sagacity and knowledge of the House are found to be markedly more superior to what he has exhibited to-day, I must warn him that he will run a very grave risk of falling into senility before he is overtaken by old age.

Commons, March 7, 1945.

Sir Stafford Cripps. Neither of his colleagues can compare with him in that acuteness and energy of mind with which he devotes himself to so many topics injurious to the strength and welfare of the State.

Commons, December 12, 1946.

Home and Abroad. When I am abroad I always make it a rule never to criticize or attack the Government of my own country. I make up for lost time when I come home.

Commons, April 18, 1947.

Expert Advice. I am a Parliamentarian myself, I have always been one. I think that a Minister is entitled to disregard expert advice. What he is not entitled to do is to pretend he is acting upon it, when, in fact, he is acting contrary to it.

Commons, May 7, 1947.

Folly. It would be a great reform in politics if wisdom could be made to spread as easily and as rapidly as folly.

Commons, August 16, 1947.

Lust for Power. No government has ever combined so passionate a lust for power with such incurable impotence in its exercise.

Commons, November 11, 1947.

History. In case of any forthcoming General Election there may be an attempt to revive these former controversies. We are taking steps to have little booklets prepared recording the utterances at different moments, of all the principal figures involved in those baffling times. For my part, I consider that it will be found much better by all Parties to leave the past to history, especially as I purpose to write that history myself.
Commons, January 23, 1948.

Dr. Hugh Dalton. Dr. Dalton, the practitioner who never cured anyone.
London, February 14, 1948.

Clement Attlee. Mr. Attlee combines a limited outlook with strong qualities of resistance.
Royal Albert Hall, London, April 27, 1951.

Political Opponents. The spectacle of a number of middle-aged gentlemen who are my political opponents being in a state of uproar and fury is really quite exhilarating to me.

Herbert Morrison. The right hon. Member for Lewisham, South, is a curious mixture of geniality and venom. The geniality, I may say after a great many years' experience, is natural to himself. The venom has to be adopted in order to keep on sides with the forces below the gangway.
Commons, May 21, 1952.

Teaching. I am always ready to learn, although I do not always like being taught.
Commons, November 4, 1952.

Motion of Censure. I have to-day to deal with a motion of censure and therefore I hope I shall be pardoned if I do not confine myself entirely to the uncontroversial methods which I usually practice.
Commons, December 4, 1952.

R. H. S. Crossman (M.P.). The hon. Member is never lucky in the coincidence of his facts with the truth.
Commons, July 14, 1954.

Judgments on His Contemporaries

General Bruce Hamilton. The hon. Member for Caernar-von Boroughs [Mr. David Lloyd George] has drawn attention to the case of one general officer, and although I deprecate debates upon the characters of individual general officers who are serving the country at this moment, because I know per-

sonally General Bruce Hamilton, whom the hon. Member with admirable feeling described as General Brute Hamilton, I feel unable to address the House without offering my humble testimony to the fact that in all His Majesty's army there are few men with better feeling, more kindness of heart, or with higher courage than General Bruce Hamilton.
Commons, February 18, 1901.

A. J. Balfour. Office at any price was his motto, at the sacrifice of any friend or colleague, at the sacrifice of any principle, by the adoption of any manoeuvre, however miserable or contemptible. *Commons, April 5, 1905.*

The hon. Gentleman looked upon the hours spent in the House as a spell upon the Parliamentary treadmill, and as part of the purchase price of office and power.
Commons, July 5, 1905.

Lord Fisher. The more Lord Fisher's contribution to our naval efficiency is studied and examined, and tested by the passage of time, the more certainly will it be established that there has been within living memory no naval administrator possessed of abilities so rare and so distinguished.
Commons, August 5, 1913.

Admiral Sir David Beatty. In Sir David Beatty we have a Commander-in-Chief who, by his gifts and also by his exceptional training, not only possesses the regular qualifications which admirals of distinction possess, but he has, perhaps, in a greater degree than almost any of the principal officers of the fleet, what may be called the "war mind." It is not only seamanship or technical attainments or even leadership of men that are required in a Commander-in-Chief, but also that feeling towards the art of war, that deep comprehension of its sombre yet simple problems, without which all other qualifications, however valuable, however laboriously attained, still only receive a limited scope.
Commons, February 21, 1917.

Sir Austen Chamberlain. The House has not always done justice to Sir Austen Chamberlain's conduct of foreign affairs. He was very much scolded and condemned at the close of the late Conservative Administration, but the Locarno Treaty and all that followed from it was a model of skillful peace-seeking diplomacy. Although other difficulties have come in other times, I cannot see that the handling of the Foreign Office since he left it should fill him with any particular feeling of humiliation. *Commons, April 13, 1933.*

Anthony Eden. I venture to suggest to my hon. Friend, in whose career the whole House has a common interest, because we do like to see new figures emerge, to be careful not to be too obliging in his departmental duties, and not to be too ready to do what is asked of him on all occasions, because he is very valuable, and we all hope that he will be associated with real success in the domain of foreign affairs.

Commons, March 14, 1934.

He is the one fresh figure of the first magnitude arising out of a generation which was ravaged by the war.

Commons, February 1938.

Sir Reginald Henderson. I should like to associate myself with the tribute . . . paid to Admiral Sir Reginald Henderson. Those of us who know that officer—and I knew him when he was gunnery lieutenant doing the gunnery trials of the ships we were building before the Great War—will realize the rare and remarkable qualities which he brought to the service of the Royal Navy. He has expended his energy, his life, his thought, his mental energy, an attribute which is rare nowadays, in the most generous manner, and if he has been stricken down by an affliction, which we all hope is only temporary, he is in exactly the same position as a brave officer who is wounded fighting for his country in action. It is well known that at the most critical period of the war this officer, then in a subordinate station, taking his career in his hands, presented facts and figures and arguments which eventually reached the highest authority—the Prime Minister —and that through that report a great change was made in our naval disposition, without which it could not be said with certainty that the submarine menace at that time would have been overcome.

Commons, March 16, 1939.

Lady Astor. When the right hon. Member for Caithness [Sir Archibald Sinclair] dwelt on the point of Russia and emphasized it, I heard a sort of commotion behind me. I heard the Noble Lady the Member for the Sutton Division of Plymouth express her dislike of any contact with Bolshevik Russia. Where was this dislike when she paid a visit to Soviet Russia with Mr. Bernard Shaw? The Noble Lady was treated with great consideration. But the point which the House should notice—it is a very serious point, and I hope I shall be able to put it without any offence, is that the time when she went to Russia and gave all her applause and credit to Russia, was a time when the influence of Russia was deeply detrimental to the interests of this country.

Commons, April 13, 1939.

Neville Chamberlain. He was, like his father and his brother Austen before him, a famous Member of the House of Commons, and we here assembled this morning, Members of all parties, without a single exception, feel that we do ourselves and our country honour in saluting the memory of one whom Disraeli would have called an "English worthy." . . .

The fierce and bitter controversies which hung around him in recent times were hushed by the news of his illness and are silenced by his death. In paying a tribute of respect and of regard to an eminent man who has been taken from us, no one is obliged to alter the opinions which he has formed or expressed upon issues which have become a part of history; but at the Lychgate we may all pass our own conduct and our own judgments under a searching review. It is not given to human beings, happily for them, for otherwise life would be intolerable, to foresee or to predict to any large extent the unfolding course of events. In one phase men seem to have been right, in another they seem to have been wrong. Then again, a few years later, when the perspective of time has lengthened, all stands in a different setting. There is a new proportion. There is another scale of values. History with its flickering lamp stumbles along the trail of the past, trying to reconstruct its scenes, to revive its echoes, and kindle with pale gleams the passion of former days. What is the worth of all this? The only guide to a man is his conscience; the only shield to his memory is the rectitude and sincerity of his actions. It is very imprudent to walk through life without this shield, because we are often mocked by the failure of our hopes and the upsetting of our calculations; but with this shield, however the fates may play, we march always in the ranks of honour. . . .

It fell to Neville Chamberlain in one of the supreme crises of the world to be contradicted by events, to be disappointed in his hopes, and to be deceived and cheated by a wicked man. But what were these wishes in which he was frustrated? What was that faith that was abused? They were surely among the most noble and benevolent instincts of the human heart—the love of peace, the toil for peace, the strife for peace, the pursuit of peace, even at great peril, and certainly to the utter disdain of popularity or clamour. Whatever else history may or may not say about these terrible tremendous years, we can be sure that Neville Chamberlain acted with perfect sincerity according to his lights and strove to the utmost of his capacity and authority, which were powerful, to save the world from the awful, devastating struggle in which we are now engaged. This alone will stand him in good stead as far as what is called the verdict of history is concerned. . . .

I do not propose to give an appreciation of Neville Chamberlain's life and character, but there were certain qualities always admired in these islands which he possessed in an altogether exceptional degree. He had a physical and moral toughness of fibre which enabled him all through his varied career to endure misfortune and disappointment without being unduly discouraged or wearied. He had a precision of mind and an aptitude for business which raised him far above the ordinary levels of our generation. He had a firmness of spirit which was not often elated by success, seldom downcast by failure, and never swayed by panic. When, contrary to all his hopes, beliefs and exertions, the war came upon him, and when, as he himself said, all that he had worked for was shattered, there was no man more resolved to pursue the unsought quarrel to the death. The same qualities which made him one of the last to enter the war, made him one of the last who would quit it before the full victory of a righteous cause was won.

Commons, November 12, 1940.

Lord Lothian. He was a man of the very highest character, and of far-ranging intellectual scope. All his life his mind played about broad issues of human progress, and, whether at home or abroad, he animated an ardent philanthropy with the keenest and brightest intellectual powers. In India his work is much respected. His work in the last war was already important, as Mr. Lloyd George—whom I am very glad to see here to-day—could no doubt remind us. But all the same, when he was appointed before the war to the Embassy in the United States, the most important of all the functions outside this country that can be discharged by any British subject, there were various opinions upon the wisdom of that choice. Very soon, however, it was seen that the new ambassador was gaining in influence every day, that his stature rose with the greatness of the topics confided to him, and that the contacts which he established, the intimate relations which he developed, with the high personnel of the United States Administration, the friendship to which the President of the United States has himself testified —all the evidence showed the remarkable efficiency and success with which he discharged his important and extremely delicate and difficult mission.

Suddenly, he is taken from us. He passes away. But I cannot help feeling that to die at the height of a man's career, the highest moment of his effort here in this world, universally honoured and admired, to die while great issues are still commanding the whole of his interest, to be taken from us at a moment when he could already see ultimate success in view—is not the most unenviable of fates. I feel that the House would have wished me to express, in these few words, the sorrow which we feel at his death, and also the very grievous and practical sense that we have of the loss we have suffered at this particular juncture in being deprived of his invaluable service.

Commons, December 19, 1940.

Lord Halifax. In Edward Halifax we have a man of light and leading, whose company is a treat and whose friendship it is an honour to enjoy. I have often disagreed with him in the twenty years I have known him in the rough and tumble of British politics, but I have always respected him and his actions because I know that courage and fidelity are the essence of his being, and that, whether as soldier with his regiment in the last war or as a ruler of, and trustee for, 400,000,000 in India, he has never swerved from the path of duty as he saw it shining out before him.

As a man of deep but unparaded and unaffected religious convictions, and as for many years an ardent lover of the chase, he has known how to get the best out of both worlds. Like all Members of the present National Government in Great Britain, most of whom seem to be gathered around this board to-day, he has vowed himself to prosecute this war against the Nazi tyranny at whatever cost until its last vestiges are destroyed.

General Auchinleck. Although the battle is not yet finished, I have no hesitation in saying that for good or ill, it is General Auchinleck's battle. Watching these affairs, as it is my duty to do, from day to day, and often from hour to hour, and seeing the seamy side of the reports as they come in, I have felt my confidence in General Auchinleck grow continually, and although everything is hazardous in war, I believe we have found in him, as we have also found in General Wavell, a military figure of the first order.

Commons, December 11, 1941.

Duke of Connaught. The late Duke of Connaught lived a life so long that it was not only a link with the tranquil days of the Victorian era, when a large number of people had persuaded themselves that most of the problems of society were solved, but also a link with the life of the Duke of Wellington. During the whole of his career, mainly in the British army, he was a devoted, faithful officer and servant of the Crown. He held a position of delicacy, not free from difficulty, beset on every side by the possibility of indiscretion when such a position is occupied by one who is a son of a queen, afterwards a brother of a king, uncle of another sovereign and the great-uncle of a fourth ruler. In that position, never did anything occur which did not make the public realize how true the Duke of Connaught was to all the constitutional implications of this position, and all who came in contact with him were impressed by his charm of manner, by his old-world courtesy, and knew that they were in the presence of a great and distinguished representative of our beloved Royal House.

Commons, January 20, 1942.

Lord Baden-Powell. I first met B.-P. many years before the birth of the Scout Movement. He was a man of character, vision and enthusiasm, and he passed these qualities on to the movement which has played, and is playing, an important part in moulding the character of our race. Sturdiness, neighbourliness, practical competence, love of country, and above all, in these times, indomitable resolve, daring and enterprise in the face of the enemy, these are the hallmarks of a scout. . . . "Be Prepared" to stand up faithfully for right and truth however the winds may blow. *London, July 16, 1942.*

Stalin. He is a man of massive outstanding personality, suited to the sombre and stormy times in which his life has been cast; a man of inexhaustible courage and will-power, and a man direct and even blunt in speech, which, having been brought up in the House of Commons, I do not mind at all, especially when I have something to say of my own. Above all, he is a man with that saving sense of humour which is of high importance to all men and all nations, but particularly to great men and great nations. Stalin also left upon me the impression of a deep, cool wisdom, and a complete absence of illusions of any kind.

Commons, September 8, 1942.

King George VI. I have seen the King, gay, buoyant and confident when the stones and rubble of Buckingham Palace lay newly scattered in heaps upon its lawns.

Edinburgh, October 12, 1942.

Jan Christiaan Smuts. He and I are old comrades. I cannot say there has ever been a kick in our gallop. I was examined by him when I was a prisoner of war, and I escaped; but we made an honourable and generous peace on both sides, and for the last forty years we have been comrades working together.

Westminster Central Hall, London, October 31, 1942.

Field-Marshal Sir Bernard Montgomery. Let me also pay my tribute to this vehement and formidable General Montgomery, a Cromwellian figure, austere, severe, accomplished, tireless, his life given to the study of war, who has attracted to himself in an extraordinary measure the confidence and the devotion of his army. *Commons, February 11, 1943.*

General Wladyslaw Sikorski. We learned yesterday that the cause of the United Nations had suffered a most grievous loss. It is my duty to express the feelings of this House, and to pay tribute to the memory of a great Polish patriot and staunch ally, General Sikorski. His death in the air crash at Gibraltar was one of the heaviest strokes we have sustained. From the first dark days of the Polish catastrophe and the brutal triumph of the German war machine until the moment of his death on Sunday night, he was the symbol and the embodiment of that spirit which has borne the Polish nation through centuries of sorrow and is unquenchable by agony.

Commons, July 6, 1943.

General Dwight D. Eisenhower. General Eisenhower assumed the command of the Expeditionary Force gathered in Britain. No man has ever laboured more skillfully or intensely for the unification and good will of the great forces under his command than General Eisenhower. He has a genius for bringing all the allies together, and is proud to consider himself an allied as well as a United States commander.

Commons, August 2, 1944.

Anthony Eden. Here is the moment when the House should pay its tribute to the work of my right hon. Friend the Foreign Secretary. I cannot describe to the House the aid and comfort he has been to me in all our difficulties. His hard life when quite young in the infantry in the last war, his constant self-preparation for the tasks which have fallen to him, his unequalled experience as a minister at the Foreign Office, his knowledge of foreign affairs and their past history, his experience of conferences of all kinds, his breadth of view, his powers of exposition, his moral courage, have gained for him a position second to none among the Foreign Secretaries of the Grand Alliance. It is not only my own personal debt but even more, that of the House to him, which I now acknowledge.

Commons, February 27, 1945.

Lloyd George. When the calm, complacent, self-satisfied tranquillities of the Victorian era had exploded into the world convulsions and wars of the terrible twentieth century, Lloyd George had another part to play on which his fame will stand with equal or even greater firmness. Although unacquainted with the military arts, although by public repute a pugnacious pacifist, when the life of our country was in peril he rallied to the war effort and cast aside all other thoughts and aims. . . .

I was his lieutenant in those bygone days, and shared in a minor way in the work. I have lived to see long strides taken, and being taken, and going to be taken, on this path of insurance by which the vultures of utter ruin are driven from the dwellings of the nation. The stamps we lick, the roads we travel, the system of progressive taxation, the principal remedies that have so far been used against unemployment—all these to a very great extent were part not only of the mission but of the actual achievement of Lloyd George; and I am sure that as time passes, his name will not only live but shine on account of the great laborious, constructive work he did for the social and domestic life of our country.

Commons, March 28, 1945.

President Franklin Delano Roosevelt. I conceived an admiration for him as a statesman, a man of affairs, and a war leader. I felt the utmost confidence in his upright, inspiring character and outlook, and a personal regard—affection I must say—for him beyond my power to express to-day. His love of his own country, his respects for its constitution, his power of gauging the tides and currents of its mobile public opinion, were always evident, but added to these were the beatings of that generous heart which was always stirred to anger and to action by spectacles of aggression and oppression by the strong against the weak. It is, indeed, a loss, a bitter loss to humanity that those heart-beats are stilled for ever. . . .

At Yalta I noticed that the President was ailing. His captivating smile, his gay and charming manner, had not deserted him, but his face had a transparency, an air of purification, and often there was a faraway look in his eyes. When I took my leave of him in Alexandria harbour I must confess that I had an indefinable sense of fear that his health and his strength were on the ebb. . . .

President Roosevelt's physical affliction lay heavily upon him. It was a marvel that he bore up against it through all the many years of tumult and storm. Not one man in ten millions, stricken and crippled as he was, would have attempted to plunge into a life of physical and mental exertion and of hard, ceaseless political controversy. Not one in ten millions would have tried, not one in a generation would have succeeded, not only in entering this sphere, not only in acting vehemently in it, but in becoming indisputable master of the scene. In this extraordinary effort of the spirit over the flesh, of will-power over physical infirmity, he was inspired and sustained by that noble woman, his devoted wife, whose high ideals marched with his own, and to whom the deep and respectful sympathy of the House of Commons flows out to-day in all fullness.

Commons, April 17, 1945.

King George VI. I do not think that any Prime Minister has ever received so much personal kindness and encouragement from his sovereign as I have. Every week I have my audience, the greater part of which occurs most agreeably at luncheon, and I have seen the King at close quarters in every phase of our formidable experiences. I remember well how in the first months of this administration the King would come in from practising with his rifle and his tommy-gun in the garden at Buckingham Palace, and if it had come to a last stand in London, a matter which had to be considered at one time, I have no doubt that His Majesty would have come very near departing from his usual constitutional rectitude by disregarding the advice of his ministers. *Commons, May 15, 1945.*

President Franklin Delano Roosevelt. When we come to speak of Franklin Roosevelt, however, we enter the sphere of British history and of world history, far above the ebb and flow of Party politics on either side of the Atlantic. And I shall not hesitate to affirm, and indeed to repeat, that he was the greatest American friend that Britain ever found, and the foremost champion of freedom and justice who has ever stretched strong hands across the oceans to rescue Europe and Asia from tyranny or destruction. *London, April 12, 1948.*

Herbert Henry Asquith. At forty, with a massive legal record behind him, he was Home Secretary. At fifty he was Prime Minister. He made his way by his distinction in the House of Commons debate, clear-cut, lucid argument, expressed in happy terms with many a glint of humour and flash of repartee, brevity as well as clarity—these were his weapons in those days of lengthy, sonorous harangues. He was no ebullient orator pouring forth his sentimental or passionate appeal. But few there were who could face him in the tense debating of issues, large or small. Here was a man who dealt in reasoned processes, who placed things in their proper scale and relation, who saw the root of the matter and simplified the tale. *Commons, December 6, 1950.*

Ernest Bevin. He takes his place among the great Foreign Secretaries of our country, and in his steadfast resistance to Communist aggression, in his strengthening of our ties with the United States and in his share of building up the Atlantic Pact, he has rendered services to Britain and to the cause of peace which will long be remembered. *London, March 17, 1951.*

Queen Mary. During six reigns, far longer, that is, than most people can remember, she has moved among us with the poise and dignity which, as age drew on, made her a figure of almost legendary distinction. . . . When she was born, Napoleon III ruled in France and Palmerston had only recently ceased to be Prime Minister of this country. Railways were comparatively new; electric light and the internal combustion engine were unknown. She knew Gladstone and Disraeli; her grandfather was the son of George III. Yet she lived into this atomic age, through two fearful wars which cast almost all the thrones of Europe to the ground, and rent but also transformed the world. The chasm which scientific invention and social change have wrought between 1867 and 1953 is so wide that it requires not only courage but mental resilience for those whose youth lay in calmer and more slowly moving times in order that they may adjust themselves to the giant outlines and harsh structure of the twentieth century.

B.B.C., March 25, 1953.

II. A WORLD CITIZEN LOOKS
AT THE WORLD

Germany and Hitler

Defeat at Sea. Defeat to Germany at sea means nothing but loss of the ships sunk or damaged in battle. Behind the German "Dreadnoughts" stand four and a half million soldiers and a narrow sea-front bristling with fortresses and batteries. Nothing we could do, after a naval victory could effect the safety or freedom of a single German hamlet.

Commons, March 17, 1914.

Defeat. While the German lines extend far beyond their frontiers, while their flag flies over conquered capitals and subjugated provinces, while all the appearances of military successes attend their arms, Germany may be defeated more fatally in the second or third year of the war than if the allied armies had entered Berlin in the first.

Commons, November 15, 1915.

Aerial Defence. In an aerial war the greatest form of defence will undoubtedly be offence.

Commons, March 21, 1922.

Mercantile Ascendancy. Absolved from all the burden of reparations, with a moratorium upon all commercial debts, with her factories equipped to the very last point of science by British and American money, freed from internal debt, mortgages, fixed charges, debentures and so forth, by the original flight from the mark, Germany only awaits trade revival to gain an immense mercantile ascendancy throughout the world.

Reparations. Let me give one striking instance which came to my notice when I was crossing the Atlantic Ocean. We and America took under the Peace Treaty three great liners from Germany. The Germans surrendered them at a valuation and then borrowed the money to build two very much better ones. They immediately captured the Blue Riband of the Atlantic, and they have it still. Now the loans with which the Germans built these ships are subject to a moratorium, while we are unable to go on with our new Cunarder because of our financial crisis. That is typical of what I mean when I say that Germany has not nearly so much reason to complain as some people suppose.

Commons, July 11, 1932.

Rearmament. Now the demand is that Germany should be allowed to rearm. Do not delude yourselves. Do not let His Majesty's Government believe—I am sure they do not believe—that all that Germany is asking for is equal status. I believe the refined term now is equal qualitative status, or, as an alternative, equal quantitative status by indefinitely deferred stages. That is not what Germany is seeking. All these bands of sturdy Teutonic youths, marching through the streets and roads of Germany, with the light of desire in their eyes to suffer for their Fatherland, when they have the weapons, believe me they will then ask for the return of lost territories and lost colonies, and when that demand is made it cannot fail to shake and possibly shatter to their foundations every one of the countries I have mentioned, and some other countries I have not mentioned.

Commons, November 23, 1932.

War Spirit. When we read about Germany, when we watch with surprise and distress the tumultuous insurgence of ferocity and war spirit, the pitiless ill-treatment of minorities, the denial of the mortal protection of civilized society to large numbers of individuals solely on the ground of race—when we see that occurring in one of the most gifted, learned, scientific and formidable nations in the world, one cannot help feeling glad that the fierce passions that are raging in Germany have not found, as yet, any other outlet but upon Germans.

Commons, March 23, 1933.

Rearmament. It is extremely dangerous for people to talk lightly about German rearmament and say that, if the Germans choose to do it, no one can stop them. I am very doubtful if Germany would rearm in defiance of the Treaty if there were a solidarity of European and world opinion that the Treaty could only be altered by discussion, and could not be altered by a violent one-sided breach. I, therefore, do not subscribe to the doctrine that we should throw up our hands and recognize the fact that Germany is going to be armed up to an equality with the neighbouring states in any period which we can immediately foresee. There may be other periods, but certainly we ought not to admit it at the moment.

Concessions. I do not think that we need break our hearts in deploring the treatment that Germany is receiving now. Germany is not satisfied; but no concession which has been made has produced any very marked appearance of gratitude.

Once it has been conceded it has seemed less valuable than when it was demanded.

Renewal of War. Nothing in life is eternal, of course, but as surely as Germany acquires full military equality with her neighbours while her own grievances are still unredressed and while she is in the temper which we have unhappily seen, so surely should we see ourselves within a measurable distance of the renewal of general European war.

Commons, April 13, 1933.

Aerial Defence. I cannot see in the present administration of Germany any assurance that they would be more nice-minded in dealing with a vital and supreme situation than was the Imperial Government of Germany, which was responsible for this procedure being adopted towards France. No, Sir, and we may, within a measurable period of time, in the lifetime of those who are here, if we are not in a proper state of security, be confronted on some occasion with a visit from an ambassador, and may have to give an answer in a very few hours; and if that answer is not satisfactory, within the next few hours the crash of bombs exploding in London and cataracts of masonry and fire and smoke will apprise us of any inadequacy which has been permitted in our aerial defences.

Commons, February 7, 1934.

New Rulers. Germany is ruled by a handful of autocrats who are the absolute masters of that gifted nation. They are men who have neither the long interests of a dynasty to consider, nor those very important restraints which a democratic Parliament and constitutional system impose upon any executive government. Nor have they the restraint of public opinion, which public opinion, indeed, they control by every means which modern apparatus renders possible. They are men who owe their power to, and are, indeed, the expression of the bitterness of defeat, and of the resolved and giant strength of that mighty German Empire.   *Commons, March 8, 1934.*

Politics. Politics in Germany are not what they are over here. There you do not leave Office to go into Opposition. You do not leave the Front Bench to sit below in the Gangway. You may well leave your high office at a quarter of an hour's notice to drive to the police station, and you may be conducted thereafter, very rapidly, to an even harder ordeal.

Commons, July 13, 1934.

Air Superiority. If Germany continues this expansion and if we continue to carry out our scheme, then some time in 1936 Germany will be definitely and substantially stronger in the air than Great Britain.   *Commons, July 30, 1934.*

Rearmament. What is the great new fact which has broken in upon us during the last eighteen months? Germany is rearming. That is the great new fact which rivets the attention of every country in Europe—indeed, in the world—and which throws almost all other issues into the background.

Strength. Beware. Germany is a country fertile in military surprises. The great Napoleon, in the years after Jena, was completely taken by surprise by the strength of the German army which fought the War of Liberation. Although he had officers all over the place, the German army which fought in the campaign of Leipzig was three or four times as strong as he expected.   *Commons, November 28, 1934.*

Armaments. Here, again, mystery shrouds all German preparations. At various points facts emerge which enable a general view to be taken. Enormous sums of money are being spent on German aviation and upon other armaments. I wish we could get at the figures which are being spent upon armaments. I believe that they would stagger us with the terrible tale they would tell of the immense panoply which that nation of nearly 70,000,000 of people is assuming, or has already assumed.   *Commons, May 19, 1935.*

Arms Production. The arms production has the first claim on the entire industry of Germany. The materials required for the production of armaments are the first charge of the German exchange. The whole of their industry is woven into an immediate readiness for war. You have a state of preparedness in German industry which was not attained by our industry until after the late War had gone on probably for two years.   *Commons, May 31, 1935.*

The German People. I bear no grudge; I have no prejudice against the German people. I have many German friends, and I have a lively admiration for their splendid qualities of intellect and valour and for their achievements in science and art. The re-entry into the European circle of a Germany at peace within itself, with a heart devoid of hate, would be the most precious benefit for which we could strive, and a supreme advantage which alone would liberate Europe from its peril and its fear, and I believe that the British and French democracies would go a long way in extending the hand of friendship to realize such a hope.

Rearmament. There is even a theory that the Germans are rearming only out of national self-respect and that they do not mean to hurt anyone at all. Whatever you believe, whatever you think, I venture to submit that we cannot have any anxieties comparable to the anxiety caused by German re-armament.

Readiness for War. Germany is already well on her way to become, and must become, incomparably the most heavily armed nation in the world and the nation most completely ready for war. *There* is the dominant factor; *there* is the factor which dwarfs all others, and affects the movements of politics and diplomacy in every country throughout Europe; and it is a melancholy reflection in the last hours of this Parliament that we have been the helpless, perhaps even the supine, spectators of this vast transformation, to the acute distress of Europe and to our own grievous disadvantage.

Commons, October 24, 1935.

War Preparations. What is the real problem, the real peril? It is not reoccupation of the Rhineland, but this enormous process of the rearmament of Germany. There is the peril. Mr. Lansbury says that in the Election I seemed to be haunted by this thought. I confess that I have been occupied with this idea of the great wheels revolving and the great hammers descending day and night in Germany, making the whole of its population into one disciplined war machine. There is the problem that lies before you. There is what is bringing war nearer. This Rhineland episode is but a step, a stage, an incident in this process. There is fear in every country, all round. Even here, in this island, with some protection from distance, there is fear, deep fear. What is the fear and what is the question which arises from that fear? It is, "How are we going to stop this war which seems to be moving towards us in so many ways?"

Commons, March 26, 1936.

Encirclement of Germany. What then, is this talk about encirclement? It is all nonsense. There is nothing that we ask for ourselves under collective security that we will not willingly concede, nay earnestly proffer, to Germany. Let her join the club, and make her great contribution and share its amenities and immunities.

Commons, November 5, 1936.

Negotiations. When we are asked whether we will grasp the proffered hand of German friendship, I think we should answer "Yes," but at the same time one wants to know what happens after that. Often when these conversations begin they go nicely for a certain time, and then it appears that what the Germans want is that peace and good will should be translated forthwith into tangible and solid immediate benefits to themselves. Very often it is suggested that we should promise to do something, or, what is perhaps even more difficult, stand by and see something or other done that may not be desirable. When the conversations reach that point, they become halting and embarrassed.

Commons, December 21, 1937.

Vain Argument. In the German view, which Herr Hitler shares, a peaceful Germany and Austria were fallen upon in 1914 by a gang of wicked designing nations, headed by Belgium and Serbia, and would have defended herself successfully if only she had not been stabbed in the back by the Jews. Against such opinions it is vain to argue.

London, April 28, 1939.

Atrocities. Field-Marshal Goering—who is one of the few Germans who has been having a pretty good time for the last few years—says that we have been spared so far because Nazi Germany is so humane. They cannot bear to do anything to hurt anybody. All they ask for is the right to live and to be let alone to conquer and kill the weak. Their humanity forbids them to apply severities to the strong. It may be true: but when we remember the bestial atrocities they have committed in Poland, we do not feel we wish to ask for any favours to be shown us. We shall do our duty as long as we have life and strength.

Commons, November 8, 1939.

Avalanche. More than a million German soldiers, including all their active divisions and armoured divisions, are drawn up ready to attack, at a few hours' notice, all along the frontiers of Luxembourg, of Belgium and of Holland. At any moment these neutral countries may be subjected to an avalanche of steel and fire; and the decision rests in the hands of a haunted, morbid being, who, to their eternal shame, the German peoples in their bewilderment have worshipped as a god.

London, March 30, 1940.

Bombing of Germany. Even if the Nazi legions stood triumphant on the Black Sea, or indeed upon the Caspian, even if Hitler was at the gates of India, it would profit him nothing if at the same time the entire economic and scientific apparatus of German war power lay shattered and pulverized at home.

Commons, August 20, 1940.

Hitler's Empire. No one can say how far Herr Hitler's empire will extend before this war is over, but I have no doubt that it will pass away as swiftly as, and perhaps more swiftly than, did Napoleon's empire, although, of course, without any of its glitter or its glory.

Commons, September 5, 1940.

Spirit of Britain. Little does he [Hitler] know the spirit of the British nation, or the tough fibre of the Londoners, whose forebears played a leading part in the establishment of Parliamentary institutions and who have been bred to value freedom far above their lives. This wicked man, the repository and embodiment of many forms of soul-destroying hatred, this monstrous product of former wrongs and shame, has now resolved to try to break our famous island race by a process of indiscriminate slaughter and destruction. What he has done is to kindle a fire in British hearts, here and all over the world, which will glow long after all traces of the conflagration he has caused in London have been removed. He has lighted a fire which will burn with a steady and consuming flame until the last vestiges of Nazi tyranny have been burnt out of Europe, and until the Old World—and the New—can join hands to rebuild the temples of man's freedom and man's honour, upon foundations which will not soon or easily be overthrown.

London, September 11, 1940.

Hitler's Resolve. Herr Hitler is not thinking only of stealing other people's territories, or flinging gobbets of them to his little confederate. I tell you truly what you must believe when I say this evil man, this monstrous abortion of hatred and defeat, is resolved on nothing less than the complete wiping out of the French nation, and the disintegration of its whole life and future. *London, October 21, 1940.*

Hatred of Germany. It will not be by German hands that the structure of Europe will be rebuilt or the union of the European family achieved. In every country into which the German armies and the Nazi police have broken there has sprung up from the soil a hatred of the German name and a contempt for the Nazi creed which the passage of hundreds of years will not efface from human memory. We cannot yet see how deliverance will come, or when it will come, but nothing is more certain than that every trace of Hitler's footsteps, every stain of his infected and corroding fingers will be sponged and purged and, if need be, blasted from the surface of the earth.

St. James's Palace, London, June 12, 1941.

Irrevocable Purpose. We have but one aim and one single, irrevocable purpose. We are resolved to destroy Hitler and every vestige of the Nazi regime. From this nothing will turn us—nothing. We will never parley, we will never negotiate with Hitler or any of his gang. We shall fight him by land, we shall fight him by sea, we shall fight him in the air, until with God's help we have rid the earth of his shadow and liberated its peoples from his yoke. Any man or state who fights on against Nazidom will have our aid. Any man or state who marches with Hitler is our foe.

London, June 22, 1941.

River of Blood. A river of blood has flowed and is flowing between the German race and the peoples of nearly all Europe. It is not the hot blood of battle, where good blows are given and returned. It is the cold blood of the execution yard and the scaffold, which leaves a stain indelible for generations and for centuries.

Mansion House, London, November 10, 1941.

German War Machine. You must never underrate the power of the German machine. It is the most terrible machine that has been created. After the last war they kept the brains of the German army together. They kept their Great Staff together. Although their weapons were taken away, this tremendous association of people who think nothing but war, studying war, ruthless scientific war, was held together, thousands of them, and they were able to train and build up an army which, as you saw, in a few weeks shattered to pieces the once famous army of France, and which has marched into country after country and laid it low, and laid low every form of opposition, and only now in the vast spaces of Russia is confronted with this immense and valiant race which has stood against them.

Westminster Central Hall, London, October 31, 1942.

Hatred of Germany. Certainly we see the Germans hated as no race has ever been hated in human history, or with such good reason. We see them sprawled over a dozen once free and happy countries, with their talons making festering wounds, the scars of which will never be effaced. Nazi tyranny and Prussian militarism, those two loathsome dominations, may well foresee and dread their approaching doom.

London, August 31, 1943.

The Germans. They combine in the most deadly manner the qualities of the warrior and the slave. They do not value freedom themselves, and the spectacle of it in others is hateful to them. Whenever they become strong they seek their prey, and they will follow with an iron discipline anyone who will lead them to it.

Commons, September 21, 1943.

German General Staff. The German General Staff system, which we failed to liquidate after the last war, represents an order comprising many thousands of highly trained officers and a school of doctrine of long, unbroken continuity. It possesses great skill, both in the handling of troops in action and in their rapid movement from place to place. The recent fighting in Italy should leave no doubt on these points.

Commons, February 22, 1944.

"Corporal" Hitler. When Herr Hitler escaped his bomb on July 20th he described his survival as providential; I think that from a purely military point of view we can all agree with him, for certainly it would be most unfortunate if the allies were to be deprived, in the closing phases of the struggle, of that form of warlike genius by which Corporal Schickelgruber has so notably contributed to our victory.

Hitler's Generalship. He has lost, or will lose when the tally is complete, nearly a million men in France and the Low Countries. Other large armies may well be cut off in the Baltic States, in Finland and in Norway. Less than a year ago, when the relative weakness of Germany was already becoming apparent, he was ordering further aggressive action in the Aegean, and the re-occupation of the islands which the Italians had surrendered, or wished to surrender. He has scattered and squandered a very large army in the Balkan Peninsula, whose escape will be very difficult; 27 divisions, many of them battered, are fighting General Alexander in Northern Italy. Many of these will not be able to recross the Alps to defend the German Fatherland. Such a vast frittering-away and dispersal of forces has never been seen, and is, of course, a prime cause of the impending ruin of Germany.

Hitler and Napoleon. I always hate to compare Napoleon with Hitler, as it seems an insult to the great Emperor and warrior to connect him in any way with a squalid caucus boss and butcher. But there is one respect in which I must draw a parallel. Both these men were temperamentally unable to give up the tiniest scrap of any territory to which the high-water mark of their hectic fortunes had carried them. Thus, after Leipzig in 1813, Napoleon left all his garrisons on the Rhine, and 40,000 men in Hamburg. He refused to withdraw many other vitally important elements of his armies, and he had to begin the campaign of 1814 with raw levies and a few seasoned troops brought in a hurry from Spain. Similarly, Hitler has successfully scattered the German armies all over Europe, and by obstination at every point from Stalingrad and Tunis down to the present moment, he has stripped himself of the power to concentrate in main strength for the final struggle. *Commons, September 28, 1944.*

Punishment of Germany. The allies are resolved that Germany shall be totally disarmed, that Nazism and militarism in Germany shall be destroyed, that war criminals shall be justly and swiftly punished, that all German industry capable of military production shall be eliminated or controlled, and that Germany shall make compensation in kind to the utmost of her ability for damage done to allied nations.

Commons, February 27, 1945.

Prostration of Germany. In the forefront of any survey of the world stands Germany, a vanquished nation. "Stands," I said—not prostrate, shattered. Seventy or eighty millions of men and women of an ancient, capable and terribly efficient race are in a ruined famished condition in the heart of Europe.

Commons, November 12, 1946.

Germany in Europe. My hope is that free, liberal civilization and democratic Parliamentary processes will win the soul of Germany for Europe and that the great underlying harmonies of the European family will predominate over the feuds that have hitherto rent our famous parent Continent and brought upon it miseries and humiliations beyond the power of statistics to measure or language to describe.

Commons, October 28, 1948.

German Principalities. I hope we shall continue to use our influence and resources, such as they are, to make the German people or the states and principalities of Germany able to govern themselves and earn good livelihood as soon as possible. I am hoping that the states of Germany—Bavaria, Saxony, Wurtemberg, Hanover and others—may regain much of their old individuality and rights. I am sure that it is along that road that both France and Britain will find it easiest to advance, and it is along that road that reconciliation and healing will, in the first instance, be most easily found across the former lines of battle. Individuality should be restored and revived before any degree of structural unity can be achieved.

Commons, December 10, 1948.

Dr. Konrad Adenauer. Dr. Adenauer may well be deemed the wisest German statesman since the days of Bismarck. . . .

I have greatly admired the perseverance, courage, composure and skill with which he has faced the complex, changing, uncertain and unpredictable situations with which he has been ceaselessly confronted.   *Commons, May 11, 1953.*

Italy and Mussolini

Friendship with Italy. As we stand to-day there is no doubt that a cloud has come over the old friendship between Great

Britain and Italy, a cloud which may very easily not pass away, although undoubtedly it is everyone's desire that it should. It is an old friendship, and we must not forget, what is a little-known fact, that at the time Italy entered into the Triple Alliance in the last century she stipulated particularly that in no circumstances should her obligations under the Alliance bring her into armed conflict with Great Britain.

Commons, July 11, 1935.

Abyssinia. I do not believe that Signor Mussolini would have embarked upon his Abyssinian venture but for the profound preoccupation of France with German rearmament, and, I must add, but for the real or supposed military and naval weakness of Great Britain. It was the fear of a rearmed Germany that led France to settle her differences with Italy at the beginning of this year, and very likely when these matters were being settled, what is called a "free hand in Abyssinia" was thrown in. We may regret it, but we must first see and consider the forces operating upon France before we presume to utter reproaches.

Commons, October 24, 1935.

Policy. What ought to be our policy towards Italy? At any rate, we can see what it ought not to be. It ought not to be a policy of nagging. Very serious antagonism existed between Great Britain, doing her part as a member of the League of Nations, and Italy over the conquest of Abyssinia. In that antagonism we have not prevailed. We have been humiliated, but we have not been dishonoured. However we may have been guided, we are not regarded either as knaves or cowards.

Commons, November 5, 1936.

Italy in Peril. Behind this fine façade, there was every sign that the Italian dictator, at any rate, was in a very difficult position: the industrious, amiable Italian people long overstrained; everything in the country eaten up in order to augment the magnificence of the state; taxes enormous; finances broken; officials abounding; all kinds of indispensable raw materials practically unpurchasable across the exchange; Abyssinia a curse, a corpse bound on the back of the killer; Libya and Spain, perhaps 400,000 men overseas, all to be maintained by a continuous drain on the hard-driven, ground-down people of Italy. One would have thought that these corrective processes upon external arrogance and ambition might have been allowed to run their course for a while; or, otherwise, how are the healing processes of human society to come into play?

Commons, February 22, 1938.

Italian Navy. We are also told that the Italian navy is to come out and gain sea superiority in these waters. If they seriously intend it, I shall only say that we shall be delighted to offer Signor Mussolini a free and safeguarded passage through the Straits of Gibraltar in order that he may play the part to which he aspires. There is a general curiosity in the British fleet to find out whether the Italians are up to the level they were at in the last war or whether they have fallen off at all.

Commons, June 18, 1940.

Mussolini. Italians, I will tell you the truth. It is all because of one man. One man and one man alone has ranged the Italian people in deadly struggle against the British Empire, and has deprived Italy of the sympathy and intimacy of the United States of America. That he is a great man I do not deny, but that after eighteen years of unbridled power he has led your country to the horrid verge of ruin can be denied by none. It is one man who, against the Crown and Royal Family of Italy, against the Pope and all the authority of the Vatican and of the Roman Catholic Church, against the wishes of the Italian people who had no lust for this war, has arrayed the trustees and inheritors of ancient Rome upon the side of the ferocious pagan barbarians.

Intervention of Italy. Where was the need for Italy to intervene? Where was the need to strike at prostrate France? Where was the need to declare war on Britain? Where was the need to invade Egypt, which is under British protection? We were content with Italian neutrality. During the first eight months of the war we paid great deference to Italian interests. But this was all put down to fear. We were told we were effete, worn out, an old chatterbox people mouthing outworn shibboleths of nineteenth-century Liberalism. But it was not due to fear. It was not due to weakness.

London, December 23, 1940.

Fall of Italian Empire. The events in Libya are only part of the story: they are only part of the story of the decline and fall of the Italian Empire, that will not take a future Gibbon so long to write as the original work.

London, February 9, 1941.

Victory over the Greeks. I daresay you have read in the newspapers that, by a special proclamation, the Italian dictator has congratulated the Italian army in Albania on the glorious laurels they had gained by their victory over the Greeks. Here surely is the world's record in the domain of the ridiculous and the contemptible. This whipped jackal, Mussolini, who to save his own skin has made all Italy a vassal state of Hitler's empire, comes frisking up at the side of the German tiger with yelpings not only of appetite—that can be understood—

but even of triumph. Different things strike different people in different ways. But I am sure there are a great many millions in the British Empire and in the United States who will find a new object in life by making sure that when we come to the final reckoning this absurd impostor will be abandoned to public justice and universal scorn.

London, April 27, 1941.

Italy at War. It is for the Italian people, forty millions of them, to say whether they want this terrible thing to happen to their country or not. One man, and one man alone, has brought them to this pass. There was no need for them to go to war; no one was going to attack them. We tried our best to induce them to remain neutral, to enjoy peace and prosperity and exceptional profits in a world of storm. But Mussolini could not resist the temptation of stabbing prostrate France, and what he thought was helpless Britain, in the back. Mad dreams of imperial glory, the lust of conquest and of booty, the arrogance of long-unbridled tyranny, led him to his fatal, shameful act. In vain I warned him: he would not harken. On deaf ears and a stony heart fell the wise far-seeing appeals of the American President. The hyena in his nature broke all bounds of decency and even common sense. To-day his empire is gone. We have over a hundred Italian generals and nearly three hundred thousand of his soldiers in our hands as prisoners of war. Agony grips the fair land of Italy. This is only the beginning, and what have the Italians to show for it? A brief promenade by German permission along the Riviera; a flying visit to Corsica; a bloody struggle with the heroic patriots of Yugoslavia; a deed of undying shame in Greece; the ruins of Genoa, Turin, Milan; and this is only a foretaste. One man and the regime he has created have brought these measureless calamities upon the hard-working, gifted and once happy Italian people, with whom, until the days of Mussolini, the English-speaking world had so many sympathies and never a quarrel. How long must this endure?

London, November 29, 1942.

Plight of Italy. No one wishes to take the native soil of Italy from the Italians, who will have their place in Europe after the war. The trouble is that they allow themselves to be held in bondage by intriguers, with the result that they are now in a terrible plight. I think they would be well advised to throw themselves upon the justice of those whom they have so grossly attacked. We shall not stain our name for posterity by any cruel, inhuman acts. It is a matter for the Italians to settle among themselves. All we can do is to apply the physical stimuli which we have at our disposal to bring

about a change of mind in these recalcitrant persons. Of this
you may be sure: we shall continue to operate on the Italian
donkey at both ends, with the carrot and with a stick.

Washington, D.C., May 25, 1943.

Liberation of Italy. We must be careful not to get ourselves into the kind of position into which the Germans have
blundered in so many countries—that of having to hold down
and administer in detail, from day to day, by a system of
gauleiters, the entire life of very large populations, thereby
becoming responsible under the hard conditions of this present period for the whole of their upkeep and well-being.
Such a course might well, in practice, turn the sense of liberation, which it may soon be in our power to bestow upon the
Italian people, into a sullen discontent against us and all our
works. The rescuers might soon, indeed, be regarded as tyrants; they might even be hated by the Italian people as much
or almost as much as their German allies. I certainly do not
wish, in the case of Italy, to tread a path which might lead
to execution squads and concentration camps, and above all
having to carry on our shoulders a lot of people who ought
to be made to carry themselves.

Commons, July 17, 1943.

Downfall of Mussolini. The end of Mussolini's long and
severe reign over the Italian people undoubtedly marks the
close of an epoch in the life of Italy. The keystone of the
Fascist arch has crumbled, and without attempting to prophesy, it does not seem unlikely that the entire Fascist edifice
will fall to the ground in ruins, if it has not already so fallen.
The totalitarian system of a single party, armed with secret
police, engrossing to itself practically all the offices, even the
humblest, under the Government; with magistrates and courts
under the control of the executive, with its whole network of
domestic spies and neighbourly informants—that system, when
applied over a long period of time, leaves the broad masses
without any influence upon their country's destinies and without any independent figures apart from the official classes.
That, I think, is a defence for the people of Italy—one defence—although there can be no really valid defence for any
country or any people which allows its freedom and inherent
rights to pass out of its own hands.

Commons, July 27, 1943.

Surrender of Italy. The Italian surrender was a windfall,
but it had nothing to do with the date fixed for harvesting the
orchard. The truth is that the Armistice announcement was

delayed to fit in with the attack, and not the attack delayed
to fit in with the announcement.

Commons, September 21, 1943.

Fate of Italy. The fate of Italy is indeed terrible, and I
personally find it very difficult to nourish animosity against
the Italian people. The overwhelming mass of the nation re-
joiced in the idea of being delivered from the subtle tyranny
of the Fascists, and they wished, when Mussolini was overthrown, to take their place as speedily as possible by the side
of the British and American armies who, it was expected,
would quickly rid the country of the Germans.

Commons, May 24, 1944.

Japan

Designs of Japan. I do not believe that Japan, deeply en-
tangled in China, nay, bleeding at every pore in China, her
strength ebbing away in a wrongful and impossible task, and
with the whole weight of Russia upon her in the north of
China, will wish to make war upon the British Empire until
she sees how matters go in Europe.

City Carlton Club, London, June 28, 1939.

Relations with Japan. I must admit that, having voted
for the Japanese alliance nearly 40 years ago, in 1902, and
having always done my very best to promote good relations
with the Island Empire of Japan, and always having been a
sentimental well-wisher to the Japanese and an admirer of
their many gifts and qualities, I should view with keen sorrow
the opening of a conflict between Japan and the English-
speaking world.

Mansion House, London, November 10, 1941.

Secret Societies. We know that for many years past the
policy of Japan has been dominated by secret societies of
subalterns and junior officers of the army and navy, who have
enforced their will upon successive Japanese Cabinets and
Parliaments by the assassination of any Japanese statesman
who opposed, or who did not sufficiently further, their aggressive policy. It may be that these societies, dazzled and
dizzy with their own schemes of aggression and the prospect
of early victories, have forced their country against its better
judgment into war. They have certainly embarked upon a very
considerable undertaking.

U. S. Congress, Washington, D. C., December 26, 1941.

War against Japan. It is no doubt true that the defeat of Japan will not necessarily entail the defeat of Hitler, whereas the defeat of Hitler would enable the whole forces of the United Nations to be concentrated upon the defeat of Japan. But there is no question of regarding the war in the Pacific as a secondary operation. The only limitation applied to its vigorous prosecution will be the shipping available at any given time.

Commons, January 29, 1942.

Japan as Foe. No one must underrate any more the gravity and efficiency of the Japanese war machine. Whether in the air or upon the sea, or man to man on land, they have already proved themselves to be formidable, deadly, and, I am sorry to say, barbarous antagonists. This proves a hundred times over that there never was the slightest chance, even though we had been much better prepared in many ways than we were, of our standing up to them alone while we had Nazi Germany at our throat and Fascist Italy at our belly.

London, February 15, 1942.

Japanese Madness. Another mistake of our foes was made by Japan when they attacked the United States at Pearl Harbour instead of attacking us alone who were already busy with Italy and Germany in Europe. It was most fortunate that, led away by their dark conspiracies and schemes, dizzy and dazzled from poring over plans, they sprang out upon a peaceful nation with whom they were at that time in peaceful parley, and were led away and tottered over the edge and, for the sake of sinking half a dozen ships of war and beating up a naval port, brought out against them the implacable energies and the measureless power of the 130 million educated people who live in the United States. We have much to be thankful for.

Westminster Central Hall, London, October 31, 1942.

Defeat of Japan. In our conferences in January 1942, between the President and myself, and between our high expert advisers, it was evident that, while the defeat of Japan would not mean the defeat of Germany, the defeat of Germany would infallibly mean the ruin of Japan.

U. S. Congress, Washington, D. C., May 19, 1943.

Japan. Japan, with all her treachery and greed, remains unsubdued. The injury she has inflicted . . . and her detestable cruelties call for justice and retribution . . .

London, May 8, 1945.

Ireland

Ireland and England. The discontent that prevailed between England and Ireland arose not so much from differences of religion and race as from the belief that the English connection was not a profitable nor paying one. If Ireland were more prosperous she would be more loyal, and if more loyal more free.
Commons, May 19, 1904.

Irish Question. There never was a time when there was a great number of moderate sensible people who were prepared to give consideration to the Irish question without passion, to see what a rotten system of government prevailed in that country, and to approach one of the most difficult, as it was one of the most attractive, questions which could occupy the minds of English politicians.

Government. Ireland was governed by neither King nor people. The system of government was not democratic, autocratic or even oligarchic.
Commons, February 20, 1905.

The Irish. Suppose there is one island in the world and one race upon the surface of the earth so curiously disposed, so strangely fashioned, that self-interest does not stir them, that the desire of prosperity does not dwell in their hearts: suppose there were a race whose two fiercest passions were, first of all, to quarrel with their own bread-and-butter, and secondly, to cut their own noses to spite their faces; suppose there were such a people, suppose that the Irish were that people, suppose they deliberately set themselves—all this concatenation of absurd suppositions must be made—to wreck and ruin the constitution they had so painfully acquired, to bring about a deadlock to infuriate or to irritate their all-powerful neighbour, to quarrel with the great protecting credit-giving, revenue-paying, and produce-purchasing power —what then? Why then, even for this inverted pyramid of absurd and unnatural assumptions, there is full provision in the Bill. The Imperial Parliament, in which the Irish will be represented, will have not only the legal but the moral right to legislate.

Home Rule for Ireland. Never before has so little been asked, and never before have so many people asked for it.

Ireland and England. I defy respectfully, and I dialectically defy you by the utmost exercise of your imagination to conjure up or picture even any set of circumstances in which the ruin of England would not mean the ruin of Ireland also.

Commons, April 30, 1912.

Unity of Ireland. If Irish unity can be achieved, it can only be because the Government of the Irish Free State will have convinced Ulster of its loyal association with the British Empire, and will have offered Ulster conditions of security and partnership in every way satisfactory to her.

Irish Prosperity. Under complete fiscal freedom England holds Irish prosperity in the hollow of her hand.

Ireland. It is a curious reflection to inquire why Ireland should bulk so largely in our lives. How is it that the great English Parties are shaken to their foundations, and even shattered, almost every generation, by contact with Irish affairs. Whence did Ireland derive its power to drive Mr. Pitt from office, to drag down Mr. Gladstone in the summit of his career, and to draw us who sit here almost to the verge of civil war, from which we were only rescued by the outbreak of the Great War. Whence does this mysterious power of Ireland come? It is a small, poor, sparsely populated island, lapped about by British sea power accessible on every side, without iron or coal. How is it she sways our councils, shakes our Parties, and infects us with her bitterness, convulses our passions, and deranges our action? How is it she has forced generation after generation to stop the whole traffic of the British Empire, in order to debate her domestic affairs? Ireland is not a daughter state. She is a parent nation. The Irish are an ancient race. "We too are," said their plenipotentiary, "a far-flung nation."

Commons, December 15, 1921.

Irish Character. No people in the world are really less likely to turn Bolshevik than the Irish. Their strong sense of personal possession, their respect for the position of women, their love of country and their religious convictions constitute them in a peculiar sense the most sure and unyielding opponents of the withering and levelling doctrines of Russia.

Commons, February 16, 1922.

Power of Ireland. If the power of Ireland to harm us will be small, the power of Ireland to help us will be very great.

Commons, March 8, 1922.

Irish Feuds. The British Empire cannot afford to be drawn continually by these brutal Irish feuds into a position dishonouring to its general and long-maintained reputation.

Commons, April 12, 1922.

Freedom of Ireland. Let us on our part be very careful that we do all we have to do in scrupulous and meticulous good faith—in scrupulous, meticulous, and even—if I may dare the word—in credulous good faith. Let us not be led by impatience, by prejudice, by vexation, by anxiety into courses which would lay us open to charges of fickleness or levity in dealing with those issues so long lasting as the relations between the two islands.   *Commons, May 31, 1922.*

Eire. For reasons of high State policy involving the position of the whole British Empire in its relation to the rest of the world, we decided to give Irishmen in the twenty-six counties their opportunity of showing what they could do to make an ordered State.   *Commons, June 26, 1922.*

Ireland and the Empire. I may cherish the hope that some day all Ireland will be loyal because it is free, will be united because it is loyal, and will be united within itself and united to the British Empire.   *Belfast, May 16, 1925.*

Dark Forces in Ireland. The dark forces in Ireland renew themselves from year to year. When some are conciliated, others present themselves. They are very powerful in Ireland now. No one has ever been brought to justice in Ireland since the Treaty for murdering an Englishman. There is a whole organization of secret men bound together on the old principle that England's danger is Ireland's opportunity.

The Case of Ireland. The case of Ireland is not comparable with the Dominions. Southern Ireland is not a Dominion; it has never accepted that position. It is a state based upon a Treaty, which Treaty has been completely demolished. Southern Ireland, therefore, becomes a state which is an undefined and unclassified anomaly. No one knows what its juridical and international rights and status are.
                       Commons, May 5, 1938.

Neutrality of Ireland. The fact that we cannot use the south and west coasts of Ireland to refuel our flotillas and aircraft and thus protect the trade by which Ireland as well as Great Britain lives, is a most heavy and grievous burden and one which should never have been placed on our shoulders, broad though they may be.   *Commons, November 5, 1940.*

Western Approaches. Owing to the action of Mr. de Valera, so much at variance with the temper and instinct of thousands of Southern Irishmen who hastened to the battlefront to prove their ancient valour, the approaches which the Southern Irish ports and airfields could so easily have guarded were closed by the hostile aircraft and U-boats. This was indeed a deadly moment in our life, and if it had not been for the loyalty and friendship of Northern Ireland we should have been forced to come to close quarters with Mr. de Valera or perish for ever from the earth. However, with a restraint and poise to which, I say, history will find few parallels, His Majesty's Government never laid a violent hand upon them, though at times it would have been quite easy and quite natural, and we left the de Valera government to frolic with the Germans and later with the Japanese representatives to their hearts' content.

London, May 13, 1945.

Irish Ports. In the case of the Irish ports, in the spring of 1938, absolutely wrong political data, in my opinion, were put before the Chiefs of Staff—another set of Chiefs of Staff —and they gave advice which nearly brought us to our ruin. [Laughter.] I have heard all this mocking laughter before in the time of a former government. I remember being once alone in the House, protesting against the cession of the Southern Irish ports. I remember the looks of incredulity, the mockery, derision and laughter I had to encounter on every side, when I said that Mr. de Valera might declare Ireland neutral.

Commons, May 24, 1946.

Soviet Russia

Bolshevism. The inherent vice of Bolshevism appears to rot simultaneously every part of the social structure of Russia, including even the military tyranny on which alone the Soviet power now depends.   *Commons, May 29, 1919.*

State Hostages. Here we have a state whose subjects are so happy that they have to be forbidden to quit its bounds under the direct penalties; whose diplomatists and agents sent on foreign missions have often to leave their wives and children at home as hostages to ensure their eventual return.

Commons, July 29, 1919.

High Priest. No sooner did Lenin arrive than he began beckoning a finger here and a finger there to obscure persons in sheltered retreats in New York, in Glasgow, in Berne and other countries, and he gathered together the leading spirits of a formidable sect, the most formidable sect in the world, of which he was the high priest and chief. With these spirits around him he set to work with demoniacal ability to tear to pieces every institution on which the Russian State and nation depended. Russia was laid low. Russia had to be laid low. She was laid low to the dust.

Lenin. Lenin was sent into Russia by the Germans in the same way that you might send a phial containing a culture of typhoid or cholera to be poured into the water supply of a great city, and it worked with amazing accuracy.

Bolsheviks. The Bolsheviks robbed Russia at one stroke of two most precious things, peace and victory—the victory that was within her grasp and the peace which was her dearest desire. Both were swept away from her. The victory was turned into defeat. As for the peace, her life ever since has been one long struggle of agonizing war.

Reactionary. In Russia a man is called a reactionary if he objects to having his property stolen and his wife and children murdered. *Commons, November 5, 1919.*

Terrorism. My hatred of Bolshevism and Bolsheviks is not founded on their silly system of economics or their absurd doctrine of an impossible equality. It arises from the bloody and devastating terrorism which they practice in every land into which they have broken, and by which alone their criminal regime can be maintained.

Commons, July 8, 1920.

Russia's Neighbours. We must also remember that the great mass of Russia, with its enormous armies and with its schools of ardent students of chemical warfare, its poison gas, its tanks and all its appliances, looms up all along the eastern frontier of Europe, and that the whole row of small states, Finland, Estonia, Latvia, Lithuania, Poland—not a small state, but for this purpose in the line—and Rumania, are under the continued preoccupation of this gigantic, and to them in many ways unfriendly, Russian power. It may well be that there is no danger, but I expect that if we lived there, we should feel rather uncomfortable about it. These grave political dangers must be faced and recognized.

Commons, May 13, 1932.

Border States. Russia has made herself an Ishmael among the nations, but she is one of the most titanic factors in the economy and in the diplomacy of the world. Russia, with her enormous, rapidly increasing armaments, with her tremendous development of poison gas, aeroplanes, tanks and every kind of forbidden fruit; Russia with her limitless manpower and her corrosive hatreds, weighs heavily upon a whole line of countries, some small, others considerable, from the Baltic to the Black Sea, all situated adjacent to Russian territory.

These countries have newly gained their independence. Their independence and nationhood are sacred to them, and we must never forget that most of them have been carved, in whole or in part, out of the old Russian Empire, the Russian Empire of Peter the Great and Catherine the Great. In some cases these countries are also in deep anxiety about Germany.

Commons, November 23, 1932.

Communism and Nazism. I will not pretend that, if I had to choose between Communism and Nazism, I would choose Communism. I hope not to be called upon to survive in the world under a government of either of those dispensations.

Commons, April 14, 1937.

Riddle of Russia. I cannot forecast to you the action of Russia. It is a riddle wrapped in a mystery inside an enigma; but perhaps there is a key. That key is Russian national interest.

Line Through Poland. Russia has pursued a cold policy of self-interest. We could have wished that the Russian armies should be standing on their present line as the friends and allies of Poland instead of as invaders. But that the Russian armies should stand on this line was clearly necessary for the safety of Russia against the Nazi menace. At any rate, the line is there, and an eastern front has been created which Nazi Germany does not dare assail. When Herr von Ribbentrop was summoned to Moscow last week, it was to learn the fact, and to accept the fact, that the Nazi designs upon the Baltic States and upon the Ukraine must come to a dead stop.

London, October 1, 1939.

Communism. Everyone can see how Communism rots the soul of a nation; how it makes it abject and hungry in peace, and proves it base and abominable in war.

Finland. Only Finland—superb, nay sublime—in the jaws of peril—Finland shows what free men can do. The service rendered by Finland to mankind is magnificent. They have exposed, for all the world to see, the military incapacity of the Red Army and of the Red Air Force. Many illusions about Soviet Russia have been dispelled in these few fierce weeks of fighting in the Arctic Circle.

London, January 20, 1940.

Invasion of Russia. The Nazi regime is indistinguishable from the worst features of Communism. It is devoid of all theme and principle except appetite and racial domination. It excels all forms of human wickedness in the efficiency of its cruelty and ferocious aggression. No one has been a more consistent opponent of Communism than I have for the last twenty-five years. I will unsay no word that I have spoken about it. But all this fades away before the spectacle which is now unfolding. The past with its crimes, its follies and its tragedies, flashes away. I see the Russian soldiers standing on the threshold of their native land, guarding the fields which their fathers have tilled from time immemorial. I see them guarding their homes where mothers and wives pray—ah yes, for there are times when all pray—for the safety of their loved ones, the return of the breadwinner, of their champion, of their protector. I see the ten thousand villages of Russia, where the means of existence was wrung so hardly from the soil, but where there are still primordial human joys, where maidens laugh and children play. I see advancing upon all this in hideous onslaught the Nazi war machine, with its clanking, heel-clicking, dandified Prussian officers, its crafty expert agents fresh from the cowing and tying-down of a dozen countries. I see also the dull, drilled, docile, brutish masses of the Hun soldiery plodding on like a swarm of crawling locusts. I see the German bombers and fighters in the sky, still smarting from many a British whipping, delighted to find what they believe is an easier and a safer prey. *London, June 22, 1941.*

Crime Without a Name. The Russian armies and all the peoples of the Russian Republic have rallied to the defence of their hearths and homes. For the first time Nazi blood has flowed in a fearful torrent. Certainly a million-and-a-half, perhaps two millions, of Nazi cannon-fodder have bit the dust of the endless plains of Russia. The tremendous battle rages along nearly two thousand miles of front. The Russians fight with magnificent devotion; not only that, our generals who have visited the Russian front line report with admiration the efficiency of their military organization and the excellence of their equipment. The aggressor is surprised, startled, staggered. For the first time in his experience mass murder has become unprofitable. He retaliates by the most frightful cruelties. As his armies advance, whole districts are being exterminated. Scores of thousands—literally scores of thousands of executions in cold blood are being perpetrated by the German police-troops upon the Russian patriots who defend their native soil. Since the Mongol invasions of Europe in the sixteenth century, there has never been methodical, merciless butchery on such a scale or approaching such a scale. And this is but the beginning. Famine and pestilence have yet to follow in the bloody ruts of Hitler's tanks. We are in the presence of a crime without a name.

London, August 24, 1941.

Survival. No government ever formed among men has been capable of surviving injuries so grave and cruel as those inflicted by Hitler upon Russia. But under the leadership of Marshal Stalin, and thanks to the stand by the British peoples when they were all alone, and to abundant British and American ammunition and supplies of all kinds, Russia has not only survived and recovered from these frightful injuries, but has inflicted, as no other force in the world could have inflicted, mortal damage on the German army machine.

London, August 31, 1943.

Changes in Soviet Russia. Profound changes have taken place in Soviet Russia. The Trotskyite form of Communism has been completely wiped out. The victories of the Russian armies have been attended by a great rise in the strength of the Russian State, and a remarkable broadening of its views. The religious side of Russian life has had a wonderful rebirth. The discipline and military etiquette of the Russian armies are unsurpassed. There is a new National Anthem, the music of which Marshal Stalin sent me, which I asked the B.B.C. to play on the frequent occasions when there are great Russian victories to celebrate. *Commons, May 24, 1944.*

Hitler's Strategy. I salute Marshal Stalin, the great champion, and I firmly believe that our twenty years' treaty with Russia will prove one of the most lasting and durable factors in preserving the peace and the good order and the progress of Europe. It may well be that Russian success has been somewhat aided by the strategy of Herr Hitler—of Corporal Hitler. Even military idiots find it difficult not to see some faults in some of his actions. Here he now finds himself with perhaps 10 divisions in the north of Finland and 20 or 30 divisions cut off in the Baltic States, all of which three or four months ago could have been transported with their matériel and their weapons to stand between Germany and the Russian advance. It is far too late for him to achieve that at the present time. Altogether, I think it is much better to let officers rise up in the proper way.

Commons, August 2, 1944.

Western Frontier of Russia. I cannot conceive that it is not possible to make a good solution whereby Russia gets the security which she is entitled to have, and which I have resolved that we will do our utmost to secure for her, on her western frontier, and, at the same time, the Polish nation have restored to them that national sovereignty and independence for which, across centuries of oppression and struggle, they have never ceased to strive.

Russo-Finnish Armistice. The armistice terms agreed upon for Finland and Rumania bear, naturally, the imprint of the Soviet will—and here I must draw attention to the restraint which has characterized the Soviet treatment of these two countries, both of which marched blithely behind Hitler in his attempted destruction of Russia, and both of which added their quota of injuries to the immense volume of suffering which the Russian people have endured, survived, and have triumphantly surmounted.

Big Three. The future of the whole world, and certainly the future of Europe, perhaps for several generations, depends upon the cordial, trustful and comprehending association of the British Empire, the United States and Soviet Russia, and no pains must be spared and no patience grudged which are necessary to bring that supreme hope to fruition.

Commons, September 28, 1944.

Good Faith of Russia. The impression I brought back from the Crimea, and from all my other contacts, is that Marshal Stalin and the Soviet leaders wish to live in honourable friendship and equality with the western democracies. I feel also that their word is their bond. I know of no government which stands to its obligations even in its own despite, more solidly than the Russian Soviet Government. I decline absolutely to embark here on a discussion about Russian good faith. It is quite evident that these matters touch the whole future of the world. Sombre indeed would be the fortunes of mankind if some awful schism arose between the western democracies and the Russian Soviet Union, if the future world organization were rent asunder, and if new cataclysms of inconceivable violence destroyed all that is left of the treasures and liberties of mankind.

Commons, February 27, 1945.

Sympathy for Russia. Any idea of Britain pursuing an anti-Russian policy, or making elaborate combinations to the detriment of Russia, is utterly opposed to British thought and conscience. Nothing but a long period of very marked injuries and antagonisms, which we all hope may be averted, could develop any such mood again in this land.

War Secrets. During the war we imparted many secrets to the Russians especially in connection with radar, but we were not conscious of any adequate reciprocity. Even in the heat of the war both countries acted under considerable reserve.

Commons, November 7, 1945.

Iron Curtain. From Stettin in the Baltic to Trieste in the Adriatic, an iron curtain has descended across the Continent. Behind that line lie all the capitals of the ancient states of central and eastern Europe. Warsaw, Berlin, Prague, Vienna, Budapest, Belgrade, Bucharest and Sofia, all these famous cities and the populations around them lie in what I must call the Soviet sphere, and all are subject in one form or another, not only to Soviet influence but to a very high and, in many cases, increasing measure of control from Moscow.

Strength and Weakness. From what I have seen of our Russian friends and allies during the war, I am convinced that there is nothing they admire so much as strength, and there is nothing for which they have less respect than weakness, especially military weakness. For that reason the old doctrine of a balance of power is unsound. We cannot afford, if we can help it, to work on narrow margins, offering temptations to a trial of strength.

Fruits of War. I do not believe that Soviet Russia desires war. What they desire is the fruits of war and the indefinite expansion of their power and doctrines.

Westminster College, Fulton, Missouri, March 5, 1946.

Communist Utopia. In the Communist sect it is a matter of religion to sacrifice one's native land for the sake of the Communist Utopia. People who, in ordinary life, would behave in a quite honourable manner, if they are infected with the disease of the mind will not hesitate a moment to betray their country or its secrets.

The American Eagle. It cannot be in the interest of Russia to go on irritating the United States. There are no people in the world who are so slow to develop hostile feelings against a foreign country as the Americans, and there are no people who, once estranged, are more difficult to win back. The American eagle sits on his perch, a large, strong bird with formidable beak and claws. There he sits motionless, and M. Gromyko is sent day after day to prod him with a sharp pointed stick—now his neck, now under his wings, now his tail feathers. All the time the eagle keeps quite still. But it would be a great mistake to suppose that nothing is going on inside the breast of the eagle.   *Commons, June 5, 1946.*

Espionage. The House may be sure that the Soviet Government know perfectly well what we have got in the navy and in the forces in Europe, and that they have got a lot of good friends moving freely about in this country who will not hesitate to tell them about any little points on which they may be short.   *Commons, March 31, 1947.*

Communist Reiteration. The Russian Bolsheviks have discovered that truth does not matter so long as there is reiteration. They have no difficulty whatever in countering a fact by a lie which, if repeated often enough and loudly enough, becomes accepted by the people.

Brighton, October 4, 1947.

Liquidation. It is part of the established technique of the "cold war" the Soviets have begun against us all, that in any country which has fallen into their power, people of character and men of heart and personality outstanding in any walk of life, from the manual worker to the university professor, shall be what is called in their savage jargon "liquidated."

Llandudno, October 9, 1948.

Bolshevism. I think the day will come when it will be recognized without doubt, not only on one side of the House but throughout the civilized world, that the strangling of Bolshevism at its birth would have been an untold blessing to the human race.

Commons, January 26, 1949.

Dealing with Communists. I tell you—it's no use arguing with a Communist. It's no good trying to convert a Communist or persuade him. You can only deal with him on the following basis . . . you can only do it by having superior force on your side on the matter in question—and they must also be convinced that you will use—you will not hesitate to use—those forces, if necessary, in the most ruthless manner. You have not only to convince the Soviet Government that you have a superior force—that they are confronted by superior force—but that you are not restrained by any moral consideration, if the case arose, from using that force with complete material ruthlessness. And that is the greatest chance of peace, the surest road to peace.

New York, March 25, 1949.

Behind the Iron Curtain. Ten ancient capitals of Europe are behind the Iron Curtain. A large part of this continent is held in bondage. They have escaped from Nazism only to fall into the other extreme of Communism. It is like making a long and agonizing journey to leave the North Pole only to find out that, as a result, you have woken up in the South Pole. All around are only ice and snow and bitter piercing winds.

Strasbourg, August 17, 1949.

Appeasement. Appeasement in itself may be good or bad according to the circumstances. Appeasement from weakness and fear is alike futile and fatal. Appeasement from strength is magnanimous and noble, and might be the surest and perhaps the only path to world peace. When nations or individuals get strong they are often truculent and bullying, but when they are weak they become better mannered. But this is the reverse of what is healthy and wise.

Commons, December 14, 1950.

Kremlin Commissars. I have had the opportunity several times of seeing in conditions of grave business some of these commissars who form the oligarchy in the Kremlin and their chiefs, and I can tell you that these men are apt to form designs and to carry them out, and that when confronted with farces and shams they very often retaliate by strong and real measures.

Commons, February 15, 1951.

France

Pacifist France. France, though armed to the teeth, is pacifist to the core.

Commons, December 23, 1932.

Disarmament of France. I read in the newspapers to-day that the Prime Minister has been giving an ultimatum or making a strong appeal to France to disarm. Whether you deal with the army or the air, you are taking an altogether undue responsibility at a time like this in tendering such advice to a friendly nation. No; I hope and trust that the French will look after their own safety, and that we shall be permitted to live our life in our island without being again drawn into the perils of the Continent of Europe.

Commons, March 14, 1933.

Shield of France. If Europe has enjoyed peace this year, it has been under the shield of France. Be careful not to break that shield. It is perhaps not the broad basis on which we should like to see the harmony of Christendom stand, but it is a shield. Beware that you do not lower it or weaken it by any action in your power before you have, at least, something which gives as good practical security erected behind it to put in its place.

Commons, March 23, 1933.

Security of France. We all know that the French are pacific. They are quite as pacific as we are. They want to be left alone, as we do, and, I would add, as the people of Soviet Russia also wish to be left alone. But the French seem much nearer to the danger than we are. There is no strip of salt water to guard their land and their liberties. We must remember that they are the only other great European country that has not reverted to despotism or dictatorship in one form or another.

Commons, October 24, 1935.

Alliance. Even an isolationist would, I think, go so far as to say: "If we have to mix ourselves up with the Continent, let us, at any rate, get the maximum of safety from our commitments."   *Commons, March 24, 1938.*

French Navy. Under the long care of Admiral Darlan and M. Campinchi, the Minister of Marine, a magnificent fighting and seafaring force has been developed. Not only have we been assisted in every way agreed upon before the war, but besides a whole set of burdens have been lifted off our shoulders by the loyal and ever-increasingly vigorous cooperation of the French fleet. It seems to me a wonderful thing that when France is making so great an effort upon land she should at the same time offer to the allied cause so powerful a reinforcement by sea.   *Commons, November 8, 1939.*

Battle of France. I am not reciting these facts for the purpose of recrimination. That I judge to be utterly futile and even harmful. We cannot afford it. I recite them in order to explain why it was we did not have, as we could have had, between twelve and fourteen British divisions fighting in the line in this great battle instead of only three. Now I put all this aside. I put it on the shelf, from which the historians, when they have time, will select their documents to tell their stories. We have to think of the future and not of the past.
Commons, June 18, 1940.

Sorrow. The House will feel sorrow at the fate of the great French nation and people, to whom we have been joined so long in war and peace, and whom we have regarded as trustees with ourselves for the progress of a liberal culture and tolerant civilization of Europe.
Commons, June 25, 1940.

Collapse. When you have a friend and comrade at whose side you have faced tremendous struggles, and your friend is smitten down by a stunning blow, it may be necessary to make sure that the weapon that has fallen from his hands shall not be added to the resources of your common enemy. But you need not bear malice because of your friend's cries of delirium and gestures of agony. You must not add to his pain; you must work for his recovery. The association of interest between Britain and France remains. The cause remains. Duty inescapable remains.

Rot. Many of these countries have been poisoned by intrigue before they were struck down by violence. They have been rotted from within before they were smitten from without. How else can you explain what has happened to

France?—to the French army, to the French people, to the leaders of the French people?

Capital Ships. During the last fortnight the British navy, in addition to blockading what is left of the German fleet and chasing the Italian fleet, has had imposed upon it the sad duty of putting effectually out of action for the duration of the war the capital ships of the French navy. These, under the Armistice terms, signed in the railway coach at Compiègne, would have been placed within the power of Germany. The transference of these ships to Hitler would have endangered the security of both Great Britain and the United States. We therefore had no choice but to act as we did, and to act forthwith. Our painful task is now complete. Although the unfinished battleship, the *Jean Bart,* still rests in a Moroccan harbour and there are a number of French warships at Toulon and in various French ports all over the world, these are not in a condition or of a character to derange our preponderance of naval power. As long, therefore, as they make no attempt to return to ports controlled by Germany or Italy, we shall not molest them in any way. That melancholy phase in our relations with France has, so far as we are concerned, come to an end.
Commons, July 14, 1940.

General de Gaulle. That General de Gaulle was right in believing that the majority of Frenchmen in Dakar was favourable to the Free French movement, I have no doubt; indeed, I think his judgment has been found extremely surefooted, and our opinion of him has been enhanced by everything we have seen of his conduct in circumstances of peculiar and perplexing difficulty. His Majesty's Government have no intention whatever of abandoning the cause of General de Gaulle until it is merged, as merged it will be, in the larger cause of France.
Commons, October 8, 1940.

Soul of France. By all kinds of sly and savage means he [Hitler] is plotting and working to quench for ever the fountain of characteristic French culture and of French inspiration to the world . . . Never will I believe that the soul of France is dead.
London, December 1, 1940.

Future of France. Many ask themselves the question: Is France finished? Is that long and famous history, adorned by so many manifestations of genius and valour, bearing with it so much that is precious to culture and civilization, and above all to the liberties of mankind—is all that now to sink for ever into the ocean of the past, or will France rise again and resume her rightful place in the structure of what may one day be again the family of Europe? I declare to you here, on this considerable occasion, even now when misguided or suborned Frenchmen are firing upon their rescuers, I declare to you my faith that France will rise again. While there are men like General de Gaulle and all those who follow him—and they are legion throughout France—and men like General Giraud, that gallant warrior whom no prison can hold, while there are men like those to stand forward in the name and in the cause of France, my confidence in the future of France is sure. *Mansion House, London, November 10, 1942.*

The Fighting French. The Germans, by their oppression, will soon procure for us the unity of Metropolitan France. That unity can now only take an anti-German form. In such a movement the spirit of the Fighting French must be continually in the ascendant. Their reward will come home on the tide. We must try to bring about as speedily as possible a working arrangement and ultimately a consolidation between all Frenchmen outside the German power. The character and constitution of Admiral Darlan's Government must be continuously modified by the introduction of fresh and, from our point of view, clean elements. We have the right and I believe we have the power to effect these necessary transformations so long as Great Britain and the United States act harmoniously together. But meanwhile, above all, let us get on with the war. . . .

The Almighty in His infinite wisdom did not see fit to create Frenchmen in the image of Englishmen.
Commons, December 10, 1942.

Restoration. I wish to make it quite clear that I regard the restoration of France as one of the great powers of Europe as a sacred duty from which Great Britain will never recede. This arises not only from the sentiments which we hold towards France, so long our comrade in victory and misfortune, but also from the fact that it is one of the most enduring interests of Great Britain in Europe that there should be a strong France and a strong French army.
Commons, September 21, 1943.

French National Committee. The French National Committee are not the owners but the trustees of the title-deeds of France. These must be restored to the French nation when freedom is achieved, for it is only on the will of the people, freely expressed under conditions of reasonable tranquillity, that in France, as in other enslaved countries, any permanent structure can be raised.
Mansion House, London, November 9, 1943.

Contribution of France. For forty years I have been a consistent friend of France and her brave army; all my life I have been grateful for the contribution France has made to the culture and glory of Europe, and above all for the sense of personal liberty and the rights of man which has radiated from the soul of France. But these are not matters of sentiment or personal feeling. It is one of the main interests of Great Britain that a friendly France should regain and hold her place among the major powers of Europe and the world. Show me a moment when I swerved from this conception, and you will show me a moment when I have been wrong.

General de Gaulle. In these last four years I have had many differences with General de Gaulle, but I have never forgotten, and can never forget, that he stood forth as the first eminent Frenchman to face the common foe in what seemed to be the hour of ruin of his country and, possibly, of ours; and it is only fair and becoming that he should stand first and foremost in the days when France shall again be raised, and raise herself, to her rightful place among the great powers of Europe and of the world.

Commons, August 2, 1944.

Alliance. For more than thirty years I have defended the cause of friendship, of comradeship, and of alliance between France and Great Britain. I have never deviated from the policy throughout the whole of my life. For so many years past have these two nations shared the glories of western Europe that they have become indispensable to each other. It is a fundamental principle of British policy that the alliance with France should be unshakable, constant and effective.

Paris, November 11, 1944.

France and Germany. I am now going to say something that will astonish you. The first step in the re-creation of the European family must be a partnership between France and Germany. In this way only can France recover the moral and cultural leadership of Europe. There can be no revival of Europe without a spiritually great France and a spiritually great Germany.

Zürich, September 19, 1946.

Poland

Poland. The Prime Minister [Ramsay MacDonald] last year, in a speech at Geneva, used a very striking phrase when he described Europe as a house inhabited by ghosts. That is to misinterpret the situation. Europe is a house inhabited by fierce, strong, living entities. Poland is not a ghost: Poland is a reincarnation. I think it is a wonderful thing that Polish unity should have re-emerged from long hideous eclipse and bondage, when the Poles were divided between three empires and made to fight one another in all the wars that took place. I rejoice that Poland has been reconstituted. I cannot think of any event arising out of the Great War which can be considered to be a more thoroughly righteous result of the struggle than the reunion of this people, who have preserved their national soul through all the years of oppression and division and whose reconstitution of their nationhood is one of the most striking facts in European history. Do not let us be led, because there are many aspects of Polish policy that we do not like or agree with, into dwelling upon the small points of disagreement, and forget what a very great work has been achieved, a work of liberation and of justice, in the reconstitution of Poland. I trust she will live long to enjoy the freedom of the lands which belong to her, a freedom which was gained by the sword of the victorious allies.

Polish Corridor. Many people would like to see, or would have liked to see a little while ago—I was one of them—the question of the Polish Corridor adjusted. For my part, I should certainly have considered that to be one of the greatest practical objectives of European peace-seeking diplomacy. There again, however, we must think of the rights of Poland. The Polish Corridor is inhabited almost entirely by Poles, and it was Polish territory before the Partition of 1772. This is a matter which in quiet times, with increasing good will, Europe should have set itself—and might well some day set itself—to solve.
Commons, April 13, 1933.

Liberation. I have always hailed the liberation of Poland from its tripartite bondage as one of the most inspiring consequences of the World War.

Commons, January 13, 1934.

Guarantee. I take a serious view of the position in which we find ourselves. It is similar to what happened last year, but with the important difference that this year no means of retreat are open to us. We had no Treaty obligations to Czechoslovakia. We had never guaranteed their security. But now we have given an absolute guarantee to Poland that if she is the object of unprovoked aggression, we in company with our French allies will be forced to declare war upon Germany. There is the brute fact which stares us in the face.
City Carlton Club, London, June 28, 1939.

Soul of Poland. Poland has been again overrun by two of the great powers which held her in bondage for 150 years but were unable to quench the spirit of the Polish nation. The heroic defence of Warsaw shows that the soul of Poland is indestructible, and that she will rise again like a rock which may for a spell be submerged by a tidal wave, but which remains a rock.   *London, October 1, 1939.*

Oppression. Everything that is happening to the Czechs pales in comparison with the atrocities which as I speak here this afternoon are being perpetrated upon the Poles. In German-occupied Poland the most hideous form of terrorism prevails. In this there are two distinct phases. In the first the Germans tried to cow the population by shooting individuals picked at random from the towns. At one place where they had decided to shoot thirty-five people they collected thirty-four, and then, finding themselves one short, went into a chemist's shop and seized the first person they saw to make up the tàlly. But later on they became more discriminating—they made careful search for the natural leaders of Polish life: the nobles, the landowners, the priests, as well as prominent workmen and peasants. It is estimated that upward of fifteen thousand intellectual leaders have been shot. These horrible mass executions are a frequent occurrence. At one place three hundred were lined up against the wall; at another a group of drunken German officers are said to have shot seventy hostages in prison; at another a hundred and thirty-six Polish students, some of whom were only twelve or thirteen years old, were butchered. Torture has been used. Press gangs seize men and women in the streets and drive them off in droves to forced labour in Germany. Famine stalks not only amid the ruins of Warsaw, but far and wide throughout that ancient country which a few months ago was the home of a people of over thirty-five millions, with a history extending back far beyond anything that Germany can boast.
        Free Trade Hall, Manchester, January 27, 1940.

Fate of Poland. What a frightful fate has overtaken Poland! Here was a community of nearly thirty-five millions of people, with all the organization of a modern government, and all the traditions of an ancient state, which in a few weeks was dashed out of civilized existence to become an incoherent multitude of tortured and starving men, women and children, ground beneath the heel of two rival forms of withering and blasting tyranny. The other day in a well-known British harbour I inspected the crew of a Polish destroyer. I have rarely seen a finer body of men. I was stirred by their discipline and bearing. Yet how tragic was their plight! Their ship was afloat, but their country had foundered. But as I looked around upon all the great ships of war which lay at their anchors, and at all the preparations which were being made on every side to carry this war forward at all costs as long as may be necessary, I comforted myself with the thought that when these Polish sailors have finished their work with the British navy, we will take particular care that they once more have a home to go to.   *London, March 30, 1940.*

Atrocities. All over Europe, races and states whose culture and history made them a part of the general life of Christendom in centuries when the Prussians were no better than a barbarous tribe, and the German Empire no more than an agglomeration of pumpernickel principalities, are now prostrate under the dark, cruel yoke of Hitler and his Nazi gang. Every week his firing parties are busy in a dozen lands. Monday he shoots Dutchmen; Tuesday, Norwegians; Wednesday, French and Belgians stand against the wall; Thursday it is the Czechs who must suffer. And now there are the Serbs and the Greeks to fill his repulsive bill of executions. But always, all the days, there are the Poles. The atrocities committed by Hitler upon the Poles, the ravaging of their country, the scattering of their homes, the affronts to their religion, the enslavement of their man-power, exceed in severity and in scale the villainies perpetrated by Hitler in any other conquered land.

Monstrous Dream. This war against the mechanized barbarians, who, slave-hearted themselves, are fitted only to carry their curse to others—this war will be long and hard. But the end is sure; the end will reward all toil, all disappointments, all suffering in those who faithfully serve the cause of European and world freedom. A day will dawn, perhaps sooner than we have now a right to hope, when the insane attempt to found a Prussian domination on racial hatred, on the armoured vehicle, on the secret police, on the alien overseer, and on still more filthy quislings, will pass like a monstrous dream. And in that morning of hope and freedom, not only the embattled and—at last—well-armed democracies, but all that is noble and fearless in the New World as well as in the Old, will salute the rise of Poland to be a nation once again.

Traditions of Poland. We in this country who are conscious that our strength is built on the broad masses of the British nation appreciate and admire the Polish nation for its noble attitude since the outbreak of the war. Mainly for geographical reasons, personal contacts between our two peoples have been restricted in the past; and fighting as we are at opposite ends of Europe against our common foe, this war has not yet provided an opportunity for personal contacts on any large scale between you and my own countrymen.

The fortunes of war have, however, brought to these shores your President, your Government and many thousands of brave Polish soldiers, airmen, sailors and merchant seamen. Their bearing has won them universal admiration in this country, and cast further lustre, if that were possible, upon the proud, heroic traditions of Poland.

London, May 3, 1941.

Future of Poland. I took occasion to raise personally with Marshal Stalin the question of the future of Poland. I pointed out that it was in fulfillment of our guarantee to Poland that Great Britain declared war upon Nazi Germany; that we had never weakened in our resolve, even in the period when we were all alone; and that the fate of the Polish nation holds a prime place in the thoughts and policies of His Majesty's Government and of the British Parliament. It was with great pleasure that I heard from Marshal Stalin that he, too, was resolved upon the creation and maintenance of a strong integral independent Poland as one of the leading powers in Europe. He has several times repeated these declarations in public, and I am convinced that they represent the settled policy of the Soviet Union.

Commons, February 22, 1944.

Poland and Russia. Our effort to bring about a renewal of relations between the Polish Government in London and Russia has not succeeded. We deeply regret that fact, and we must take care to say nothing that would make any agreement more difficult in the future. I must repeat that the essential part of any arrangement is regulation of the Polish eastern frontiers, and that, in return for any withdrawal made by Poland in that quarter, she should receive other territories at the expense of Germany, which will give her an ample seaboard and a good, adequate and reasonable homeland in which the Polish nation may safely dwell. Nothing can surpass the bravery of our Polish allies in Italy and elsewhere daily on the sea and in the air, and in the heroic resistance of the Underground Movement to the Germans. I have seen here men who came a few days ago out of Poland, who told me about it, and who are in relation with, and under orders of, the present Polish Government in London. They are most anxious that this Underground Movement should not clash with the advancing Russian army but should help it, and orders have been sent by the Polish Government in London that the Underground Movement should help the Russian armies in as many ways as possible. There are many ways in which guerrillas can be successful, and we must trust that statesmanship will yet find some way through. *Commons, May 24, 1944.*

Liberation. The Russian armies now stand before the gates of Warsaw. They bring the liberation of Poland in their hands. They offer freedom, sovereignty and independence to the Poles. They ask that there should be a Poland friendly to Russia. This seems to me very reasonable, considering the injuries which Russia has suffered through the Germans marching across Poland to attack her.

Commons, August 2, 1944.

Britain and Poland. It would be affectation to pretend that the attitude of the British, and, I believe, the United States Governments towards Poland is identical with that of the Soviet Union. Every allowance must be made for the different conditions of history and geography which govern the relationship of the Western democracies on the one hand and the Soviet Government on the other with the Polish nation. Marshal Stalin has repeatedly declared himself in favour of a strong, friendly Poland, sovereign and independent. In this our great Eastern Ally is in the fullest accord with His Majesty's Government, and also, judging from American public statements, with the United States. We in this island and throughout our Empire who drew the sword against mighty Germany, on account of her aggression against Poland, have sentiments and duties towards Poland which deeply stir the British race. Everything in our power has been and will be done to achieve, both in the letter and in the spirit, the declared purposes towards Poland of the three great allies.

Commons, September 28, 1944.

Polish Home Army. I am sure I am expressing the feelings of the House, as well as those of His Majesty's Government, in paying tribute to the heroic stand of the Polish Home Army and of the Polish civilian population of Warsaw. Their resistance to overwhelming odds, under inconceivable conditions of hardship, came to an end on October 3rd, after a fight which lasted 63 days. Despite all the efforts of the Soviet army, the strong German positions on the Vistula could not be taken, and relief could not come in time. British, American, Polish and Soviet airmen did what they could to succour the Poles at Warsaw, but although this sustained the Polish resistance beyond what could have seemed possible, it could not turn the tide. In the battle for Warsaw, terrible damage has been inflicted upon that noble city, and its heroic population has undergone sufferings and privations unsurpassed even among the miseries of this war.

Commons, October 5, 1944.

Home for Poland. It is our persevering and constant aim that the Polish people, after their sufferings and vicissitudes, shall find in Europe an abiding home and resting-place, which though it may not entirely coincide or correspond with the pre-war frontiers of Poland, will, nevertheless, be adequate for the needs of the Polish nation and not inferior in character and quality, taking the picture as a whole, to what they previously possessed.   *Commons, October 27, 1944.*

Poland Restored. We have never weakened in any way in our resolve that Poland shall be restored and stand erect as a sovereign, independent nation, free to model her social institutions or any other institutions in any way her people choose, provided, I must say, that these are not on Fascist lines, and provided that Poland stands loyally as a barrier and friend of Russia against German aggression from the west.

Eastern Frontier. I am absolutely convinced that it is in the profound future interest of the Polish nation that they should reach agreement with the Soviet Government about their disputed frontiers in the east before the march of the Russian armies through the main part of Poland takes place. This is the great gift they have to make to Russia, a settlement now at this time which gives the firm title of mutual agreement to what might otherwise be disputed at the Peace Conference. I must, however, say, because I am most anxious the House should understand the whole position, speaking on behalf of His Majesty's Government in a way which I believe would probably be held binding by our successors, that at the Conference we shall adhere to the lines which I am now unfolding to the House, and shall not hesitate to proclaim that the Russians are justly treated, and rightly treated, in being granted the claim they make to the eastern frontier along the Curzon Line as described.   *Commons, December 15, 1944.*

Citizenship for Poles. His Majesty's Government will never forget the debt they owe to the Polish troops who have served so valiantly, and to all those who have fought under our command. I earnestly hope it may be possible to offer citizenship and freedom of the British Empire, if they so desire. I am not able to make a declaration on that subject to-day, because all matters affecting citizenship require to be discussed between this country and the Dominions, and that takes time. But so far as we are concerned we should think it an honour to have such faithful and valiant warriors dwelling among us as if they were men of our own blood.

Problem of Poland. For more than a year past, and since the tide of war has turned so strongly against Germany, the

Polish problem has been divided into two main issues—the frontiers of Poland and the freedom of Poland.

Solemn Declarations. Most solemn declarations have been made by Marshal Stalin and the Soviet Union that the sovereign independence of Poland is to be maintained, and this decision is now joined in both by Great Britain and the United States. Here also, the world organization will in due course assume a measure of responsibility. The Poles will have their future in their own hands, with the single limitation that they must honestly follow, in harmony with their allies, a policy friendly to Russia. That is surely reasonable.

Commons, February 27, 1945.

New Frontiers. It is not in the power of any British government to bring home solutions which would be regarded as perfect by the great majority of Members of this House wherever they may sit. I must put on record my own opinion that the provisional western frontier agreed upon for Poland, running from Stettin on the Baltic, along the Oder and its tributary, the western Neisse, comprising as it does one quarter of the arable land of all Germany, is not a good augury for the future map of Europe. We always had in the Coalition Government a desire that Poland should receive ample compensation in the west for the territory ceded to Russia east of the Curzon Line. But here I think a mistake has been made, in which the Provisional Government of Poland have been an ardent partner, by going far beyond what necessity or equity required. . . .

There are few virtues that the Poles do not possess—and there are few mistakes they have ever avoided.

Commons, August 16, 1945.

New Domination. Poland is denied all free expression of her national will. Her worst appetites of expansion are encouraged. At the same time, she is held in strict control by a Soviet-dominated government who do not dare have a free election under the observation of representatives of the three or four great powers. The fate of Poland seems to be an unending tragedy, and we, who went to war all ill-prepared on her behalf, watch with sorrow the strange outcome of our endeavours. I deeply regret that none of the Polish troops—and I must say this—who fought with us on a score of battlefields, who poured out their blood in the common cause, are to be allowed to march in the Victory Parade. They will be in our thoughts on that day. We shall never forget their bravery and martial skill, associated with our own glories at Tobruk, at Cassino and at Arnhem.

Commons, June 5, 1946.

Satellite. We must be very careful to distinguish in our minds between the present Polish Government, and the heart of the Polish nation, to whose sorrows and sufferings there seems never to be an end.   *Commons, October 23, 1946.*

The Boers

The Boer. The Boer is a curious combination of the squire and the peasant, and under the rough coat of the farmer there are very often to be found the instincts of the squire. . . .

No people in the world received so much verbal sympathy and so little practical support as the Boers. If I were a Boer fighting in the field—and if I were a Boer I hope I should be fighting in the field—I would not allow myself to be taken in by any message of sympathy, not even if it were signed by a hundred hon. Members.   *Commons, February 18, 1901.*

Co-operation. It must be self-evident to everyone who had studied the South Africa question that the loyal co-operation of the Boers in the settlement of South Africa would be such a dazzling bribe, such an enormous advantage, that it would be inconceivable that any government acquainted with the conditions should refuse to make any considerable sacrifices to secure so desirable an end.   *Commons, January 21, 1902.*

General Louis Botha. As a matter of principle General Botha would be the last person to avail himself of the influence of a Member of Parliament in order to obtain for himself special terms which other Boers did not get.   *Commons, March 26, 1906.*

Indentured Labour. If we were able by some good fortune to make a settlement in the Transvaal between the two races which would be lasting, which would give the Boers direct partnership in the British Empire so that both races might work and live together and wrangle together in the rough-and-tumble of representative institutions, then I say we should have achieved a work which would linger in the minds of the people of South Africa long after every trace of this hideous Chinese monstrosity has been effaced from human recollection.   *Commons, June 8, 1906.*

Asiatics. All Asiatic races are subject to certain disabilities which do not apply to Europeans. [In South Africa.]   *Commons, July 16, 1906.*

Africander Nation. If the near future should unfold to our eyes a tranquil, prosperous, consolidated Africander nation under the protecting aegis of the British Crown, then, the good also will not be confined to South Africa; then the cause of the poor and the weak all over the world will have been sustained; and everywhere small peoples will get more room to breathe, and everywhere great empires will be encouraged by our example to step forward—and it only needs a step— into the sunshine of a more gentle and more generous age. . . .

The people of these colonies, and, in a special measure, the Boers, will become the trustees of freedom all over the world. We have tried to act with fairness and good feeling. If by any chance our counsels of reconciliation should come to nothing, if our policy should end in mocking disaster, then the resulting evil would not be confined to South Africa. Our unfortunate experience would be trumpeted forth all over the world wherever despotism wanted a good argument for bayonets, whenever an arbitrary Government wished to deny or curtail the liberties of imprisoned nationalities.

Colonial Policy. It has always been the settled and successful colonial policy of this country during the last fifty years to allow great liberties of self-government to distant communities under the Crown, and no responsible statesman, and no British Cabinet, so far as I know, ever contemplated any other solution of the South African problem but that of full self-government.   *Commons, December 17, 1906.*

The Empire and the Dominions

French Canadians. The French Canadians derived greater pleasure from singing "God Save the King" than from singing "Rule Britannia."   *Commons, July 19, 1904.*

Exploitation of Natives. All forms of cruelty to natives are to be reprobated, but there is one form of cruelty which is especially odious; it is when it takes the form of the exploitation of natives for the purpose of gain.
      Commons, February 28, 1906.

Empire as Family. The British Empire existed on the principles of a family and not on those of a syndicate.

Colonial Affairs. Colonial affairs suffer very much when brought into the arena of British Party politics.
Imperial Conference, Downing Street, London, May 7, 1907.

Inclusive Empire. Let us then seek to impress year after year upon the British Empire an inclusive and not an exclusive character. We who sit on this side of the House, who look forward to larger brotherhoods and more exact standards of social justice, value and cherish the British Empire because it represents more than any other similar organization has ever represented, the peaceful co-operation of all sorts of men in all sorts of countries, and because we think it is, in that respect at least, a model of what we hope the whole world will some day become.   *Commons, July 15, 1907.*

National Satiation. We have got all we want in territory, but our claim to be left in undisputed enjoyment of vast and splendid possessions, largely acquired by war and largely maintained by force, is one which often seems less reasonable to others than to us.   *Commons, March 17, 1914.*

Britain's Work in India. The reason why, in my judgment, Lord Irwin, for all his virtue and courage has not succeeded in India as he deserved to, is that he has been proceeding upon a wrong mental theme. His attitude towards India has throughout been an apology. He has not shown sufficient confidence in the indispensable work which our country has done, and is doing, for India, or in British resolution that it shall not be interrupted or destroyed. That is the sole foundation upon which the peaceful and successful administration of India can be used.

Dominion Status for India. You will ask me what, then, are we to make of our promises of Dominion status and responsible government. Surely we cannot break our word! There I agree. The formal, plighted word of the King-Emperor is inviolable. It does not follow, however, that every Socialist jack-in-office can commit this great country by his perorations. . . . Except as an ultimate visionary goal, Dominion status like that of Canada or Australia is not going to happen in India in any period which we can even remotely foresee.   *Manchester, January 30, 1931.*

Price of Empire. Already Mr. Gandhi moves about surrounded by a circle of wealthy men, who see at their finger-tips the acquisition of an Empire on cheaper terms than were ever yet offered in the world. Sir, the Roman senator, Didius Julianus, was dining in a restaurant when they told him that the Praetorian Guard put the Empire up to auction and were selling it in the ditch in their camp; he ran out, and, according to Gibbon, bought it for £200 sterling per soldier. That was fairly cheap; but the terms upon which the Empire is being

offered to this group surrounding Mr. Gandhi are cheaper still.
Commons, March 12, 1931.

Nehru. If in the sacrifice of every British interest and of all the necessary safeguards and means of preserving peace and progress in India you came to terms with Gandhi, Gandhi would at that selfsame moment cease to count any more in the Indian situation. Already Nehru, his young rival in the Indian Congress, is preparing to supersede him the moment that he has squeezed his last drop from the British lemon.

Provincial Government for India. We believe that the next forward step is the development of Indian responsibility in the provincial government of India. Efforts should be made to make them more truly representative of the real needs of the people. Indians should be given ample opportunities to try their hand at giving capable government in the provinces; and meanwhile the central Imperial executive, which is the sole guarantee of impartiality between races, creeds and classes, should preserve its sovereign power intact, and allow no derogation from its responsibility to Parliament. . . .

It makes me sick when I hear the Secretary of State saying of India *"she* will do this," and *"she* will do that!" India is an abstraction . . . India is no more a political personality than Europe. India is a geographical term. It is no more a united nation than the Equator.

Departure from India. There can be no doubt, therefore, that the departure of the British from India, which Mr. Gandhi advocates, and which Mr. Nehru demands, would be followed first by a struggle in the North and thereafter by a reconquest of the South by the North and of the Hindus by the Moslems. This danger has not escaped the crafty foresight of the Brahmins. It is for that reason that they wish to have control of a British army, or failing that, a white army of Janissaries officered, as Mr. Gandhi has suggested, by Germans or other Europeans.

A Derelict Empire. All sorts of greedy appetites have been excited and many itching fingers are stretching and scratching at the vast pillage of a derelict Empire.
Royal Albert Hall, London, March 18, 1931.

Concessions to India. Where there have been differences between Indians and Great Britain, some adjustment has been made by Great Britain giving way; but as to differences between Indians themselves, there has not been one concession, not one difficulty has been solved or surmounted. Nevertheless, on we go, moving slowly, in a leisurely manner, jerkily onwards, towards an unworkable conclusion, crawling me-

thodically towards the abyss which we shall reach in due course.
Commons, July 9, 1931.

Canada. Canada is the linchpin of the English-speaking world. Canada, with those relations of friendly affectionate intimacy with the United States on the one hand and with her unswerving fidelity to the British Commonwealth and the Motherland on the other, is the link which, spanning the oceans, brings the continents into their true relation and will prevent in future generations any growth of division between the proud and the happy nations of Europe and the great countries which have come into existence in the New World.
Mansion House, London, September 4, 1941.

Canada occupies a unique position in the British Empire because of its unbreakable ties with Britain and its ever-growing friendship and intimate association with the United States. Canada is a potent magnet, drawing together those in the New World and in the Old whose fortunes are now united in a deadly struggle for life and honour against the common foe.
Ottawa, Canada, December 30, 1941.

Liquidation of Empire. We mean to hold our own. I have not become the King's First Minister in order to preside over the liquidation of the British Empire.
Mansion House, London, November 10, 1942.

Indian Army. All the great countries in this war count their armies by millions, but the Indian Army has a peculiar characteristic not found in the armies of Britain or the United States or Russia or France or in the armies of our foes, in that it is entirely composed of volunteers. No one has been conscripted or compelled. The same thing is broadly true throughout our great Colonial Empire.
Guildhall, London, June 30, 1943.

Canadian Ships. Canada has become in the course of this war an important seafaring nation, building many scores of warships and merchant ships, some of them thousands of miles from salt water, and sending them forth manned by hardy Canadian seamen to guard the Atlantic convoys and our vital lifeline across the ocean. The munition industries of Canada have played a most important part in our war economy. Last, but not least, Canada has relieved Great Britain of what would otherwise have been a debt for these munitions of no less than $2,000,000,000.
London, August 31, 1943.

Anxiety about the Empire. There were, when I was young, some statesmen whose names are honoured, who spoke of the Colonies as burdens, and of the Dominions as fruit which would fall from the tree when ripe. I did not live myself in days when those speeches were made, but I remember well times of great anxiety about the Empire, at the end of the last century.

Solidarity of the Empire. I remember coming out of the Cabinet meeting on an August afternoon in 1914, when war was certain, and the fleet was already mobilized, with this feeling: "How are we to explain it all to Canada, Australia, South Africa and New Zealand; nay, how are we to explain it all to our own people in the short time left?" But, when we came out from the fierce controversy of the Cabinet room into the open air, the whole of the peoples of the British Empire, of every race and every clime, had already sprung to arms. Our old enemies, recent enemies, Generals Botha and Smuts, were already saddling their horses to rally their commandos to the attack on Germany, and Irishmen, whose names I always bear in my memory with regard, John Redmond and his brother, and others of the old Irish Parliamentary Party which fought us for so many years in this House, pleading the cause of Ireland, with great eloquence and Parliamentary renown; there they were, making these speeches of absolute support and unity with this country until everybody said everywhere: "The brightest spot in the world is Ireland." It may be that a grand opportunity was lost then. We must keep our eyes open. I always keep mine open on the Irish question.

Commons, April 21, 1944.

The Empire and the War. Once again the British Commonwealth and Empire emerges safe, undiminished, and united from a mortal struggle. Monstrous tyrannies which menaced our life have been beaten to the ground in ruin, and a brighter radiance illumines the Imperial Crown than any which our annals record. The light is brighter because it comes not only from the fierce but fading glow of military achievements . . . but because there mingle with it in mellow splendour the hopes, joys and blessings of almost all mankind. This is the true glory, and long will it gleam upon our forward path.

Commons, August 15, 1945.

Unity of India. India is a continent as large and more populous than Europe, and not less deeply divided by racial and religious differences than Europe. India has no more unity than Europe, except that superficial unity which has been created by our rule and guidance in the last 150 years.

Westminster, May 7, 1946.

India and the Empire. No one will doubt the sincerity and the earnestness with which the Cabinet ministers concerned and the viceroy [Lord Wavell] have laboured to bring about the solution of Indian disagreement. They have worked for that solution with the zeal that would be natural if it were to gain an empire and not to cast one away.

Commons, May 16, 1946.

Withdrawal from India. Take stock round the world at the present moment; after all we are entitled to survey the whole field. We declare ourselves ready to abandon the mighty Empire and Continent of India with all the work we have done in the last 200 years, territory over which we possess unimpeachable sovereignty. The Government are, apparently, ready to leave the 400 million Indians to fall into all the horrors of sanguinary civil war—civil war compared to which anything that could happen in Palestine would be microscopic; wars of elephants compared with wars of mice.

Commons, August 1, 1946.

Censure for Empire. What has been the effect of our immense act of surrender in India? On the morrow of our victory and of our services, without which human freedom would not have survived, we are divesting ourselves of the mighty and wonderful empire which had been built up in India by two hundred years of effort and sacrifice, and the number of the King's subjects is being reduced to barely a quarter of what it has been for generations. Yet at this very moment and in the presence of this unparalleled act of voluntary abdication, we are still ceaselessly abused by the Soviet wireless and by certain unfriendly elements in the United States for being a land-grabbing Imperialistic power seeking expansion and aggrandizement. While Soviet Russia is expanding or seeking to expand in every direction, and has already brought many extra scores of millions of people directly or indirectly under the despotic control of the Kremlin and the rigours of Communist discipline, we who sought nothing from this war but to do our duty and are in fact reducing ourselves to a fraction of our former size and population, are successfully held up to world censure.

Blackpool, October 5, 1946.

Incongruity. To abandon India, with all the dire consequences that would follow therefrom, but to have a war with the Jews in order to give Palestine to the Arabs amid the execration of the world, appears to carry incongruity of thought and policy to levels which have rarely been attained in human history.

Commons, November 12, 1946.

Choices in India. In all this confusion, uncertainty and gathering storm, which those who have studied the Indian problem over long years might well have foreseen, there ap-

pear at the present time to be three choices—the proverbial three choices—before the British Parliament. The first is to proceed with ruthless logic to quit India regardless of what may happen there. This we can certainly do. Nothing can prevent us, if it be the will of Parliament, from gathering together our women and children and unarmed civilians, and marching under strong rearguards to the sea. That is one choice. The second is to assert the principle, so often proclaimed, that the King needs no unwilling subjects and that the British Commonwealth of Nations contemplates no compulsory partnership, that, in default of real agreement, the partition of India between the two different races and religions, widely differing entities, must be faced: that those who wish to make their own lives in their own way may do so, and the gods be with them; and that those who desire to find, in a variety of systems, a means of association with our great free Commonwealth may also be permitted to take the course which, ultimately, they may show themselves ready to take.
Commons, December 12, 1946.

Parties in India. The Indian political Parties and political classes do not represent the Indian masses. It is a delusion to believe that they do. I wish they did. They are not as representative of them as the movements in Britain represent the surges and impulses of the British nation.
Commons, March 6, 1947.

Nehru. It was a cardinal mistake to entrust the government of India to the caste Hindu, Mr. Nehru. He has good reason to be the most bitter enemy of any connection between India and the British Commonwealth.

Loss of India. In this melancholy tale of the casting away of the British Empire in India and of the misfortunes and slaughter which are falling upon its peoples, all the blame cannot be thrown on one Party. But the Socialist Government on gaining power threw themselves into the task of destroying our long-built-up and splendid structure in the East with zeal and gusto, and they certainly have brought widespread ruin, misery and bloodshed upon the Indian masses to an extent no man can measure, by the methods with which they have handled the problem. *Brighton, October 4, 1947.*

Canada. There are no limits to the majestic future which lies before the mighty expanse of Canada with its virile, aspiring, cultured and generous-hearted people. Canada is the vital link in the English-speaking world and joins across the Atlantic Ocean the vast American democracy of the

United States with our famous old island and the fifty millions who keep the flag flying here.

Guildhall, London, November 19, 1951.

International Co-operation

League of Nations. I hope that the League of Nations is not going to be asked now to do the impossible. Those who believe, as I do sincerely, that the League of Nations is a priceless instrument of international comity, which may play as great a part as the most daring, hopeful founders ever forecast for it, should be especially careful not to put upon the League strains which in its present stage it is utterly incapable of bearing. . . .

I have sympathy with, and respect for, the well-meaning, loyal-hearted people who make up the League of Nations Union in this country, but what impresses me most about them is their long-suffering and inexhaustible gullibility. Any scheme of any kind for disarmament put forward by any country, so long as it is surrounded by suitable phraseology, is hailed by them, and the speeches are cheered, and those who speak gain the need of their applause.

Commons, November 23, 1932.

International Force. I do not believe you will ever succeed in building up an international force in a vague and general manner, or that it can be created in cold blood. But it might well be that an international force would come into being by an alliance of national forces for a particular emergency or for particular purposes, and once having been started, it might give the security to the world which would avert the approaching curse of war.

Commons, March 21, 1934.

Mainstay of Peace. I have been trying to seek out for myself what would be the best way of preventing war, and it has seemed to me that the League of Nations should be the great instrument upon which all those resolves to maintain peace should centre, and that we should all make our contribution to the League of Nations.

Commons, July 13, 1934.

Pacifists. When I hear extreme pacifists denouncing this act of the League of Nations I am left wondering what foundations these gentlemen offer to countries for abandoning national armaments.

Commons, May 2, 1935.

Naval Treaty with Germany. We have, however, unintentionally, nullified and stultified the League of Nations' condemnation of treaty-breaking in respect of armaments, in which we were ourselves concerned, in which, indeed, we took a leading part. We have, it seems to me, revealed, again quite unintentionally, a very considerable measure of indifference to the interests of other powers, particularly powers in the Baltic, who were encouraged by our example to join with us in the League of Nations in condemning treaty-breaking. In the name of what is called practical realism we have seemed to depart from the principle of collective security in a very notable fashion. [By concluding the Treaty with Germany.]
Commons, July 11, 1935.

Perseverance. We have moved on and we are not going to move back. The League of Nations has passed from shadow into substance, from theory into practice, from rhetoric into reality. We see a structure always majestic, but hitherto shadowy, which is now being clothed with life and power, and endowed with coherent thought and concerted action. We begin to feel the beatings of a pulse which may, we hope and we pray, one day—and the sooner for our efforts—restore a greater measure of health and strength to the whole world. We can see these difficulties and dangers for ourselves, but if we confront them with a steady eye, I believe the House and the country will reach the conclusion that the case for perseverance holds the field. . . .

Some people say: "Put your trust in the League of Nations." Others say: "Put your trust in British rearmament." I say we want both. I put my trust in both. . . .

It is quite certain that the British Empire will never fight a war contrary to the Covenant of the League of Nations. Any attempt to embark upon a war of aggrandizement or pride or ambition would break the British Empire into fragments, and any Government that was even suspected of such a motive would be chased from power long before its machinations could become effective. . . .

If I am asked, "How far will you go in support of the Covenant of the League of Nations?" I shall say we ought to go the whole way with the whole lot.
Commons, October 24, 1935.

Moral Force. I think we ought to place our trust in those moral forces which are enshrined in the Covenant of the League of Nations. Do not let us mock at them, for they are surely on our side. Do not mock at them, for this may well be a time when the highest idealism is not divorced from strategic prudence. Do not mock at them, for these may be years, strange as it may seem, when Right may walk hand in hand with Might. . . .

Let us, therefore, do everything in our power to add to our strength and use that strength for the purpose of helping the gathering together of the nations upon the basis of the Covenant of the League. Upon the rock of the Covenant many nations, great and small, are drawing constantly and swiftly together. In spite of the disappointments of the past, in spite of many misgivings, difficulties and ridiculings, that process is continuing, and these nations are welding themselves into what will some day be a formidable yet benignant alliance, pledged to resist wrong-doing and the violence of an aggressor.   *Commons, March 4, 1937.*

Grand Alliance. If a number of states were assembled around Great Britain and France in a solemn treaty for mutual defence against aggression; if they had their forces marshalled in what you may call a Grand Alliance; if they had their staff arrangements concerted; if all this rested, as it can honourably rest, upon the Covenant of the League of Nations, in pursuance of all the purposes and ideals of the League of Nations; if that were sustained, as it would be, by the moral sense of the world; and if it were done in the year 1938—and, believe me, it may be the last chance there will be for doing it—then I say that you might even now arrest this approaching war. Then perhaps the curse which overhangs Europe would pass away. Then perhaps the ferocious passions which now grip a great people would turn inwards and not outwards in an internal rather than an external explosion, and mankind would be spared the deadly ordeal towards which we have been sagging and sliding month by month.

                                        Commons, March 14, 1938.

League of Peoples. If the League of Nations has been mishandled and broken, we must rebuild it. If a League of peace-seeking people is set at naught, we must convert it into a League of armed peoples, too faithful to molest others, too strong to be molested themselves. . . .

It is no use espousing a cause without having also a method and a plan by which that cause may be made to win. I would not affront you with generalities. There must be the vision. There must be a plan, and there must be action following upon it. We express our immediate plan and policy in a single sentence: "Arm, and stand by the Covenant." In this alone lies the assurance of safety, the defence of freedom, and the hope of peace.

Free Trade Hall, Manchester, May 9, 1938.

Council of Europe. One can imagine that under a world institution embodying or representing the United Nations, and some day all nations, there should come into being a Council of Europe and a Council of Asia. As, according to the forecast I am outlining, the war against Japan will still be raging, it is upon the creation of the Council of Europe and the settlement of Europe that the first practical task will be centred. Now this is a stupendous business. In Europe lie most of the causes which have led to these two world wars. In Europe dwell the historic parent races from whom our western civilization has been so largely derived. I believe myself to be what is called a good European, and deem it a noble task to take part in reviving the fertile genius and in restoring the true greatness of Europe.

London, March 21, 1943.

Failure. It is said that the League of Nations failed. If so, that is largely because it was abandoned, and later on betrayed: because those who were its best friends were till a very late period infected with a futile pacifism: because the United States, the originating impulse, fell out of the line: because, while France had been bled white and England was supine and bewildered, a monstrous growth of aggression sprang up in Germany, in Italy and Japan.

Harvard University, September 6, 1943.

Brotherhood among Men. I rejoice in the prospect, now becoming sure and certain, that the Nazi ideology, enforced in a hideous manner upon a vast population, will presently be beaten to the ground. These facts and manifestations, which I see taking place continually as the world war crashes onwards to its close, make me increasingly confident that when it is won, when the hateful aggressive Nazi and Fascist systems have been laid low, and when every precaution has been taken against their ever rising again, there may be a new brotherhood among men which will not be based upon crude antagonisms of ideology but upon broad, simple, homely ideals of peace, justice and freedom. Therefore, I am glad that the war is becoming less an ideological war between rival systems and more and more the means by which high ideals and solid benefits may be achieved by the broad masses of the people in many lands and ultimately in all.

Commons, August 2, 1944.

Lack of Concerted Action. The League of Nations did not fail because of its principles or conceptions. It failed because these principles were deserted by those states who had brought it into being. It failed because the governments of those days feared to face the facts, and act while time remained. This disaster must not be repeated.

Zürich University, September 19, 1946.

Britain and the United States

America and Britain. I have always thought that it ought to be the main end of English state-craft over a long period of years to cultivate good relations with the United States.

Commons, June 22, 1903.

Anglo-American Destiny. These are not the days when you can order the British nation or the British Empire about as if it were a pawn on the chessboard of Europe. You cannot do it. Of course, if the United States were willing to come into the European scene as a prime factor, if they were willing to guarantee to those countries who take their advice that they would not suffer for it, then an incomparably wider and happier prospect would open to the whole world. If they were willing not only to sign, but to ratify, treaties of that kind, it would be an enormous advantage. It is quite safe for the British Empire to go as far in any guarantee in Europe as the United States is willing to go, and hardly any difficulty in the world could not be solved by the faithful co-operation of the English-speaking peoples. But that is not going to happen to-morrow.

Commons, November 23, 1932.

Anglo-American Navies. I have always thought that the union of these two great forces [the British and American navies], not for purposes of aggression or narrow selfish interests, but in an honourable cause, constitutes what I may call the sheet-anchor of human freedom and progress.

Corn Exchange, Cambridge, May 19, 1939.

American Bases. His Majesty's Government are entirely willing to accord defence facilities to the United States on a 99 years' leasehold basis, and we feel sure that our interests no less than theirs, and the interests of the Colonies themselves, and of Canada and Newfoundland, will be served thereby.

American Destroyers. Undoubtedly this process [fifty American destroyers handed over to Britain] means that these two great organizations of the English-speaking democracies—the British Empire and the United States—will have to be somewhat mixed up together in some of their affairs for mutual and general advantage. For my own part, looking out upon the future, I do not view the process with any misgivings. I could not stop it if I wished—no one can stop it. Like the Mississippi, it just keeps rolling along. Let it roll! Let it roll on in full flood, inexorable, irresistible, benignant, to broader lands and better days.

Commons, August 20, 1940.

Anglo-American Unity. It is no exaggeration to say that the future of the whole world and the hopes of a broadening civilization founded upon Christian ethics depend upon the relation between the British Empire or Commonwealth of Nations and the U.S.A. The identity of purpose and persistence of resolve prevailing throughout the English-speaking world will, more than any other single fact, determine the way of life which will be open to the generations and perhaps to the centuries which follow our own.

London, January 9, 1941.

Action of the United States. During the last year we have gained by our bearing and conduct a potent hold upon the sentiments of the people of the United States. Never, never in our history, have we been held in such admiration and regard across the Atlantic Ocean. In that great Republic, now in much travail and stress of soul, it is customary to use all the many valid, solid arguments about American interests and American safety, which depend upon the destruction of Hitler and his foul gang and even fouler doctrines. But in the long run—believe me, for I know—the action of the United States will be dedicated, not by methodical calculations of profit and loss, but by moral sentiment, and by that gleaming flash of resolve which lifts the hearts of men and nations, and springs from the spiritual foundations of human life itself. . . .

The President and Congress of the United States, having newly fortified themselves by contact with their electors, have solemnly pledged their aid to Britain in this war because they deem our cause just, and because they know their own interests and safety would be endangered if we were destroyed. They are taxing themselves heavily. They have passed great legislation. They have turned a large part of their gigantic industry to making munitions which we need. They have even given us or lent us valuable weapons of their own.

London, April 27, 1941.

Lend and Lease. By very severe measures we had been able to gather and spend in America about £500,000,000 sterling, but the end of our financial resources was in sight—

nay, had actually been reached. All we could do at that time a
year ago was to place orders in the United States without being
able to see our way through, but on a tide of hope and not
without important encouragement.

Then came the majestic policy of the President and Congress
of the United States in passing the Lend and Lease Bill, under
which in two successive enactments about £3,000,000,000
sterling were dedicated to the cause of world freedom without
—mark this, for it is unique—the setting up of any account in
money. Never again let us hear the taunt that money is the
ruling thought or power in the hearts of the American democracy. The Lend and Lease Bill must be regarded without question as the most unsordid act in the whole of recorded history.
Mansion House, London, November 10, 1941.

Solidarity with America. Should the United States become
involved in war with Japan, the British declaration will follow
within the hour.   *Commons, November 10, 1941.*

Anglo-American Solidarity. Prodigious hammer-strokes
have been needed to bring us together again, or if you will
allow me to use other language, I will say that he must indeed
have a blind soul who cannot see that some great purpose and
design is being worked out here below, of which we have the
honour to be the faithful servants. It is not given to us to peer
into the mysteries of the future. Still, I avow my hope and
faith, sure and inviolate, that in the days to come the British
and American peoples will, for their own safety and for the
good of all, walk together side by side in majesty, in justice,
and in peace.

Speech to Congress, Washington, December 26, 1941.

Comradeship. The other day I crossed the Atlantic again
to see President Roosevelt. This time we met not only as
friends, but as comrades, standing side by side and shoulder to
shoulder, in a battle for dear life and dearer honour, in the
common cause, and against a common foe. When I survey and
compute the power of the United States and its vast resources
and feel that they are now in with us, with the British Commonwealth of Nations all together, however long it lasts, till
death or victory, I cannot believe there is any other fact in
the whole world which can compare with that. That is what
I have dreamed of, aimed at and worked for, and now it has
come to pass.   *London, February 15, 1942.*

Peaceful Nations. When peaceful nations like the British
and the American, very careless in peacetime about their
defences, care-free, unsuspecting nations, peoples who have

never known defeat—improvident nations I will say, feckless nations, nations who despise the military art and thought war so wicked that it could never happen again—when nations like these are set upon by highly organized, heavily armed conspirators, planning and calculating in secret for years on end, exalting war as the highest form of human effort, glorifying slaughter and aggression, prepared and trained to the last point science and discipline can carry them, is it not natural that the peaceful, unprepared, improvident peoples should suffer terribly and that the wicked, scheming aggressors should have their reign of savage exaltation?

Usher Hall, Edinburgh, October 12, 1942.

Home Guard. Our eyes are fixed upon the future, but we may spare a moment to glance back to those past days of 1940, which are so strangely imprinted upon our memories that we can hardly tell whether they are near or far away. In those days of May and June, and July, in that terrible summer, when we stood alone, and as the world thought, forlorn, against the all-powerful aggressor with his vast armies and masses of equipment, Mr. Anthony Eden, as Secretary of State for War, called upon the local Defence Volunteers to rally round the searchlight positions. Shotguns, sporting rifles, and staves, were all they could find for weapons; it was not until July that we ferried safely across the Atlantic the 1,000,000 rifles and 1,000 field guns, with ammunition proportionable, which were given to us by the Government and people of the United States by an act of precious and timely succour.

London, May 14, 1943.

Britain and America. The experience of a long life and the promptings of my blood have wrought in me the conviction that there is nothing more important for the future of the world than the fraternal association of our two peoples in righteous work both in war and peace.

Broadcast from the Capitol, Washington, D. C.,
May 19, 1943.

Atlantic Charter. Upon the fraternal association and intimate alignment of policy of the United States and the British Commonwealth and Empire depends, more than on any other factor, the immediate future of the world. If they walk, or if need be march, together in harmony and in accordance with the moral and political conceptions to which the English-speaking peoples have given birth, and which are frequently referred to in the Atlantic Charter, all will be well. If they fall apart and wander astray from the commanding beacon-light of their destiny, there is no end or measure to the miseries and confusion which await modern civilization.

Guildhall, London, June 30, 1943.

Price of Greatness. The price of greatness is responsibility. If the people of the United States had continued in a mediocre station, struggling with the wilderness, absorbed in their own affairs and a factor of no consequence in the movement of the world, they might have remained forgotten and undisturbed beyond their own protecting oceans: but one cannot rise to be in many ways the leading community in the civilized world without being involved in its problems, without being convulsed by its agonies and inspired by its causes.

America and Europe. Twice in my lifetime the long arm of destiny has reached across the oceans and involved the entire life and manhood of the United States in a deadly struggle. There was no use in saying: "We don't want it; we won't have it; our forebears left Europe to avoid these quarrels; we have founded a new world which has no contact with the old." There was no use in that. The long arm reaches out remorselessly, and everyone's existence, environment, and outlook undergo a swift and irresistible change.

Harvard University, September 6, 1943.

Co-operation. I would turn aside for a moment to emphasize how perfect is the co-operation between the commanders of the British and American Armies. Nothing like it has ever been seen before among allies. No doubt language is a great help, but there is more in it than that. In all previous alliances the staffs have worked with opposite numbers in each department and liaison officers, but in Africa General Eisenhower built up a uniform staff, in which every place was filled with whoever was thought to be the best man, and they all ordered each other about according to their rank, without the slightest regard to what country they belonged to. The same unity and brotherhood is being instituted here throughout the Forces which are gathering in this country, and I cannot doubt that it will be found most serviceable, and unique also in all the history of alliances.

Commons, February 22, 1944.

American Achievement. I must pay my tribute to the United States Army, not only in their valiant and ruthless battle-worthy qualities, but also in the skill of their commanders and the excellence of their supply arrangements. When one remembers that the United States four or five years ago was a peace-loving power, without any great body of troops, munitions, and with only a very small regular army to draw their commanders from, the American achievement is truly amazing. After the intense training they have received for nearly three years, or more than three years in some cases, their divisions are now composed of regular professional soldiers whose military quality is out of all comparison with hurriedly-raised war-time levies.

American War Effort. When I think of the measureless output of ships, munitions and supplies of all kinds with which the United States has equipped herself and has sustained all the fighting allies in generous measure, and of the mighty war she is conducting, with troops of our Australian and New Zealand Dominions, over the spaces of the Pacific Ocean, this House may indeed salute our sister nation as being at the highest pinnacle of her power and fame.

Commons, September 28, 1944.

English-speaking Peoples. Neither the sure prevention of war nor the continuous use of world organization will be gained without . . . the fraternal association of the English-speaking peoples. This means a special relationship between the British Commonwealth and Empire and the United States. . . . Eventually there may come principles of common citizenship, but that we may be content to leave to destiny, whose outstretched arm so many of us can clearly see. I feel eventually this will come.   *Fulton, Missouri, March 3, 1946.*

Joint Inheritance. We must never cease to proclaim in fearless tones the great principles of freedom and the rights of man which are the joint inheritance of the English-speaking world and which through Magna Charta, the Bill of Rights, the Habeas Corpus, trial by jury, and the English common law find their most famous expression in the American Declaration of Independence. . . .

If the population of the English-speaking Commonwealth be added to that of the United States with all that such co-operation implies in the air, on the sea, all over the globe and in science and in industry and in moral force, there will be no quivering, precarious balance of power to offer its temptation to ambition or adventure. On the contrary, there will be an overwhelming assurance of security.

Westminster College, Fulton, Missouri, March 5, 1946.

Greatheart. It is in the years of peace that wars are prevented and that those foundations are laid upon which the noble structures of the future can be built. But peace will not be preserved without the virtues that make victory possible in war. Peace will not be preserved by pious sentiments expressed in terms of platitudes or by official grimaces and diplomatic correctitude, however desirable this may be from time to time. It will not be preserved by casting aside in dangerous years the panoply of warlike strength. There must be earnest thought. There must also be faithful perseverance and foresight. Greatheart must have his sword and armour to guard the pilgrims on their way. Above all, among the English-speaking peoples, there must be the union of hearts based upon conviction and common ideals. That is what I offer. That is what I seek.

General Assembly of Virginia, Richmond, March 8, 1946.

American Army. There have been many occasions when a powerful state has wished to raise great armies, and with money and time and discipline and loyalty that can be accomplished. Nevertheless the rate at which the small American Army of only a few hundred thousand men, not long before the war, created the mighty force of millions of soldiers, is a wonder in military history.

The Pentagon, Washington, March 9, 1946.

Monroe Doctrine. For at least two generations we were, as the American writer Walter Lippman has reminded us, a guardian, and almost a guarantor, of the Monroe Doctrine upon which, as Canning's eye foresaw, the free development of South America was founded. We and the civilized world owe many blessings to the United States, but we have also in later generations made our contribution to their security and splendour.

London, May 7, 1946.

Foundation of British Policy. The foundation of British poilcy must be an ever-closer association with the United States. I have never asked at any time for an alliance. I want something much more than that. We must seek something less precise and far more potent. The whole English-speaking world must move forward together in fraternal association along the lines of destiny. This will be the greatest hope of peace among nations and of the freedom and dignity of ordinary men and women over the largest portion of the globe.

Blenheim Palace, August 4, 1947.

Identity of Ideals. At this point I must turn to the United States with whom our fortunes and interests are intertwined. I was sorry that the hon. Member for Nelson and Colne [Mr. S. Silverman], whom I see in his place, said some weeks ago that they were "shabby moneylenders." That is no service to our country nor is it true. The Americans took little when they emigrated from Europe except what they stood up in and what they had in their souls. They came through, they tamed the wilderness, they became what old John Bright called "A refuge for the oppressed from every land and clime." They have become to-day the greatest state and power in the world, speaking our own language, cherishing our common law, and pursuing, like our great Dominions, in broad principle, the same ideals. *Commons, October 28, 1947.*

American Millionaires. Nor should it be supposed as you would imagine, to read some of the Left-wing newspapers, that all Americans are multi-millionaires of Wall Street. If they were all multi-millionaires that would be no reason for condemning a system which has produced such material results.
The Royal Albert Hall, London, April 21, 1948.

Denouncing Capitalism. When I see the present Socialist Government denouncing capitalism in all its forms, mocking with derision and contempt the tremendous free enterprise capitalist system on which the mighty production of the United States is founded, I cannot help feeling that as a nation we are not acting honourably or even honestly.
Woodford Green, July 10, 1948.

Fraternal Association. The drawing together in fraternal association of the British and American peoples, and of all the peoples of the English-speaking world may well be regarded as the best of the good things that have happened to us and to the world in this century of tragedy and storm.
Dorchester Hotel, London, July 4, 1950.

III. THE MAN OF ACTION

On the Nature of War

War and Chance. War is a game with a good deal of chance in it, and, from the little I have seen of it, I should say that nothing in war ever goes right except occasionally by accident.

Commons, March 12, 1901.

European War. A European war can end only in the ruin of the vanquished and the scarcely less fatal commercial dislocation and exhaustion of the conquerors. Democracy is more vindictive than cabinets. The wars of peoples will be more terrible than those of kings.

Commons, May 12, 1901.

Price of War. Once you are so unfortunate as to be drawn into a war, no price is too great to pay for an early and victorious peace. . . .

A European war cannot be anything but a cruel, heartrending struggle which, if we are ever to enjoy the bitter fruits of victory, must demand, perhaps for several years, the whole manhood of the nation, the entire suspension of peaceful industry, and the concentrating to one end of every vital energy of the community.

Commons, May 13, 1901.

Illusion of War. The utility of war even to the victor may in most cases be an illusion. Certainly all wars of every kind will be destitute of any positive advantage to the British Empire, but war itself, if ever it comes, will not be an illusion —even a single bullet will be found real enough.

Modern Naval Engagement. Indeed, the more we force ourselves to picture the hideous course of a modern naval engagement, the more one is inclined to believe that it will resemble the contest between Manulius and Herminius at the battle of Lake Regillus, or the still more homely conflict of the Kilkenny cats. That is a very satisfactory reflection for the stronger naval power.

Commons, March 18, 1912.

Future Naval Warfare. We are increasingly convinced of the power of the submarine and the decisive part which this weapon, aided perhaps in some respects by the seaplane, may play in the naval warfare of the future.

Modern Battleships. The offensive power of modern battleships is out of all proportion to their defensive power. Never was the disproportion so marked. If you want to make a true picture in your mind of a battle between great modern ironclad ships you must not think of it as if it were two men in armour striking at each other with heavy swords. It is more like a battle between two egg-shells striking each other with hammers. *Commons, March 17, 1914.*

Naval Warfare. There is a difference between military and naval anxiety, which the House will appreciate. A division of soldiers cannot be annihilated by a cavalry patrol. But at any moment a great ship, equal in war power, and a war unit, to a division or an army may be destroyed without a single opportunity of its fighting strength being realized, or a man on board having a chance to strike a blow in self-defence. *Commons, November 27, 1914.*

Game of War. In war, if you are not able to beat your enemy at his own game, it is nearly always better to adopt some striking variant, and not to be content merely with doing the same thing as your enemy is doing, only not doing it quite so well or on quite so large a scale.
Commons, May 12, 1916.

Horrors of War. The whole business of war is beyond all words horrible, and the nations are filled with the deepest loathing of it, but if wars are going to take place, it is by no means certain that the introduction of chemical warfare is bound to make them more horrible than they have been.
Commons, May 13, 1932.

Wars Do Not Wait. Wars do not always wait until all the combatants are ready. Sometimes they come before they are ready, sometimes when one nation thinks itself less unready than another, or when one nation thinks it is likely to become not stronger, but weaker, as time passes.
Commons, March 10, 1936.

Lunacy of War. Five years ago all felt safe; five years ago all were looking forward to peace, to a period in which mankind would rejoice in the treasures which science can spread to all classes if conditions of peace and justice prevail. Five years ago to talk of war would have been regarded not only as a folly and a crime, but almost as a sign of lunacy. Look at the difference in our position now! We find ourselves compelled once again to face the hateful problems and ordeals which those of us who worked and toiled in the last struggle hoped were gone for ever.

Commons, March 26, 1936.

Just War. When Herr Goebbels's Nazi propaganda blares and blethers upon the ether that Britain and France have lost the capacity to make war if it is forced upon them, we do not get angry because we know it is not true. We know that our sufferings will be very hard and we are determined not to be guilty of bringing about a crash, the consequences of which no man can measure. We know also that we could only throw ourselves into such a struggle if our consciences were clear.

City Carlton Club, London, June 28, 1939.

War Waste. There is bound to be both extravagance and waste in time of war. In our country, accustomed to strict Parliamentary supervision, this waste arises very rarely from fraud or corruption. It arises sometimes from inefficiency, and is capable of correction. It arises most of all, I think, from excessive zeal in preparing against dangers which often change, and sometimes fade as soon as they are faced; and still more from the well-intentioned desire of every branch and section to reach 100 per cent standard of safety, which, of course, is never attainable in war.

Commons, February 27, 1940.

Hazards of War. It often happens in war that an operation which is successful on a small scale becomes vicious if it is multiplied by three, four or five times.

Commons, May 8, 1940.

Universal War. There is another more obvious difference from 1914. The whole of the warring nations are engaged, not only soldiers, but the entire population, men, women and children. The fronts are everywhere. The trenches are dug in towns and streets. Every village is fortified. Every road is barred. The front line runs through the factories. The workmen are soldiers with different weapons but the same courage. These are great and distinctive changes from what many of us saw in the struggle of a quarter of a century ago.

Commons, August 20, 1940.

Certainty about War. There is only one thing certain about war, that it is full of disappointments and also full of mistakes.

London, April 27, 1941.

Military Operations. Military operations must be judged by the success which attends them rather than by the sentiments which inspired them, though these, too, may play their part in the verdict of history and in the survival of races. *Commons, May 7, 1941.*

Desert Warfare. The desert warfare has to be seen to be believed. Large armies, with their innumerable transport and tiny habitations, are dispersed and scattered as if from a pepper-pot over the vast indeterminate slopes and plains of the desert, broken here and there only by a sandy crease or track in the ground or an outcrop of rock. The ground in most places, especially on all commanding eminences, is rock with only an inch or two of sand on the top, and no cover can be obtained for guns or troops except by blasting. Scattered though the troops are, there is an elaborate system of signalling, the enormous development of which is incredible. The more improvements there are in our means of communication, the more people are required to serve the Signal Branch. But owing to this elaborate system of signalling, in which tens of thousands of people are engaged, this army, scattered over the vast areas, can be moved and brought into action with extraordinary rapidity, and enormous distances can be covered by either side in what would have seemed a few years ago to be an incredibly short space of time. *Commons, September 8, 1942.*

Curtain of Battle. I have often thought that it is sometimes unwise of generals to try to foresee with meticulous exactness just what will happen after a battle has been fought. A battle hangs like a curtain across the future. Once that curtain is raised or rent we can all see how the scenery is arranged, what actors are left upon the scene, and how they appear to be related to one another.
Commons, October 31, 1944.

Belligerents. There is nothing improper in belligerents meeting to discuss their affairs even while actual battles are going on. All history abounds in precedents.
Commons, February 25, 1954.

World War I

Defence of Britain. In order that our naval defence shall be fully effective, there must be sufficient military force in this country to make it necessary for an invader to come in

such large numbers that he will offer a target to the N
and certainly would be intercepted if he embarked. . .

By a sober and modest conduct, by a skillful diplom
we can in part disarm and in part divide the elements of
tential danger. But two things have to be considered: F
that our diplomacy depends in great part for its effective
upon our naval position; and that our naval strength is
one great balancing force which we can contribute to
own safety and to the peace of the world. Secondly, we
not a young people with a blank record and a scanty inh
ance. We have won for ourselves, in times when o
powerful nations were paralysed by barbarism or inte
war, an exceptional share of the wealth and traffic of
world.   *Commons, March 17, 1*

Constantinople. All this year I have offered the s
counsel to the Government—undertake no operation in
west which is more costly to us in life than to the ene
in the east, take Constantinople; take it by ship, if you
take it by soldiers if you must; take it whichever plan,
tary or naval, commends itself to your military experts,
take it, and take it soon, and take it while time remains.

Gallipoli. I will not have it said that this was a civi
plan, foisted by a political amateur, upon reluctant offi
and experts. . . .

I am concerned to make it clear to the House, and
only to the House but to the navy, that this enterprise
profoundly, maturely and elaborately considered, that t
was a great volume of expert opinion behind it, that it
framed entirely by expert and technical minds, and tha
no circumstances could it have been regarded as ha
been undertaken with carelessness or levity. . . .

It seems to me that if there were any operations in
history of the world which, having been begun, it was w
while to carry through with the utmost vigour and fury,
a consistent flow of reinforcements, and an utter disre
of life, it was the operation so daringly and brilliantly
gun by Sir Ian Hamilton in the immortal landing of A
25.

Tendencies in War. There is no reason to be discour
about the progress of the war. We are passing through a
time now, and it will probably be worse before it is be
but it will be better, if we only endure and persever
have no doubt whatever. The old wars were decided by t
episodes rather than by their tendencies. In this war

tendencies are far more important than the episodes. Without winning any sensational victories we may win this war. We may win it even during the continuance of extremely disappointing and vexatious events. It is not necessary for us, in order to win the war, to push the German lines back over all the territory they have absorbed, or to pierce them. While the German lines extend far beyond their frontiers, while their flag flies over conquered capitals and subjugated provinces, while all the appearances of military success attend their arms, Germany may be defeated more fatally in the second or third year of the war than if the allied army had entered Berlin in the first.

Commons, November 15, 1915.

Zeppelins. No responsible officer at the War Office or at the Admiralty whom I ever met before the war anticipated that Zeppelins would be used to drop bombs indiscriminately on undefended towns and the countryside. This was not because of any extravagant belief in human virtue in general, or in German virtue in particular, but because it is reasonable to assume that your enemy will be governed by good sense and by a lively regard for his own interests.

Commons, May 17, 1916.

Infantry. This war proceeds along its terrible path by the slaughter of infantry. It is this infantry which is the most difficult to replenish, which is continually worn away on both sides, and though all the other services of the army are necessary to its life, and to its maintenance . . . it is this fighting part that is the true measure of your military power, and the only true measure. *Commons, May 23, 1916.*

War Effort. We cannot go on treating the war as if it were an emergency which can be met by makeshifts. It is, until it is ended, the one vast, all-embracing industry of the nation, and it is until it is ended the sole aim and purpose of all our lives. *Commons, August 22, 1916.*

Nation at War. This nation at war is an army; it must be looked upon as an army; it must be organized like an army; it must be directed like an army; and it ought to be rationed and provided and supplied like an army.

Commons, September 16, 1916.

Dardanelles. The light of victory was shining clearly before us, and the path was clearly illuminated, yet we could not get the strength, the power, and the driving force to follow it. We could not get the strength and the resources which were needed to carry it through. It will always be incredible to future ages that every man in this country did not rally to an enterprise which carried with it such immense possibilities, and which required such limited resources to carry it into effect. It will always be incredible that for the sake of a dozen old ships and half a dozen extra divisions, more or less, and a few hundred thousand rounds of high-explosive shells we failed to gain a prize specially adapted to our Oriental interests and our amphibious power, and which by cutting Turkey out of the war, and uniting in one federation the states of the Balkan Peninsula, would have brought us within measurable distance of lasting success.

Commons, March 20, 1917.

Nitrates. It is a very strange thing to reflect that but for the invention of Professor Haber the Germans could not have continued the war after their original stock of nitrates was exhausted. The invention of this single man has enabled them, utilizing the interval in which their accumulations were used up, not only to maintain an almost unlimited supply of explosives for all purposes, but to provide amply for the needs of agriculture in chemical manures. It is a remarkable fact, and shows on what obscure and accidental incidents the fortunes possibly of the whole world may turn in these days of scientific discovery.

Commons, April 25, 1918.

Legitimate War Gamble. After weighing and sifting all the expert evidence with the personal knowledge I had of all the officers concerned, I recommended it [Gallipoli breakthrough] to the Prime Minister and the War Council in the presence of my principal naval advisers, believing, as did everyone there, that I carried them with me, and I pressed it with all the resources at my disposal. I recommended it to the War Council, and to the French Government, not as a certainty, but as a legitimate war gamble, with stakes that we could afford to lose for a prize of unestimable value —a prize which, in the opinion of the highest experts, there was a fair reasonable chance of our winning, a prize which at that time could be won by no other means. On that basis clearly understood it was accepted by all concerned.

Commons, November 15, 1918.

Fear of Retribution. The most dangerous form of air attack is the attack by incendiary bombs. Such an attack was planned by the Germans for the summer of 1918, I think for the time of the harvest moon. The argument in favour of such an attack was that if in any great city there are, we will say, fifty fire-brigades, and you start simultaneously one hundred fires and the wind is high, an almost incalculable conflagration may result. The reason why the Germans did not carry out that attack in 1918 must be stated. It was not at all, as Lord Mottistone suggested in another place, that our air defense had become so excellent that we were protected against it. It was because the advance of the allied armies, with the British army in the van, already confronted the Imperial Government of Germany with the prospect of impending defeat, and they did not wish to incur the fury of retribution which would follow from such a dreadful act of power and terror as would have been involved in such a raid. *Commons, November 28, 1934.*

Glut of Victory. During the war [1914–1918] we repeatedly asked ourselves the question: How are we going to win? and no one was able to answer it with much precision, until at the end, quite suddenly, quite unexpectedly, our terrible foe collapsed before us, and we were so glutted with victory that in our folly we threw it away.
Commons, June 18, 1940.

War Casualties. In the last war [1914–1918] millions of men fought by hurling enormous masses of steel at one another. "Men and shells" was the cry, and prodigious slaughter was the consequence. In this war nothing of this kind has yet appeared. It is a conflict of strategy, of organization, of technical apparatus, of science, mechanics and morale. The British casualties in the first 12 months of the Great War amounted to 365,000. In this war, I am thankful to say, British killed, wounded, prisoners and missing, including civilians, do not exceed 92,000, and of these a large proportion are alive as prisoners of war. Looking more widely around, one may say that throughout Europe for one man killed or wounded in the first year perhaps five were killed or wounded in 1914–1915.

Commons, August 20, 1940.

Lloyd George Cabinet. It is now the fashion to speak of the Lloyd George War Cabinet as if it gave universal satisfaction and conducted the war with unerring judgment and unbroken success. On the contrary, complaints were loud and clamant. Immense disasters, such as the slaughter of Passchendale, the disaster at Caporetto in 1917, the destruction of the Fifth Army after March 21, 1918—all these and others befell that rightly famous Administration. It made numerous mistakes. No one was more surprised than its Members when the end of the war came suddenly in 1918, and there have even been criticisms about the character of the peace which was signed and celebrated in 1919.
Commons, February 24, 1942.

Between Two Wars

Mesopotamia Mandate. I am quite certain that the loose talk indulged in in the newspapers about the speedy exacuation of Mesopotamia earlier in the year was a factor which provoked and promoted the rebellion. Whatever your policy might be, it would certainly be in the highest degree imprudent to let it be thought that this country, having accepted the mandate, having entered into territory of that kind, having incurred, accepted and shouldered responsibilities towards every class inhabiting it, was in a moment of irritation or weakness going to cast down those responsibilities, to leave its obligations wholly undischarged, and to scuttle from the country regardless of what might occur.

Commons, December 15, 1920.

The New Century. Undoubtedly, this new twentieth century is not in many ways so favorable to us as the nineteenth century. A new world is growing up around us, far larger than anything previously seen, and filled with giant states and competitors.

Commons, July 24, 1928.

Disarmament. Once upon a time all the animals in the zoos decided that they would disarm, and they arranged to have a conference to arrange the matter. So the Rhinoceros said when he opened the proceedings that the use of teeth was barbarous and horrible and ought to be strictly prohibited by general consent. Horns, which were mainly defensive weapons, would, of course, have to be allowed. The Buffalo, the Stag, the Porcupine, and even the little Hedgehog all said they would vote with the Rhino, but the Lion and the Tiger took a different view. They defended teeth and even claws, which they described as honourable weapons of immortal antiquity. The Panther, the Leopard, the Puma, and the whole tribe of small cats all supported the Lion and the Tiger. Then the Bear spoke. He proposed that both teeth and horns should be banned and never used again for fighting by any animal. It would be quite enough if animals were allowed to give each other a good hug when they quarrelled. No one could object to that. It was so fraternal, and that would be a great step towards peace. However, all the other animals were very offended with the Bear, and the Turkey fell into a perfect panic.

The discussion got so hot and angry, and all those animals began thinking so much about horns and teeth and hugging when they argued about the peaceful intentions that had brought them together that they began to look at one another in a very nasty way. Luckily the keepers were able to calm them down and persuade them to go back quietly to their cages, and they began to feel quite friendly with one another again.

Aldersbrook Road, West Essex, October 25, 1928.

Qualitative Disarmament. I come now to the proposals of qualitative disarmament about which the Foreign Secretary was so insistent. He told us that it was difficult to divide weapons into offensive and defensive categories. It certainly is, because almost every conceivable weapon may be used either in defence or offence; it all depends upon the circumstances; and every weapon, whether offensive or defensive, may be used either by an aggressor or by the innocent victim of his assault. . . .

This attempt to employ the energies of Geneva upon discriminating between offensive and defensive weapons will only lead to rigmarole and delay, and is in itself a silly expedient. The adoption of such topics for discussion casts a certain air of insincerity over the proceedings at Geneva.

Commons, May 13, 1932.

Carthaginian Peace. What, then, has become of the Carthaginian peace of which we used to hear so much? That has gone. Some of it may have been written down in the Versailles Treaty, but its clauses have never been put into operation. There has been no Carthaginian peace. Neither has there been any bleeding of Germany white by the conquerors. The exact opposite has taken place. The loans which Britain and the United States particularly, and also other countries, have poured into the lap of Germany since the firing stopped, far exceed the sum of reparations which she had paid; indeed, they have been nearly double. If the plight of Germany is hard—and the plight of every country is hard at the present time—it is not because there has been any drain of her life's blood or of valuable commodities from Germany to the victors. It is Germany that has received an infusion of blood from the nations with whom she went to war and by whom she was decisively defeated.

Commons, July 11, 1932.

Lausanne Conference. Everything which has happened since July last shows how unwise it was to bring the Lausanne Conference to a conclusion, and to trumpet its results all round the globe. If we look back on those July days, when the Prime Minister [Mr. Ramsay MacDonald] was welcomed in triumph on his return, with all the Cabinet and under-secretaries drawn up like a row of Grenadiers of varying sizes at the railway station, we can see how absurd were the claims which were then advanced that Lausanne had "saved Europe" and that a "new era" had opened for the world. There is quite a lot still to be done in Europe, and for many people it is very much the same old era in the world.

War Debts. There is no doubt whatever that harm was done to the prospect of the settlement of the war debts by what happened at Lausanne. I ventured to warn the Government before this happened, in May or June of last year, of the extreme unwisdom of making the Debt Settlement an issue at the American elections. The consequences of Lausanne have been to force all the candidates for Congress and the Senate, on both sides of politics, to give specific pledges and to make definite declarations upon this subject. We all know what happens at elections.

Failure of Disarmament. The expectation of general disarmament upon a great scale has failed; the hope of one nation being able to disarm its rival has been frustrated by the very stout and stubborn resistance which every nation makes to that process. Now I am afraid that a large part of the object of every country is to throw the blame for an impending failure upon some other country while willing, if possible, to win the Nobel Peace Prize for itself. . . .

I have watched the Disarmament Conferences which have now been going on for many years, and I have formed certain opinions about them. Disarmament divides itself into disarmament by scale and disarmament by ratio. Disarmament by scale is not so important, but disarmament by ratio, the altering of the relative positions of nations, is the part of the problem which excites the most intense anxiety and even passion.

Entanglement. It must be remembered that Great Britain will have more power and will run far less risk in pressing for the redress of grievances than in pressing for disarmament. We can only promote disarmament by giving further guarantees of aid. We can press for the redress of grievances by merely threatening, if our counsels are not attended to, to withdraw ourselves at the proper time from our present close entanglement in European affairs. The first road of pressing for disarmament and offering more aid only leads us deeper and deeper into the European situation. The second either removes the cause of danger or leads us out of the danger zone.   *Commons, November 23, 1932.*

Supreme Object of Policy. Our first supreme object is not to go to war. To that end we must do our best to prevent others from going to war. But we must be very careful that, in so doing, we do not increase the risk to ourselves of being involved in a war if, unfortunately, our well-meant efforts fail to prevent a quarrel between other powers.

Limits of Disarmament. I am very doubtful whether there is any use in pressing national disarmament to a point where nations think their safety is compromised, while the quarrels which divide them and which lead to their armaments and their fears are still unadjusted. The elaborate process of measuring words around the table at Geneva, which has gone on for so many years, stirs all the deepest suspicions and anxieties of the various powers, and forces all the statesmen to consider many hypothetical contingencies which but for this prolonged process perhaps would not have crossed their minds and would only have remained buried in the archives of some general staff.

Technique. All the nations at Geneva have developed a very elaborate technique in dealing with disarmament proposals which do not suit their needs or which they think are dangerous or inconvenient. They have learned very well to talk the language which is agreeable to the League of Nations Union. They think they do it very well there. They have had a lot of practice at it. They never refuse at first sight any proposal, however injurious, visionary or foolish they may think it. On the contrary, they make praiseworthy speeches. They interchange agreeable compliments—"How interesting!" "How hopeful!" "What a meeting of our point of view is embodied in this!" "It is the first time we have really had a helping hand in this difficult situation." "What noble sentiments have inspired this theme for which we are indebted to the genius of England!" And then, having read it a second time, to use our Parliamentary forms, amid prolonged enthusiasm, they adjourn to the banqueting hall and leave it to be killed in committee by a lot of minor objections to detail, or by putting forward counter-proposals which only make confusion worse confounded.

Commons, March 23, 1933.

Leadership of Europe. It is easy to talk about the moral leadership of Europe. That great prize still stands before the statesmen of all countries, but it is not to be achieved merely by making speeches of unexceptionable sentiments. If it is to be won by any nation it will only be by an immense amount of wise restraint and timely, discreet action which, over a period of years, has created a situation where speeches are not merely fine exhortations but record the unity and conciliation which have been achieved. There is the moral leadership of Europe. It is not to be won by such easy methods as merely making speeches which will arouse the applause of every good-hearted person in this country.

Disarmament. It may be very virtuous and high-minded to press disarmament upon nations situated as these nations are, but if not done in the right way and in due season, and in moderation, with regard for other people's points of view as well as our own sentiments, it may bring war nearer rather than peace, and may lead us to be suspected and hated instead of being honoured and thanked as we should wish to be.

Nationalism. I have heard, as everyone has of late years, a great deal of condemnation of the treaties of peace, of the Treaties of Versailles and of Trianon. I believe that that denunciation has been very much exaggerated, and in its effect harmful. These treaties, at any rate, were founded upon the strongest principle alive in the world to-day, the principle of nationalism, or, as President Wilson called it, self-determination. The principle of self-determination or of nationalism was applied to all the defeated powers over the whole area of middle and eastern Europe. Europe to-day corresponds to its ethnological groupings as it has never corresponded before. You may think that nationalism has been excessively manifested in modern times. That may well be so. It may well be that it has a dangerous side, but we must not fail to recognize that it is the strongest force now at work. . . .

In applying this principle of nationalism to the defeated states after the war it was inevitable that mistakes and some injustices should occur. There are places where the populations are inextricably inter-mingled. There are some countries where an island of one race is surrounded by an area inhabited by another. There were all kinds of anomalies, and it would have defied the wit of man to make an absolutely perfect solution.

Four Power Pact. The Pact or Agreement so incontinently accepted [Mussolini's proposals of the Four Power Pact] has to be amended, has to be modified to fit the views of the small nations in the League. It has to be modified again to meet special claims. It has to be modified again to meet the requirements of France, and it very soon reaches the point where it loses the adherence of Germany. It is no good saying it is merely "much ado about nothing." That is not so. Harm has been done, disturbance has been created, suspicion has been spread, and English influence has lost a measure of its virtue and added a measure to its responsibility.

Commons, April 13, 1933.

Concert of Europe. I believe that we shall find our greatest safety in co-operating with the other powers of Europe, not taking a leading part but coming in with all the neutral states and the smaller states of Europe which will gather together anxiously in the near future at Geneva. We shall make a great mistake to separate ourselves entirely from them at this juncture. Whatever way we turn there is risk. But the least risk and the greatest help will be found in re-creating the Concert of Europe through the League of Nations, not for the purpose of fiercely quarrelling and haggling about the details of disarmament, but in an attempt to address Germany collectively, so that there may be some redress of the grievances of the German nation and that that may be effected before this peril of [German] rearmament reaches a point which may endanger the peace of the world.   *Commons, November 7, 1933.*

Covert Armaments. A new situation has been created, mainly in the last three or four years, by rubbing this sore of the Disarmament Conference until it has become a cancer, and also by the sudden uprush of Nazism in Germany, with the tremendous covert armaments which are proceeding there to-day.   *Commons, February 7, 1934.*

Air Disarmament. I have not been able to convince myself that the policy which the Government have pursued has been in sufficiently direct contact with the harsh realities of the European situation, but, of course, I admit most fully that they have made it clear before all the world, not only by words, which are so easy, but by actions, which are so hard, and by inaction, which is so questionable, how sincere has been, and still is, our desire to bring about a general measure of disarmament, especially in the air.   *Commons, March 8, 1934.*

Disarmament and Peace. I am very glad that the Disarmament Conference is passing out of life into history. One of the greatest mistakes that can be made is to point to the failure of the Disarmament Conference as if it were really the failure of the League of Nations, and to mix up disarmament with peace. When you have peace you will have disarmament. But there has been during these years a steady deterioration in the relations between different countries and a rapid increase in armaments that has gone on in spite of the endless flow of oratory, of well-meaning sentiments, of perorations, and of banquets. Europe will be secure when nations no longer feel themselves in danger as many of them do now. Then the pressure and the burden of armaments will fall away automatically, as they ought to have done in a long peace, and it might be quite easy to seal a movement of that character by some general agreement.

Commons, July 13, 1934.

Sanctions Against Italy. Here are fifty sovereign states solemnly sitting down together to devise and concert hostile economic action against a great power, prohibiting the export of arms to Italy, encouraging such exports to Italy's enemy, taking concerted measures to destroy Italian credit and financial strength in every quarter of the globe, laying an embargo on many kinds of exports to Italy, and even attempting a complete boycott of Italian imports into each country. When we are told that there are leakages and loopholes, that difficulties will arise and disputes will break out between the boycotters, and so forth, that may all be true, but these are, to anyone who views things in their true proportion, only the exceptions which are proving a most impressive rule. Such a system of pains and penalties has never been proclaimed against a single state, as far as I am aware, in the whole history of the world. If we could get away a little further from the scene and take a more general view than is possible to us living through events from day to day, I am sure we should see that we are already in the presence of a memorable event.

Abyssinia. No one can keep up the pretence that Abyssinia is a fit, worthy and equal member of a league of civilized nations. The wisdom of the British policy was shown in our opposing her admission to the League, and the unwisdom of Continental countries, who now bitterly regret what they did, was shown in their consenting to it. It was a mistake. . . .

I share the feeling common throughout the country of sympathy for the primitive feudal people of Abyssinia who are fighting for their hearths and homes and for the ancient freedom of their mountains against a scientific invader. The native independence of Abyssinia cannot be made a matter for compromise or barter.

Commons, October 24, 1935.

Reoccupation of Rhineland. We have managed to secure the disadvantages of all the courses without the advantages of any. We have pressed France into a course of action which did not go far enough to help the Abyssinians, but went far enough to sever her from Italy, with the result that the occasion was given to Herr Hitler to tear up treaties and reoccupy the Rhineland.

Abyssinia. The League of Nations—fifty nations led by one, as Signor Mussolini said, in a phrase of formidable significance —will have been unable to do anything of the slightest use to the Abyssinians. Indeed, all we have done for them, as far as I can remember, is to put an embargo on their obtaining arms before they are attacked. Otherwise we have done nothing for them at all—except, of course, the speeches which have been made. . . .

Now, Sir, I say it was a very grievous thing to lead these fifty nations up the blind alley of fatuity and frustration. It was a grievous thing also to encourage, however indirectly, a primitive population to a desperate resistance and then, in the event, to leave them to their fate. We cannot undo the past, but we are bound to pass it in review in order to draw from it such lessons as may be applicable to the future, and surely the conclusion from this story is that we should not intervene in these matters unless we are in earnest and prepared to carry out intervention to all necessary lengths.

Commons, April 6, 1936.

Locust Years. The Government can not simply make up their minds, or they cannot get the Prime Minister to make up his mind. So they go on in strange paradox, decided only to be undecided, resolved to be irresolute, adamant for drift, solid for fluidity, all-powerful to be impotent. So we go on preparing more months and years—precious, perhaps vital, to the greatness of Britain—for the locusts to eat.

Commons, November 12, 1936.

Air Parity. We have been most solemnly promised parity. We have not got parity. Would the right hon. Gentleman rise in his place and say he could contend that we have parity at the present time with this Power which is in striking distance of our shores in first-line strength? I say we have not got the parity which we were promised. We have not nearly got it, we have not nearly approached it. Nor shall we get it during the whole of 1937, and I doubt whether we shall have it, or anything approaching it, during 1938. I feel bound to make these statements.

Commons, January 27, 1937.

Civil War in Spain. Of course, neither of the two Spanish sides can afford to say that it would tolerate the idea of a settlement. They are fighting for life; they are desperate men, and all their lives are at stake. They dare not show the slightest sign of weakness, but they have their seconds, they have their friends in these great powers who are in close touch with them. Is it not time when this horrible duel might for the moment be considered by the seconds and not necessarily only by the principal parties, and when the seconds could decide, as they often did in private duels, that honour is satisfied, or if you like to put it more truthfully, that dishonour is gorged?

Commons, April 14, 1937.

Conquest of Austria. The public mind has been concentrated upon the moral and sentimental aspects of the Nazi conquests of Austria—a small country brutally struck down, its Government scattered to the winds, the oppression of the Nazi party doctrine imposed upon a Catholic population, and upon the working classes of Austria and of Vienna, the hard ill-usage of persecution which indeed will ensue—which is probably in progress at the moment—of those who, this time last week, were exercising their undoubted political rights, discharging their duties faithfully to their own country. . . .

We are not in a position to say to-night, "The past is the past." We cannot say, "The past is the past," without surrendering the future.   *Commons, March 14, 1938.*

Threat to Czechoslovakia. Then we come to the case of Czechoslovakia. There has been a lot of talk about giving a guarantee, but I should be sorry if the grave issue now open in Europe were to turn solely on that point, cardinal though it be. Far wider decisions are called for; far larger interests are at stake. I listened with the utmost attention to all that the Prime Minister said about our relations to Czechoslovakia, and it seems to me that he has gone a long way in making a commitment. First, I was very glad to hear him reaffirm his adherence and that of the Government to the obligations of the Covenant of the League. Under the Covenant of the League we are obliged not to be neutral, in the sense of being indifferent, if Czechoslovakia is the victim of unprovoked aggression.   *Commons, March 24, 1938.*

Intrusions in Spain. The agony of the Civil War [in Spain] continues. Had it been only a Spanish quarrel fought out by Spaniards, we might have averted our eyes from its horrors; but the shameful intrusions of Dictator powers with organized troops and masses of munitions under the deceitful masquerade of Non-Intervention, has invested their struggles with an added bitterness and a significance which extends far outside the Spanish Peninsula.

Free Trade Hall, Manchester, May 9, 1938.

Sacrifice of Czechoslovakia. No one has been a more resolute and uncompromising struggler for peace than the Prime Minister. Everyone knows that. Never has there been such intense and undaunted determination to maintain and secure peace. That is quite true. Nevertheless, I am not quite clear why there was so much danger of Great Britain or France being involved in a war with Germany at this juncture if, in fact, they were ready all along to sacrifice Czechoslovakia. The terms which the Prime Minister brought back with him could easily have been agreed, I believe, through the ordinary diplomatic channels at any time during the summer. And I will say this, that I believe the Czechs, left to themselves and told they were going to get no help from the Western Powers, would have been able to make better terms than they got after all this tremendous perturbation; they could hardly have had worse. . . .

I venture to think that in future the Czechoslovak State cannot be maintained as an independent entity. I think you will find that in a period of time which may be measured by years, but may be measured only by months, Czechoslovakia will be engulfed in the Nazi regime. Perhaps they may join it in despair or in revenge. At any rate, that story is over and told. All is over. Silent, mournful, abandoned, broken Czechoslovakia recedes into the darkness. She has suffered in every respect by her association with the western democracies and with the League of Nations, of which she has always been an obedient servant. She has suffered in particular from her association with France, under whose guidance and policy she has been actuated for so long.

Sudetenland. We in this country, as in other Liberal and democratic countries, have a perfect right to exalt the principle of self-determination, but it comes ill out of the mouths of those in Totalitarian States who deny even the smallest element of toleration to every section and creed within their bounds. But, however you put it, this particular block of land, this mass of human beings to be handed over, has never expressed the desire to go into the Nazi rule. I do not believe that even now, if their opinion could be asked, they would exercise such an opinion.

Opportunities Lost. When I think of the fair hopes of a long peace which still lay before Europe at the beginning of 1933 when Herr Hitler first obtained power, and of all the opportunities of arresting the growth of the Nazi power which have been thrown away, when I think of the immense combinations and resources which have been neglected or squandered, I cannot believe that a parallel exists in the whole course of history. So far as this country is concerned the responsibility must rest with those who have had the undisputed control of our political affairs. They neither prevented Germany from rearming, nor did they rearm ourselves in time. They quarrelled with Italy without saving Ethiopia. They exploited and discredited the vast institution of the League of Nations and they neglected to make alliances and combinations which might have repaired previous errors, and thus they left us in the

hour of trial without adequate national defence or effective international security.
Commons, October 5, 1938.

Anglo-Italian Agreement. The Agreement, of course, has been violated in every material respect by Italy, but I do not feel that anything would be gained by a denouncement with bell, book and candle at this juncture. It certainly represents a sincere, if hitherto unrequited, attempt on the part of Great Britain to dwell on terms of friendship with Italy and with the Italian people in the Mediterranean Sea.
Commons, April 13, 1939.

Sense of Responsibility. In this free, old, independent Island we are not living in the Middle Ages. We see great hopes for the future of all the world. We see the opportunity of lifting, through the aid of science, all the men in all the lands to a far higher level of well-being and culture than was ever possible before. It is an opportunity which has never come to mankind before, and which may not come to them again if it is cast away till generations and perhaps centuries have passed. We are determined that there shall not rest upon us the guilt and the shame of standing between the toiling masses of the world and the ever-brightening prospects which are at last within their reach. It is this sense of responsibility before the high monuments of history which has governed our policy and conduct, and no taunts or insults will move us from this determination.
Commons, June 28, 1939.

The Threat from the Air

Bombing. The hon. Gentleman opposite made our flesh creep the other night by suggesting the dropping of bombs from airships on the House of Commons. If that event should happen, I am confident that the Members of this House would gladly embrace the opportunity of sharing the perils which the soldiers and the sailors have to meet. . . .

If war breaks out to-morrow foreign airships, no doubt, might do a certain amount of mischief and damage before they got smashed up, which would not be very long, but it is foolish to suppose that in their present stage of development they could produce results which would decisively influence the course of events.
Commons, March 26, 1913.

Anti-aircraft Defence. Passive defence against such an attack is perfectly hopeless and endless. You would have to roof in the world to be quite sure. Something may be done, and something has been done by the provision of guns which fire upwards, and by searchlights which train throughout the entire arc, but the only real security upon which sound military principles will rely is that you should be master of your own air.

Commons, March 17, 1914.

Insularity of Britain. We are no longer an island. When once the navigation of the air has been brought to a high degree of perfection as it must undoubtedly be in the generation which lies in front of us, we have lost to a very considerable extent that distinctive insular position on which our safety and our greatness have hitherto depended.

Commons, March 21, 1922.

Detrimental Weapons. I agree with what I imagine were his feelings when he [Stanley Baldwin] wished that neither aeroplanes nor submarines had ever been invented. I am sure they have both been deeply detrimental to the special interests and security of this Island; and I agree also with his general theme that the air power may either end war or end civilization.

Discriminate Bombing. If all of a sudden two powers with equal forces went to war, and one threw its bombs upon cities so as to kill as many women and children as possible, and the other threw its bombs on the aerodromes and air bases and factories and arsenals and dockyards and railway focal points of the other side, can anyone doubt that next morning the one who had committed the greatest crime would not be the one who had reaped the greatest advantage?

Air Defence. Why should we fear the air? We have as good technical knowledge as any country. There is no reason to suppose that we cannot make machines as good as any country. We have—though it may be thought conceited to say so—a particular vein of talent in air piloting which is in advance of that possessed by other countries. There is not the slightest reason to suppose that we are not capable of producing as good results for money put into action as any other country. That being so, I ask the Government to consider profoundly and urgently the whole position of our air defence.

Commons, March 14, 1933.

War from the Air. This cursed, hellish invention and development of war from the air has revolutionized our position. We are not the same kind of country we used to be when we were an island, only twenty-five years ago. That is borne in upon me more than anything else. It is not merely a question of what we like and what we do not like, of ambitions and desires, of rights and interests, but it is a question of safety and independence. That is involved now as never before.

Commons, February 7, 1934.

Perils of Air War. There seem to me to be four lines of protection by which we can secure the best chance, and a good chance, of immunity for our people from the perils of air war—a peaceful foreign policy; the convention regulating air warfare; the parity in air power to invest that convention with validity; and, arising out of that parity, a sound system of home defence—in addition to all these other arrangements if they all fail.   *Commons, March 8, 1934.*

Bombing of London. No one can doubt that a week or ten days' intensive bombing attack upon London would be a very serious matter indeed. One could hardly expect that less than 30,000 or 40,000 people would be killed or maimed. The most dangerous form of air attack is the attack by incendiary bombs.
                                   Commons, November 8, 1934.

Vulnerable Britain. When one considers the enormous range of aeroplanes and the speeds at which they travel—230 and 240 miles an hour—it is evident that every part of this small Island is almost equally within range of attack. . . .

Certainly nothing is more necessary, not only to this country but to all peace-loving and peace-interested powers in the world and to world civilization, than that the good old earth shoul1 acquire some means or methods of destroying sky marauders.   *Commons, November 28, 1934.*

Ground Against Air. I was very glad indeed that the Prime Minister to-day, in answer to Sir Austen Chamberlain, spoke about the committee which is to examine defensive measures against aeroplane attacks. That is a matter in which all countries, in my opinion, have a similar interest—all peaceful countries. It is a question not of one country against another, but of the ground against the air, and unless the dwellers upon the earth can manage to secure the air above their heads, it is almost impossible to forecast the misfortunes and fears which this invention, of which the world has proved itself so utterly unworthy, may bring upon them.
                                   Commons, March 19, 1935.

Anti-aircraft Defence. It is only in the twentieth century that this hateful conception of inducing nations to surrender by terrorizing the helpless civil population and by massacring the women and children has gained acceptance and countenance amongst men. If it continues, one can clearly see that the conquest of the air may mean the subjugation of mankind and the destruction of our civilization. This is not the cause of any one nation. No; every country would feel safer if once it were found that the bombing aeroplane was at the mercy of appliances erected on the earth, and the haunting fears and suspicions which are leading nations nearer and nearer to the brink of another catastrophe would be abated. But this island people more than any other nation would gain by such a discovery.

Fragility of Aeroplanes. After all, an aeroplane, though a very formidable engine of war, is also a very fragile structure, and an explosive charge no bigger than a small cigar is sufficient to bring down the most powerful aeroplane if it strikes a spar or the propeller: even a bird has been the cause of fatal accidents. Merely to fire at an aeroplane in the air is like trying to shoot a flying duck with a pea-rifle. What must be aimed at is not the hitting of the aeroplane, but the creation of conditions in the air around the aeroplane which are extremly noxious if not destructive to it. For that purpose it is clear that this effect of the shell which is fired should not be momentary. . . .

I wonder that the League of Nations at Geneva does not offer an enormous monetary prize to incite inventors of all countries to discover methods of bringing down the marauding aeroplane.   *Commons, June 7, 1935.*

Ordeals from the Air. It may be that great ordeals are coming to us in this Island from the air. We shall do our best to give a good account of ourselves; and we must always remember that the command of the seas will enable us to bring the immense resources of Canada and the New World into play as a decisive ultimate air factor, a factor beyond the reach of what we have to give and take over here.

London, October 1, 1939.

Knights of the Air. The great French army was very largely, for the time being, cast back and disturbed by the onrush of a few thousands of armoured vehicles. May it not also be that the cause of civilization itself will be defended by the skill and devotion of a few thousand airmen. There never had been, I suppose, in all the world, in all the history of war, such an opportunity for youth. The Knights of the Round Table, the Crusaders, all fall back into the past, not only distant but prosaic; these young men, going forth every morn to guard their native land and all that we stand for, holding in their hands these instruments of colossal and shattering power, of whom it may be said that "Every morn brought forth a noble chance, and every chance brought forth a noble knight," deserve our gratitude, as do all of the brave men who, in so many ways and on so many occasions, are ready, and continue ready, to give life and all for their native land.

Commons, June 4, 1940.

Airborne Invasion. It seems quite clear that no invasion on a scale beyond the capacity of our land forces to crush speedily is likely to take place from the air until our air force has been definitely overpowered. In the meantime, there may be raids by parachute troops and attempted descents of airborne soldiers.
Commons, June 18, 1940.

The R.A.F. The gratitude of every home in our Island, in our Empire, and indeed throughout the world, except in the abodes of the guilty, goes out to the British airmen who, undaunted by odds, unwearied in their constant challenge and mortal danger, are turning the tide of the world war by their prowess and by their devotion. Never in the field of human conflict was so much owed by so many to so few. All hearts go out to the fighter pilots, whose brilliant actions we see with our own eyes day after day.
Commons, August 20, 1940.

Battle of Britain. The three great days of August 15th, September 15th and September 27th have proved to all the world that here at home over our own Island we have the mastery of the air. That is a tremendous fact. It marks the laying down of the office [of Chief of the Air Staff] which he has held with so much distinction for the last three years by Sir Cyril Newall, and it enables us to record our admiration to him for the services he has rendered. It also marks the assumption of new and immense responsibilities by Sir Charles Portal, an officer who, I have heard from every source and every side, commands the enthusiastic support and confidence of the Royal Air Force.
Commons, October 8, 1940.

Malta Air Force. Malta is the first instance of an air force being maintained against odds often of ten to one from a few airfields, all under constant bombardment. . . . It may be that presently the German air forces attacking Malta will have to move eastward to sustain the impending offensive against Southern Russia. If so, we shall have topped the ridge. . . .
For now nearly two years Malta has stood against the enemy. What a thorn it has been in their side! What toll it has taken of their convoys! Can we wonder that a most strenuous effort has been made by Germany and Italy to rid themselves of this fierce, aggressive foe. For the last six weeks over 450 German first-line strength in aircraft, and perhaps 200 Italian, have been venting their fury on Malta. An unending intermittent bombardment has fallen upon the harbour and city, and sometimes as many as 300 aircraft have attacked in a single day. The terrific ordeal has been borne with ex-

emplary fortitude by the garrison and people. Very heavy losses have been inflicted upon the enemy's air strength.

Commons, April 23, 1942.

Demon of the Air. Hitler made a contract with the demon of the air, but the contract ran out before the job was done, and the demon has taken on an engagement with the rival firm. How truly it has been said that nations and people very often fall by the very means which they have used, and built their hopes upon, for their rising-up.

Commons, July 2, 1942.

Flying Bombs. The House will, I think, be favourably surprised to learn that the total number of flying bombs launched from the enemy's stations have killed almost exactly one person per bomb. That is a very remarkable fact, and it has kept pace roughly week by week. Actually the latest figures are 2,754 flying bombs launched and 2,752 fatal casualties sustained. They are the figures up to six o'clock this morning. Well, I am bound to say I was surprised when, some time ago, I perceived this wonderful figure. This number of dead will be somewhat increased by people who die of their injuries in hospital. Besides these there has been a substantially larger number of injured, and many minor injuries have been caused by splinters of glass.

Commons, July 6, 1944.

Conquest of the Air. The conquest of the air and the perfection of the art of flying fulfilled the dream which for thousands of years had glittered in human imagination. Certainly it was a marvellous and romantic event. Whether the bestowal of this gift upon an immature civilization composed of competing nations, whose nationalization grew with every advance of democracy, and who were as yet devoid of international organization, whether this gift was a blessing or a curse has yet to be proved.

Massachusetts Institute of Technology, Boston, March 31, 1949.

Cassandra of the Coming Storm

Retribution. The great liner is sinking in a calm sea. One bulkhead after another gives way; one compartment after another is bilged, the list increases; she is sinking, but the captain and the officers and the crew are all in the saloon dancing to the jazz band. But wait till the passengers find out what is their position!

Commons, January 26, 1931.

Balance of Power. I say quite frankly, though I may shock the House, that I would rather see another ten or twenty years of one-sided armed peace than see a war between equally well-matched powers or combinations of power—and that may be the choice.   *Commons, November 23, 1932.*

German Rearmament. Mr. Lansbury said just now that he and the Socialist Party would never consent to the rearming of Germany. But is he quite sure that the Germans will come and ask him for his consent before they rearm? Does he not think they might omit that formality and go ahead without even taking a card vote of the T.U.C.?
Commons, November 7, 1933.

War Production. We ought to begin the reorganization of our civil factories so that they can be turned over rapidly to war purposes. All over Europe that is being done, and to an amazing extent. This process is incomparably more efficient than anything that existed in the days of Prussian Imperialism before the war. Every factory in those countries is prepared to turn over to the production of some material for the deplorable and melancholy business of slaughter. What have we done? There is not an hour to lose. Those things cannot be done in a moment. The process should be started, and the very maximum of money that can be usefully spent will be spent from to-day on—if we act with wisdom.

Air Power. I cannot conceive how, in the present state of Europe and of our position in Europe, we can delay in establishing the principle of having an air force at least as strong as that of any power that can get at us. I think that is a perfectly reasonable thing to do. It would only begin to put us back to the position in which we were brought up. We have lived under the shield of the navy. To have an air force as strong as the air force of France or Germany, whichever is the stronger, ought to be the decision which Parliament should take, and which the National Government should proclaim.
Commons, February 7, 1934.

Preservation of Peace. Putting the preservation of peace in the first place, what is the next great object that we must have in view? It is to secure our national freedom of choice to remain outside a European war, if one should break out. That I put as the more direct and more practical issue, subordinate to, but not less important than, the preservation of peace.   *Commons, March 8, 1934.*

Inversion. The Romans had a maxim: "Shorten your weapons and lengthen your frontiers." But our maxim seems to be, "Diminish your weapons and increase your obligations." Aye, and "diminish the weapons of your friends."

Commons, March 14, 1934.

British Armaments. I am not to be understood to mean that the possibilities of a gigantic war are nearer, but the actual position of Great Britain is much less satisfactory than it was this time twenty years ago, for then at least we had a supreme fleet; nobody could get at us in this island; and we had powerful friends on the Continent of Europe, who were likely to be involved in any quarrel before we were. But today, with our aviation in its present condition, we are in a far worse position. The Disarmament Conference has been carried out year after year *ad nauseam*. It must no longer delay our taking the necessary measures ourselves.

Balance of Power. There is no greater danger than equal forces. If you wish to bring about war, you bring about such an equipoise that both sides think they have a chance of winning. If you want to stop war, you gather such an aggregation of force on the side of peace that the aggressor, whoever he may be, will not dare to challenge.

Commons, July 13, 1934.

Myopia. Eight years ago we were told that disarmament had been discussed at Geneva. For two and a half years the actual conference has been proceeding. The leader of the Liberal Opposition [Sir Herbert Samuel] has, therefore, had a good run for his experiment. His hope has been abounding. It has preserved him at every stage from seeing the facts.

Commons, July 30, 1934.

German Rearmament. The German munition factories are working practically under war conditions, and war matériel is flowing out from them, and has been for the last twelve months, in an ever broadening flow. Much of this is undoubtedly in violation of the treaties which were signed. Germany is rearming on land; she is rearming also to some extent at sea; but what concerns us most of all is the rearmament of Germany in the air. . . .

The danger which might confront us would expose us not only to hideous suffering, but even to mortal peril, by which I mean peril of actual conquest and subjugation. It is just as well to confront those facts while time remains to take proper measures to cope with them. I may say that all these possibilities are perfectly well known abroad, and no doubt every one of them has been made the subject of technical study.

Commons, November 28, 1934.

Stitch in Time. Even at this time last year, if a resolve had been taken, as I urged, to double and redouble the British air force as soon as possible—Sir Herbert Samuel described me as a Malay run amok because I made such a suggestion—very much better results would have been yielded in 1935, and we should not find ourselves in our present extremely dangerous position.   *Commons, March 19, 1935.*

Repetition of History. When the situation was manageable it was neglected, and now that it is thoroughly out of hand we apply too late the remedies which then might have effected a cure. There is nothing new in the story. It is as old as the Sibylline Books. It falls into that long, dismal catalogue of the fruitlessness of experience and the confirmed unteachability of mankind. Want of foresight, unwillingness to act when action would be simple and effective, lack of clear thinking, confusion of counsel until the emergency comes, until self-preservation strikes its jarring gong—these are the features which constitute the endless repetition of history.

Armaments and Policy. It used to be said that armaments depend on policy. It is not always true, but I think that at this juncture it is true to say that policy depends, to a large extent, upon armaments. It is true to say that we have reached a position where the choice of policy is dictated by considerations of defence.   *Commons, May 2, 1935.*

German Air Superiority. We are entering upon a period of danger and difficulty. And how do we stand in this long period of danger? There is no doubt that the Germans are superior to us in the air at the present time, and it is my belief that by the end of the year, unless their rate of construction and development is arrested by some agreement, they will be possibly three, and even four, times our strength. . . .

For the first time for centuries we are not fully equipped to repel or to retaliate for an invasion. That to an island people is astonishing. Panic indeed! The position is the other way round. We are the incredulous, indifferent children of centuries of security behind the shield of the Royal Navy, not yet able to wake up to the woefully transformed conditions of the modern world.   *Commons, May 22, 1935.*

Air Equality. Speeches are made in the country by leading Ministers, saying that we have decided that we must have air equality, that we cannot accept anything less. We have not got it. We are already decidedly inferior to Germany, and, it must be said, of course to France. . . .

Air armaments are not expressed merely by the air squadrons in existence or the aeroplanes which have been made; they cannot be considered apart from the capacity to manufacture. If, for instance, there were two countries which each had 1,000 first-line aeroplanes, but one of which had the power to manufacture at the rate of 100 a month and the other at the rate of 1,000 a month, it is perfectly clear that air parity would not exist between those two countries very long.

Corridor of Danger. It would be folly for us to act as if we were swimming in a halcyon sea, as if nothing but balmy breezes and calm weather were to be expected and everything were working in the most agreeable fashion. By all means follow your lines of hope and your paths of peace, but do not close your eyes to the fact that we are entering a corridor of deepening and darkening danger, and that we shall have to move along it for many months and possibly for years to come.   *Commons, May 31, 1935.*

German Battleships. We always believed before the war that battleships could never be laid down without our knowledge. The Germans were entitled to build 10,000-ton ships according to the Treaty, but they, by a concealment which the Admiralty were utterly unable to penetrate, converted these into 26,000-ton ships. Let us be careful when we see all these extremely awkward incidents occurring.
                                       Commons, July 22, 1935.

Armaments' Race. Let us see what we are doing. It is a general impression that we are overhauling Germany now; that we started late, it is true, but we are making up for lost time, and that every month our relative position will improve. That is delusion. It is contrary to the truth this year, and probably for many months next year. I am not saying anything which is not known in every country of the world. These matters are thoroughly understood. Germany will be outstripping us more and more even if our new programmes are accepted, and we shall be worse off at the end of this year than we are now, in spite of all our exertions. . . .

Will there be time to put our defences in order? We live in contact with the unknown, but we are not defenceless now. Will there be time to make these necessary efforts, or will the awful words "too late" be recorded? I will never despair that we can make ourselves secure. The Royal Navy, especially after the toning up which it has received, is unsurpassed in the world, and is still the main bulwark of our security; and even at this eleventh hour, if the right measures are taken and if the right spirit prevails in the British nation and the British

Empire, we may surround ourselves with other bulwarks equally sure, which will protect us against whatever storms may blow.

Commons, March 10, 1936.

Collective Forces of the World. The whole history of the world is summed up in the fact that when nations are strong they are not always just, and when they wish to be just they are often no longer strong. I desire to see the collective forces of the world invested with overwhelming power. If you are going to depend on a slight margin, one way or the other, you will have war. But if you get five or ten to one on one side, all bound rigorously by the covenant and the conventions which they own, then you may have an opportunity of a settlement which will heal the wounds of the world. Let us have this blessed union of power and justice: "Agree with thine adversary quickly, while thou art in the way with him." Let us free the world from the reproach of a catastrophe carrying with it calamity and tribulation beyond the tongue of man to tell.

Commons, March 26, 1936.

German Fortifications. Germany is now fortifying the Rhine zone, or is about to fortify it. No doubt it will take some time. We are told that in the first instance only field entrenchments will be erected, but those who know to what perfection the Germans can carry field entrenchments like the Hindenburg Line, with all the masses of concrete and the underground chambers included—those who remember that will realize that field entrenchments differ only in degree from permanent fortifications, and work steadily up from the first cutting of the sods to their final and perfect form.

Commons, April 6, 1936.

Climax in Europe. Europe is approaching a climax. I believe that climax will be reached in the lifetime of the present Parliament. Either there will be a melting of hearts and a joining of hands between great nations which will set out upon realizing the glorious age of prosperity and freedom which is now within the grasp of the millions of toiling people, or there will be an explosion and a catastrophe the course of which no imagination can measure, and beyond which no human eye can see. I believe also that a strongly armed Britain, resolutely and valiantly led, seeking peace but ready to run risks for peace, may conceivably turn the scale between the blessing and the cursing of mankind.

Commons, April 23, 1936.

Alarm. We are told that we must not interfere with the normal course of trade, that we must not alarm the easy-going voter and the public. How thin and paltry these arguments will sound if we are caught a year or two hence, fat, opulent, free-spoken—and defenceless. I do not ask that war conditions should be established in order to execute these programmes. All I ask is that these programmes to which the Government have attached their confidence shall be punctually executed, whatever may be the disturbance of our daily life.

Commons, May 21, 1936.

Machine Tools. We know now that these machine tools which we are about to order should have been ordered then, but were overlooked.

That is the kind of thing that has happened, and my right hon. Friend now exhibits it to the whole world. As we see by the telegrams from different countries, it produced a shock, because while everyone knows that the industry of Britain is vast and flexible, if it has not these particular appliances it cannot manifest itself. A hideous hiatus of eight months must elapse before it can manifest itself, and after that it takes another eight months to make a gun. So that an enormous vista of anxiety lies before us, what I may call this valley of the shadow that we are going to move through for a long time—month after month of deep anxiety, when efforts will be made increasingly every month, every week, when anxiety will grow in the nation, when my right hon. Friend will be exerting himself night and day, I have no doubt. God speed him in it! But, all the same, he will be paying the penalty of these previous neglects.

Commons, May 29, 1936.

Worsening Conditions. The Secretary of State for War [Mr. Duff Cooper] has told us that conditions are worse than in 1914. How, then, can it be argued that conditions of emergency have not supervened? I do not ask that war conditions should be established for the production of munitions; it would not be necessary or helpful. All I ask is that the intermediate stage between ordinary peacetime and actual war should be recognized, that a state of emergency preparation should be proclaimed, and that the whole spirit and atmosphere of our rearmament should be raised to a higher pitch; that we should lay aside a good deal of the comfort and smoothness of our ordinary life, that we should not hesitate to make an inroad into our industry, and that we should make the most strenuous efforts in our power to execute the programmes that the Government have in mind at such pace as would make them relevant to the ever-growing dangers that gather round us.

Air Force Miscalculation. My right hon. Friend [Sir Thomas Inskip, Minister for the Co-ordination of Defence] used an extraordinary argument. He said that, if we had begun to expand our air force three years ago, or words to that effect, we should be worse off than we are now—we should be cumbered with a mass of inferior machines. This is an altogether new defence for the miscalculation which the Government have admitted in respect of the relative strength of the British and German air forces. In fact, I do not know why, on this basis, the Prime Minister ever needed at all to stand in the most handsome way in a white sheet, because apparently this was not an oversight; it was not an accident: this was some deep design, a truly Machiavellian stroke of policy, which enabled us to pretend that a miscalculation had been made while all the time we were holding back in order to steal a march on other countries by the production of great numbers of machines of the latest type. That is a most remarkable defence.

Commons, July 20, 1936.

The Tank. The tank was a British invention. This idea, which has revolutionized the conditions of modern war, was a British idea forced on the War Office by outsiders. Let me say they would have just as hard work to-day to force a new idea on it. I speak from what I know. During the war we had almost a monopoly, let alone the leadership, in tank warfare, and for several years afterwards we held the foremost place. To England all eyes were turned. All that has gone now. Nothing has been done in "the years that the locust hath eaten" to equip the Tank Corps with new machines.

Commons, November 12, 1936.

Armageddon. When a whole continent is arming feverishly, when mighty nations are laying aside every form of ease and comfort, when scores of millions of men and weapons are being prepared for war, when whole populations are being led forward or driven forward under conditions of exceptional overstrain, when the finances of the proudest dictators are in the most desperate condition, can you be sure that all your programmes so tardily adopted will, in fact, be executed in time? . . .

Time passes quickly. Everything is in constant change. When the first beginnings of evil which may subsequently challenge peace and freedom and even the life of the State make their appearance on the horizon, it is right then to sound the alarm and to try, even by frantic exertions, to arouse somnolent authority to novel dangers; but once we are in the danger zone, once everybody can see that we are marching through that long, dark valley of which I spoke to the House two years ago, then a mood of coolness and calmness is enjoined.

Commons, March 4, 1937.

Drift. We seem to be moving, drifting, steadily, against our will, against the will of every race and every people and every class, towards some hideous catastrophe. Everybody wishes to stop it, but they do not know how.

Commons, April 14, 1937.

Foreign Policy. The peace of Europe rests to-day upon the French army. That army at the present time is the finest in Europe, but with every month that passes its strength is being outmatched by the ceaseless development of the new formations into which the vastly superior manhood of Germany is being cast. Almost any foreign policy is better than duality or continual chops and changes. It is strange that the British people, who have such a reputation for stability in other matters, should have been in the last few years pursuing a foreign policy so baffling by its shift and twists that foreign countries have been unable to keep step with us, while the little nations who are indirectly affected by our changes are thrown into the utmost bewilderment and confusion.

Commons, February 22, 1938.

Occupation of Austria. The gravity of the event of the 11th of March cannot be exaggerated. Europe is confronted with a programme of aggression, nicely calculated and timed, unfolding stage by stage, and there is only one choice open, not only to us, but to other countries who are unfortunately concerned—either to submit, like Austria, or else to take effective measures while time remains to ward off the danger and, if it cannot be warded off, to cope with it.

Intentions of Britain. Everyone remembers the controversy, which has dragged on for many years, about whether we could have stopped the Great War in 1914 if Sir Edward Grey had made plain declarations a week beforehand. I myself am of opinion that he did all it was possible for him to do in the circumstances, and I doubt very much whether the event would have been averted even if he had made such a declaration. But still there is a weight of historic judgment piling up that in all these matters of international strife and danger, it is most necessary that nations should declare plainly where they stand, and of all nations which should so declare itself our country, with her insular characteristics still partially remaining to her, has an obligation to give a perfectly plain statement of what she will or will not do in certain contingencies when those contingencies approach the threshold of reality.

Commons, March 14, 1938.

The Abyss. For five years I have talked to the House of these matters—not with very great success. I have watched this famous Island descending incontinently, recklessly, the stairway which leads to a dark gulf. It is a fine broad stairway at the beginning, but after a bit, the carpet ends. A little further on there are only flagstones, and, a little further on still, these break beneath your feet.

Punic Wars. Look back upon the last five years—since, that is to say, Germany began to rearm in earnest and openly to seek revenge. If we study the history of Rome and Carthage, we can understand what happened and why. It is not difficult to form an intelligent view about the three Punic Wars; but if mortal catastrophe should overtake the British nation and the British Empire, historians a thousand years hence will still be baffled by the mystery of our affairs. They will never understand how it was that a victorious nation with everything in hand suffered themselves to be brought low, and to cast away all that they had gained by measureless sacrifice and absolute victory—gone with the wind.

Dictators. If we do not stand up to the dictators now, we shall only prepare the day when we shall have to stand up to them under far more adverse conditions. Two years ago it was safe, three years ago it was easy, and four years ago a mere dispatch might have rectified the position. But where shall we be a year hence?

Eleventh Hour. Now is the time at last to rouse the nation. Perhaps it is the last time it can be roused with a chance of preventing war, or with a chance of coming through to victory should our efforts to prevent war fail. We should lay aside every hindrance and endeavour by uniting the whole force and spirit of our people to raise again a great British nation standing up before all the world; for such a nation, rising in its ancient vigour, can even at this hour save civilization.

Commons, March 24, 1938.

Basis of Foreign Policy. There must be a moral basis for British foreign policy. People in this country, after all we have gone through, do not mean to be drawn into another terrible war in the name of old-world alliances or diplomatic combinations. If deep causes of division are to be removed from our midst, if all our energies are to be concentrated upon the essential task of increasing our strength and security, it can only be because of lofty and unselfish ideals which command the allegiance of all classes here at home, which rouse their echoes in the breasts even of dictator-ridden peoples themselves, and stir the pulses of the English-speaking race in every quarter of the globe.

Trembling Balance. Never before has the choice of blessings or curses been so plainly, vividly, even brutally offered to mankind. The choice is open. The dreadful balance trembles. It may be that our Island and all the Commonwealths it has gathered around it may, if we are worthy, play an important, perhaps even a decisive part in turning the scales of human fortune from bad to good, from fear to confidence, from miseries and crimes immeasurable to blessings and gains abounding.

Ideologies. We are told that we must not involve ourselves in a quarrel about ideologies. If this means that we are not to back Communism against Nazism or vice versa, we all agree. Both doctrines are equally obnoxious to the principles of freedom. Certainly we should not back one against the other. But surely we must have an opinion between Right and Wrong? Surely we must have an opinion between Aggressor and Victim?

Common Bond. However we may differ in political opinion, however divergent our Party interests, however diverse our callings and stations, we have this in common. We mean to defend our Island from tyranny and aggression, and so far as we can, we mean to hold out a helping hand to others who may be in an even more immediate danger than at this moment we are ourselves. *Free Trade Hall, Manchester, May 9, 1938.*

Subjugation of Czechoslovakia. The Government which allowed Czechoslovakia to be broken and disarmed was suddenly surprised and horrified that Herr Hitler should march into Prague and actually subjugate the Czech people. This damnable outrage opened the eyes of the blind, made the deaf hear, and even in some cases the dumb speak.
Corn Exchange, Cambridge, May 19, 1938.

Deficiencies in Armaments. We are now in the third year of openly avowed rearmament. Why is it, if all is going well, there are so many deficiencies? Why, for instance, are the Guards drilling with flags instead of machine-guns? Why is it that our small Territorial Army is in a rudimentary condition? Is that all according to schedule? Why should it be, when you consider how small are our forces? Why should it be impossible to equip the Territorial Army simultaneously with the Regular Army? . . .

You ought now—I said this two years ago, but it is still true to-day—to have every factory in the country planned out, not only on paper, but with the necessary jigs, gauges and appliances handy, hung up on the spot, so that they could turn over at once in time of war to some form of war production. . . .

The more you are prepared and the better you are known to be prepared, the greater is the chance of staving off war and of saving Europe from the catastrophe which menaces it.

Commons, May 25, 1938.

Survival of Civilization. Civilization will not last, freedom will not survive, peace will not be kept, unless a very large majority of mankind unite together to defend them and show themselves possessed of a constabulary power before which barbaric and atavistic forces will stand in awe.

University of Bristol, July 2, 1938.

Munich. I will begin by saying what everybody would like to ignore or forget but which must nevertheless be stated, namely, that we have sustained a total and unmitigated defeat, and that France has suffered even more than we have. The utmost my right hon. Friend the Prime Minister [Mr. Neville Chamberlain] has been able to secure by his immense exertions, by all the great efforts and mobilization which took place in this country, and by all the anguish and strain through which we have passed in this country, the utmost he has been able to gain for Czechoslovakia in the matters which were in dispute has been that the German dictator, instead of snatching the victuals from the table, has been content to have them served to him course by course. . . .

I do not grudge our loyal, brave people, who were ready to do their duty no matter what the cost, who never flinched under the strain of last week—I do not grudge them the natural, spontaneous outburst of joy and relief when they learned that the hard ordeal would no longer be required of them at the moment; but they should know the truth. They should know that there has been gross neglect and deficiency in our defences; they should know that we have sustained a defeat without a war, the consequences of which will travel far with us along our road; they should know that we have passed an awful milestone in our history, when the whole equilibrium of Europe has been deranged, and that the terrible words have for the time being been pronounced against the western democracies: "Thou art weighed in the balance and found wanting." . . .

The Chancellor of the Exchequer [Sir John Simon] said it was the first time Herr Hitler had been made to retract—I think that was the word—in any degree. We really must not waste time after all this long debate upon the difference between the positions reached at Berchtesgaden, at Godesberg and at Munich. They can be very simply epitomized, if the House will permit me to vary the metaphor. £1 was demanded at the pistol's point. When it was given, £2 were demanded at the pistol's point. Finally, the dictator consented to take £1 17s. 6d. and the rest in promises of good will for the future. . . .

Do not suppose that this is the end. This is only the beginning of the reckoning. This is only the first sip, the first foretaste of a bitter cup which will be proffered to us year by year unless by a supreme recovery of moral health and martial vigour we arise again and take our stand for freedom as in the olden time.

Improvident Stewardship. We cannot consider the abandonment and ruin of Czechoslovakia in the light only of what happened only last month. It is the most grievous consequence of what we have done and of what we have left undone in the last five years—five years of futile good intentions, five years of eager search for the line of least resistance, five years of uninterrupted retreat of British power, five years of neglect of our air defences. Those are the features which I stand here to expose and which marked an improvident stewardship for which Great Britain and France have dearly to pay. We have been reduced in those five years from a position where the very word "war" was considered one which could be used only by persons qualifying for a lunatic asylum. We have been reduced from a position of safety and power—power to do good, power to be generous to a beaten foe, power to make terms with Germany, power to give her proper redress for her grievances, power to stop her arming if we chose, power to take any step in strength or mercy or justice which we thought right—reduced in five years from a position safe and unchallenged to where we stand now. . . .

Many people, no doubt, honestly believe that they are only giving away the interests of Czechoslovakia, whereas I fear we shall find that we have deeply compromised, and perhaps endangered, the safety and even the independence of Great Britain and France. This is not merely a question of giving up the German colonies, as I am sure we shall be asked to do. Nor is it a question only of losing influence in Europe. It goes far deeper than that. You have to consider the character of the Nazi movement and the rule which it implies. . . .

We are in the presence of a disaster of the first magnitude which has befallen Great Britain and France. Do not let us blind ourselves to that. It must now be accepted that all the countries of central and eastern Europe will make the best terms they can with the triumphant Nazi power. The system of alliances in central Europe upon which France has relied for her safety has been swept away, and I can see no means by which it can be reconstituted.

Air Supremacy. The sole method that is open, is for us to regain our old island independence by acquiring that supremacy in the air which we were promised, that security in our air defences which we were assured we had, and thus to make ourselves an island once again. That, in all this grim outlook, shines out as the overwhelming fact. An effort at rearmament the like of which has not been seen, ought to be made forthwith, and all the resources of this country and all its united strength should be bent to that task.

Commons, October 5, 1938.

Czechoslovakia. All the world wishes for peace and security. Have we gained it by the sacrifice of the Czechoslovak Republic? Here was the model democratic state of Central Europe, a country where minorities were treated better than anywhere else. It has been deserted, destroyed and devoured. It is now being digested. The question which is of interest to a lot of ordinary, common people is whether this destruction of the Czechoslovak Republic will bring upon the world a blessing or a curse. . . .

I hold to the conviction I expressed some months ago, that if in April, May or June, Great Britain, France and Russia had jointly declared that they would act together upon Nazi Germany if Herr Hitler committed an act of unprovoked aggression against this small state [Czechoslovakia], and if they had told Poland, Yugoslavia and Rumania what they meant to do in good time and invited them to join the combination of peace-defending powers, I hold that the German dictator would have been confronted with such a formidable array that he would have been deterred from his purpose.

London, October 16, 1938.

Healthy Growl. One healthy growl from those benches three years ago—and how different to-day would be the whole lay-out of our armaments production! Alas, that service was not forthcoming. We have drifted on in general good-natured acquiescence for three whole years—not for three whole years of ignorance or unawareness, but for three whole years with the facts glaring us full in the face.

Defence of London. Take the astounding admission that modern guns available for the defence of London would have been doubled in number but for the bankruptcy of a small firm charged with an essential part. I beg the Prime Minister to face the force of that admission. He is a businessman of high competence himself. Is it not shocking that such a thing should have happened?

Bren Gun. Now the Secretary of State for War [Mr. Hore Belisha], I will not say incorrigible, but impenitent, tells us the new Bren gun is being produced at a maximum. What does that mean? What is the maximum? The wit of man, of a man in a fix, could not devise a more vague and misleading phrase.
Commons, November 17, 1938.

Battleships. I am horrified to learn that the Admiralty propose to scrap the five 15-inch battleships of the Royal Sovereign class, one in 1942, one in 1943 and the rest, I suppose, in the following year. The House would hardly gather from the euphemistic phrase the Parliamentary Secretary employed—"replacement"—that these two ships are to be destroyed. That does not tell us what one would expect, that until the new ships are in commission the old ones will be kept in reserve. In other days I used to say that when the ace is out the king is the best card.

Anglo-German Naval Agreement. Under the Anglo-German Agreement no provision was made, as some of us suggested, that old ships should be counted at a lower tonnage than new ships in estimating the tonnage of German naval construction. If we keep the Royal Sovereigns, Germany would be entitled under the Treaty to build two additional battleships in the four-year period in question, and they have asked us to state in advance, as they have a right to ask, what we propose to do. We have promised to scrap or sink the first two Royal Sovereigns, and I presume that there is no hope now of rescuing the others from that imprudent decision.

Command of the Baltic. The German navy in the next few years will not be able to form a line of battle for a general engagement. One would expect that cruisers and submarines would be sent out to attack commerce, but I think you may take it as absolutely certain that the prime object of the German navy will be to preserve command of the Baltic, which is of supreme consequence to Germany, not only because of the supplies she can obtain from the Scandinavian countries, and the influence she can exert over them, but because the loss of naval command in the Baltic would lay the whole of the Baltic shores of Germany open to attack or possible invasions from other Baltic powers, of which the largest and most important is, of course, the Soviet Union.
Commons, March 16, 1939.

Example of Britain. When we aspire to lead all Europe back from the verge of the abyss on to the uplands of law and peace, we must ourselves set the highest example. We must keep nothing back. How can we bear to continue to lead our comfortable, easy life here at home, unwilling even to pronounce the word "compulsion," unwilling even to take the necessary measure by which the armies that we have promised can alone be recruited and equipped? How can we continue—let me say it with particular frankness and sincerity—with less than the full force of the nation incorporated in the governing instrument? These very methods, which the Government owe it to the nation and to themselves to take, are not only indispensable to the duties that we have accepted but, by their very adoption, they may rescue our people and the people of many lands from the dark, bitter waters which are rising fast on every side.

Commons, April 13, 1939.

British Empire. If the British Empire is fated to pass from life into history, we must hope it will not be by the slow process of dispersion and decay, but in some supreme exertion for freedom, for right and for truth.

Canada Club, London, April 20, 1939.

Aggressors. They [Hitler and Mussolini] cannot pursue their course of aggression without bringing about a general war of measureless devastation. To submit to their encroachments would be to condemn a large portion of mankind to their rule; to resist them, either in peace or war, will be dangerous, painful and hard. There is no use at this stage in concealing these blunt facts from anyone. No one should go forward in this business without realizing plainly both what the cost may be, and what are the issues at stake.

Corn Exchange, Cambridge, May 19, 1939.

Before the Storm. I have been a persistent critic of the present Government, both in their foreign policy and in their measures for defence. My warnings and censures for the last six years are on record, and to-day no one is asking me to take one word back. If I support the Government to-day, it is not because I have changed my views. It is because the Government have in principle and even in detail adopted the policy I have urged. I only hope they have not adopted it too late to prevent war.

When danger is at a distance, when there is plenty of time to make the necessary preparations, when you can bend twigs instead of having to break massive boughs—it is right, indeed it is a duty, to sound the alarm. But when danger comes very near, when it is plain that not much more can be done in the time that may be available, it is no service to dwell upon the shortcomings or neglects of those who have been responsible. The time to be frightened is when evils can be remedied; when they cannot be fully remedied they must be faced with courage.   *Commons, June 28, 1939.*

We are an old nation. It is nearly a thousand years since we were conquered. We have built up our state and way of life slowly and gradually, across the centuries. Therefore we can afford to make exertions for peace which would not be easy in a race less sure of itself and of its duty. . . .

The forces of aggression are gradually gathering, have, indeed, already been to a large extent gathered. Many people say that nothing will happen till the harvest has been garnered, and perhaps they are right, but personally I always distrust dates which are mentioned beforehand, because they may so easily be antedated, and after all, the harvest itself is not far off. I think we must consider July, August and September as months in which the tension of Europe will become most severe. . . .

Where is it all to end? To try to buy off Nazidom, or any other sign of moral weakness, would only be to bring near the very thing we still hope may be averted. We certainly cannot go on like this. Throughout the whole country people of all classes and Parties have the same feelings. Business is at a standstill. The progress of the whole world is blocked. All its resources are being devoured by armaments. No one can plan ahead. We live from crisis to crisis. There is a profound and almost universal conviction throughout the land that we shall not escape our dangers by recoiling from them.

              City Carlton Club, London, June 28, 1939.

All plans and preparations may be perfected, and yet the fateful signal may not be given. Whether it will be given or not depends on the mood, temperament and decision of a single man, who has raised himself from an obscure position to a grisly summit from which he can perhaps let loose, upon the greater part of mankind, immeasurable catastrophe and tribulation. If my words could reach him, as indeed they may, I would say "Pause, consider well before you take a plunge into the terrible unknown. Consider whether your life's work, which might now be famous in the eyes of history, in raising Germany from prostration and defeat to a point where all the world is waiting anxiously upon her actions—consider whether all this may not be irretrievably cast away."

                                 Commons, June 28, 1939.

The Conflict and the Victory

Perseverance. No doubt at the beginning we shall have to suffer, because of having too long wished to lead a peaceful life. Our reluctance to fight was mocked at as cowardice. Our desire to see an unarmed world was proclaimed as the proof of our decay. Now we have begun. Now we are going on. Now, with the help of God, and with the conviction that we are the defenders of civilization and freedom, we are going to persevere to the end.
London, October 1, 1939.

Liberation of Europe. In the bitter and increasingly exacting conflict which lies before us we are resolved to keep nothing back, and not to be outstripped by any in service to the common cause. Let the great cities of Warsaw, of Prague, of Vienna, banish despair even in the midst of their agony. Their liberation is sure. The day will come when the joybells will ring again throughout Europe, and when victorious nations, masters not only of their foes, but of themselves, will plan and build in justice, in tradition, and in freedom, a house of many mansions where there will be room for all.
London, January 20, 1940.

Criticism. We do not resent the well-meant criticism of any man who wishes to win the war. We do not shrink from any fair criticism, and that is the most dangerous of all. On the contrary, we take it earnestly to heart and seek to profit by it. Criticism in the body politic is like pain in the human body. It is not pleasant, but where would the body be without it? No health or sensibility would be possible without continued correctives and warnings of pain.
Commons, January 27, 1940.

Clarion Call. Come then: let us to the task, to the battle, to the toil—each to our part, each to our station. Fill the armies, rule the air, pour out the munitions, strangle the U-boats, sweep the mines, plough the land, build the ships, guard the streets, succour the wounded, uplift the downcast and honour the brave. Let us go forward together in all parts of the Empire, in all parts of the Island. There is not a week, nor a day, nor an hour to lose.
Free Trade Hall, Manchester, January 27, 1940.

Clinch of the War. The very recklessness with which Hitler and his advisers have cast the interests of the German navy upon the wild waters to meet all that moves thereon—this very

158

recklessness makes me feel that these audacious, costly operations may be only the prelude to far larger events which impend
on land. We have probably arrived now at the first main clinch
of the war. But we certainly find no reason in the fact of what
has just happened, and still less in our own hearts, to deter us
from entering upon any further trials that may lie before us.
While we will not prophesy or boast about battles still to be
fought, we feel ourselves ready to encounter the utmost malice
of the enemy and to devote all our life strength to achieve
the victory in what is a world cause.

Commons, April 11, 1940.

Before the Battle. In that supreme emergency we shall not
hesitate to take every step, even the most drastic, to call forth
from our people the last ounce and the last inch of effort of
which they are capable. The interests of property, the hours of
labour, are nothing compared with the struggle for life and
honour, for right and freedom, to which we have vowed
ourselves.

Sublime Hour. This is one of the most awe-striking periods
in the long history of France and Britain. It is also beyond
doubt the most sublime. Side by side, unaided except by their
kith and kin in the great Dominions and by the wide empires
which rest beneath their shield—side by side, the British and
French peoples have advanced to rescue not only Europe but
mankind from the foulest and most soul-destroying tyranny
which has ever darkened and stained the pages of history.
Behind them—behind us, behind the armies and fleets of
Britain and France—gather a group of shattered states and
bludgeoned races: the Czechs, the Poles, the Norwegians, the
Danes, the Dutch, the Belgians—upon all of whom the long
night of barbarism will descend, unbroken even by a star of
hope, unless we conquer, as conquer we must; as conquer we
shall.

London, May 19, 1940.

Surrender of Belgium. The House will be aware that the
King of the Belgians yesterday sent a plenipotentiary to the
German Command asking for a suspension of arms on the
Belgian front. The British and French Governments instructed
their generals immediately to dissociate themselves from this
procedure and to persevere in the operations in which they
are now engaged. However, the German Command has agreed
to the Belgian proposals and the Belgian army ceased to resist
the enemy's will at four o'clock this morning. . . .

The Belgian Government has dissociated itself from the
action of the King and declaring itself to be the only legal
Government of Belgium, has formally announced its resolve

to continue the war at the side of the Allies who have come to the aid of Belgium at her urgent appeal. Whatever our feelings may be upon the facts so far as they are known to us, we must remember that the sense of brotherhood between the many peoples who have fallen into the power of the aggressor and those who still confront him will play its part in better days than those through which we are passing.

Commons, May 28, 1940.

German Breakthrough. The German eruptions swept like a sharp scythe around the right and rear of the armies of the north. Eight or nine armoured divisions, each of about four hundred armoured vehicles of different kinds, but carefully assorted to be complementary and divisible into small self-contained units, cut off all communications between us and the main French armies. It severed our own communications for food and ammunition, which ran first to Amiens and afterwards through Abbeville, and it shore its way up the coast to Boulogne and Calais, and almost to Dunkirk. Behind this armoured and mechanized onslaught came a number of German divisions in lorries, and behind them again there plodded comparatively slowly the dull brute mass of the ordinary German army and German people, always so ready to be led to the trampling down in other lands of liberties and comforts which they have never known in their own.

Military Disaster. Our thankfulness at the escape of our army and so many men whose loved ones have passed an agonizing week, must not blind us to the fact that what has happened in France and Belgium is a colossal military disaster. The French army has been weakened, the Belgian army has been lost, a large part of those fortified lines upon which so much faith had been reposed is gone, many valuable mining districts and factories have passed into the enemy's possession, the whole of the Channel ports are in his hands, with all the tragic consequences that follow from that, and we must expect another blow to be struck almost immediately at us or at France.

We Shall Go On . . . Even though large tracts of Europe and many old and famous states have fallen or may fall into the grip of the Gestapo and all the odious apparatus of Nazi rule, we shall not flag or fail. We shall go on to the end, we shall fight in France, we shall fight on the seas and oceans, we shall fight with growing confidence and growing strength in the air, we shall defend our Island, whatever the cost may be, we shall fight on the beaches, we shall fight on the landing grounds, we shall fight in the fields and in the streets, we shall fight in the hills; we shall never surrender, and even if, which

I do not for a moment believe, this Island or a large part of it were subjugated and starving, then our Empire beyond the seas, armed and guarded by the British fleet, would carry on the struggle, until, in God's own time, the New World, with all its power and might, steps forth to the rescue and the liberation of the Old.

Commons, June 4, 1940.

Capitulation of France. The news from France is very bad and I grieve for the gallant French people who have fallen into this terrible misfortune. Nothing will alter our feelings towards them or our faith that the genius of France will rise again. What has happened in France makes no difference to our actions and purpose. We have become the sole champions now in arms to defend the world cause. We shall do our best to be worthy of this honour. We shall defend our Island home, and with the British Empire we shall fight on unconquerable until the curse of Hitler is lifted from the brows of mankind. We are sure that in the end all will come right.

London, June 17, 1940.

Their Finest Hour. I expect that the Battle of Britain is about to begin. Upon this battle depends the survival of Christian civilization. Upon it depends our own British life, and the long continuity of our institutions and our Empire. The whole fury and might of the enemy must very soon be turned on us. Hitler knows that he will have to break us in this Island or lose the war. If we can stand up to him, all Europe may be free and the life of the world may move forward into broad, sunlit uplands. But if we fail, then the whole world, including the United States, including all that we have known and cared for, will sink into the abyss of a new Dark Age made more sinister, and perhaps more protracted, by the lights of perverted science. Let us therefore brace ourselves to our duties, and so bear ourselves that, if the British Empire and its Commonwealth last for a thousand years, men will say, "This was their finest hour."

Commons, June 18, 1940.

Ordeal by Battle. And now it has come to us to stand alone in the breach, and face the worst that the tyrant's might and enmity can do. Bearing ourselves humbly before God, but conscious that we serve an unfolding purpose, we are ready to defend our native land against the invasion by which it is threatened. We are fighting by ourselves alone; but we are not fighting for ourselves alone. Here in this strong City of Refuge which enshrines the title-deeds of human progress and is of deep consequence to Christian civilization; here, girt about by the seas and oceans where the navy reigns; shielded from above by the prowess and devotion of our airmen—we await undismayed the impending assault. Perhaps it will come to-night. Perhaps it will come next week. Perhaps it will never come. We must show ourselves equally capable of meeting a sudden violent shock, or what is perhaps a harder test, a prolonged vigil. But be the ordeal sharp or long, or both, we shall seek no terms, we shall tolerate no parley; we may show mercy— we shall ask for none. . . .

We would rather see London laid in ruins and ashes than that it should be tamely and abjectly enslaved.

Commons, July 14, 1940.

British at War. When the British people make up their minds to go to war they expect to receive terrible injuries. That is why we tried to remain at peace as long as possible.

Commons, September 5, 1940.

Inspiration. It is a message of good cheer to our fighting forces on the seas, in the air, and in our waiting armies in all their posts and stations, that we send them from this capital city. They know that they have behind them a people who will not flinch or weary of the struggle—hard and protracted though it be; but that we shall rather draw from the heart of suffering itself the means of inspiration and survival, and of a victory won not only for ourselves but for all; a victory won not only for our own time, but for the long and better days that are to come.

London, September 11, 1940.

Ordeals. I must appeal to the House to show its consideration for ministers, and for a Government in whom it has recorded its confidence almost unanimously. We are really doing our very best. There are no doubt many mistakes and shortcomings. A lot of things are done none too well. Some things that ought to be done have not yet been done. Some things have been done that had better have been left undone. But looking broadly at the whole picture as it is viewed by any impartial eye, the way in which our system of government and society is standing up to its present ordeals, which will certainly increase in severity, constitutes a magnificent achievement, and has justly commanded the wonder and admiration of every friendly nation in the world.

Threat of Invasion. The shipping available and now assembled is sufficient to carry in one voyage nearly half a million men. We should, of course, expect to drown a great many on the way over, and to destroy a large proportion of their vessels. But when you reflect upon the many points from which they could start, and upon the fact that even the most likely sector of invasion, i.e., the sector in which enemy fighter support is available for their bombers and dive-bombers, extending from the Wash to the Isle of Wight, is nearly as long as the whole front in France from the Alps to the sea, and also upon the dangers of fog or artificial fog, one must expect many lodgements or attempted lodgements to be made on our Island simultaneously. These we shall hope to deal with as they occur, and also to cut off the supply across the sea by which the enemy will seek to nourish his lodgements.

Commons, September 17, 1940.

Supreme Exertion. Because we feel easier in ourselves and see our way more clearly through our difficulties and dangers than we did some months ago, because foreign countries, friends and foes, recognize the giant, enduring, resilient strength of Britain and the British Empire, do not let us dull for one moment the sense of the awful hazards in which we stand. Do not let us lose the conviction that it is only by supreme and superb exertions, unwearying and indomitable, that we shall save our souls alive. No one can predict, no one can even imagine, how this terrible war against German and Nazi aggression will run its course or how far it will spread or how long it will last. Long, dark months of trials and tribulations lie before us. Not only great dangers, but many more misfortunes, many shortcomings, many mistakes, many disappointments will surely be our lot. Death and sorrow will be the companions of our journey; hardship our garment; constancy and valour our only shield. We must be united, we must be undaunted, we must be inflexible. Our qualities and deeds must burn and glow through the gloom of Europe until they become the veritable beacon of its salvation.

Commons, October 8, 1940.

Invasion of Britain. The plain fact that an invasion, planned on so vast a scale, has not been attempted in spite of the very great need of the enemy to destroy us in our citadel and that all these anxious months, when we stood alone and the whole of the world wondered, have passed safely away—that fact constitutes in itself one of the historic victories of the British Isles and is a monumental milestone on our onward march.

Commons, November 5, 1940.

Survival of Britain. The outside world which a little while ago took only a moderate view of our prospects, now believes that Britain will survive. But between immediate survival and lasting victory there is a long road to tread. In treading it, we shall show the world the perseverance and steadfastness of the British race and the glorious resilience and flexibility of our ancient institutions.

Mansion House, London, November 9, 1940.

Surrender of Liberties. Immense surrenders of their hard-won liberties have been voluntarily made by the British people in order in time of war to serve the better the cause of freedom and fair play, to which, keeping nothing back, they have devoted all that they have and all that they are. Parliament stands custodian of these surrendered liberties, and its most sacred duty will be to restore them in their fullness when victory has crowned our exertions and our perseverance.

Commons, November 21, 1940.

Struggle for Liberty. We know that other hearts in millions and scores of millions beat with ours; that other voices proclaim the cause for which we strive; other strong hands wield the hammers and shape the weapons we need; other clear and gleaming eyes are fixed in hard conviction upon the tyrannies that must and shall be destroyed.

London, March 18, 1941.

Air War. There is a sensible improvement in our means of dealing with German raids upon this Island, and a very great measure of security has been given to this country in day-time—and we are glad that the days are lengthening. But now the moonlight periods are also looked forward to by the Royal Air Force as an opportunity for inflicting severe deterrent losses upon the raiders, as well as for striking hard at the enemy in his own territory. The fact that our technical advisers welcome the light—daylight, moonlight, starlight—and that we do not rely for protection on darkness, clouds and mists, as would have been the case some time ago, is pregnant with hope and meaning.

Commons, April 9, 1941.

Spirit. I go about the country whenever I can escape for a few hours or for a day from my duty at headquarters, and I see the damage done by the enemy attacks; but I also see side by side with the devastation and amid the ruins quiet, confident, bright and smiling eyes, beaming with a consciousness of being associated with a cause far higher and wider than any human or personal issue. I see the spirit of an unconquerable people. I see a spirit bred in freedom, nursed in a tradition which has come down to us through the centuries, and which will surely at this moment, this turning-point in the history of the world, enable us to bear our part in such a way that none of our race who come after us will have any reason to cast reproach upon their sires.

Bristol University, April 12, 1941.

Criticism. I am not one, and I should be the last, unduly to resent unfair criticism, or even fair criticism, which is so much more searching. I have been a critic myself—I cannot at all see how I should have stood the test of being a mere spectator in the drama which is now passing. But there is a kind of criticism which is a little irritating. It is like a bystander who, when he sees a team of horses dragging a heavy waggon painfully up a hill, cuts a switch from the fence, and there are many switches, and belabours them lustily. He may well be animated by a benevolent purpose, and who shall say the horses may not benefit from his efforts, and the waggon get quicker to the top of the hill.

Profession of Faith. I ask you to witness, Mr. Speaker, that I have never promised anything or offered anything but blood, tears, toil and sweat, to which I will now add our fair share of mistakes, shortcomings and disappointments, and also that this may go on for a very long time, at the end of which I firmly believe—though it is not a promise or a guarantee, only a profession of faith—that there will be complete, absolute and final victory. *Commons, May 7, 1941.*

If. I give no guarantee, I make no promise or prediction for the future. But if the next six months, during which we must expect even harder fighting and many disappointments, should find us in no worse position than that in which we stand to-day; if, after having fought so long alone, single-handed against the might of Germany, and against Italy, and against the intrigues and treachery of Vichy, we should still be found the faithful and unbeaten guardian of the Nile Valley and of the regions that lie about it, then I say that a famous chapter will have been written in the martial history of the British Empire and Commonwealth of Nations. *Commons, June 10, 1941.*

Responsibilities. A wonderful story is unfolding before our eyes. How it will end we are not allowed to know. But on both sides of the Atlantic we all feel, I repeat, all, that we are a part of it, that our future and that of many generations is at stake. We are sure that the character of human society will be shaped by the resolves we take and the deeds we do. We need not bewail the fact that we have been called upon to face such solemn responsibilities. We may be proud, and even rejoice amid our tribulations, that we have been born at this cardinal time for so great an age and so splendid an opportunity of service here below.

Barbarism. Wickedness, enormous, panoplied, embattled, seemingly triumphant, casts its shadow over Europe and Asia. Laws, customs and traditions are broken up. Justice is cast from her seat. The rights of the weak are trampled down. The grand freedoms of which the President of the United States has spoken so movingly are spurned and chained. The whole stature of man, his genius, his initiative and his nobility, is ground down under systems of mechanical barbarism and of organized and scheduled terror.   *London, June 16, 1941.*

London. The administration of London in all its branches was confronted with problems hitherto unknown and un-measured in all the history of the past. Public order, public health, the maintenance of all the essential services, the han-dling of the millions of people who came in and out of London every day; the shelter—not indeed from the enemy's bombs, for that was beyond us, but from their blast and splinters—the shelter of millions of men and women, and the removal of the dead and wounded from the shattered buildings; the care of the wounded when hospitals were being ruthlessly bombed, and the provision for the homeless—sometimes amounting to many thousands in a single day, and accumulating to many more after three or four days of successive attacks—all these things, with the welfare and the education amid these scenes of our great numbers of children here—all these presented tasks which, viewed in cold blood beforehand, might well have seemed overwhelming.

Londoners. I remember one winter evening travelling to a railway station—which still worked—on my way north to visit troops. It was cold and raining. Darkness had almost fallen on the blacked-out streets. I saw everywhere long queues of people, among them hundreds of young girls in their silk stockings and high-heeled shoes, who had worked hard all day and were waiting for bus after bus, which came by already overcrowded, in the hope of reaching their homes for the night. When at that moment the doleful wail of the siren betokened the approach of the German bombers, I confess to you that my heart bled for London and the Londoner.
        County Hall, London, July 14, 1941.

Temptations to Optimism. We must be on our guard equally against pessimism and against optimism. There are, no doubt, temptations to optimism. It is the fact that the mighty Russian State, so foully and treacherously assaulted, has struck back with magnificent strength and courage, and is inflicting pro-digious and well-deserved slaughter for the first time upon the Nazi armies. It is the fact that the United States, the greatest single power in the world, is giving us aid on a gigantic scale and advancing in rising wrath and conviction to the very verge of war. It is the fact that the German air superiority has been broken, and that the air attacks on this country have for the time being almost ceased. It is a fact that the Battle of the Atlantic, although far from won, has, partly through American intervention, moved impressively in our favour. It is the fact that the Nile Valley is now far safer than it was twelve months ago or three months ago. It is the fact that the enemy has lost all pretence of theme or doctrine, and is sunk ever deeper in moral and intellectual degradation and bankruptcy, and that almost all his conquests have proved burdens and sources of weakness.   *Commons, July 29, 1941.*

Atlantic Meeting. This was a meeting [with President Roosevelt] which marks for ever in the pages of history the taking-up by the English-speaking nations, amid all this peril, tumult and confusion, of the guidance of the fortunes of the broad, toiling masses in all the continents; and our loyal effort, without any clog of selfish interest, to lead them forward out of the miseries into which they have been plunged back to the broad highroad of freedom and justice. This is the highest honour and the most glorious opportunity which could ever have come to any branch of the human race. . . .

The meeting was therefore symbolic. That is its prime importance. It symbolizes, in a form and manner which everyone can understand in every land and in every clime, the deep underlying unities which stir, and at decisive moments rule, the English-speaking peoples throughout the world. Would it be presumptuous for me to say that it symbolizes something even more majestic—namely, the marshalling of the good forces of the world against the evil forces which are now so formidable and triumphant, and which have cast their cruel spell over the whole of Europe and a large part of Asia?
London, August 24, 1941.

Mood of Britain. Thus far then have we travelled along the terrible road we chose at the call of duty. The mood of Britain is wisely and rightly averse from every form of shallow or premature exultation. This is no time for boasts or glowing prophecies, but there is this—a year ago our position looked forlorn and well nigh desperate to all eyes but our own. To-day we may say aloud before an awe-struck world, "We are still masters of our fate. We still are captains of our soul."
Commons, September 9, 1941.

Supreme Effort. Provided that every effort is made, that nothing is kept back, that the whole man-power, brain-power, virility, valour and civic virtue of the English-speaking world with all its galaxy of loyal, friendly, associated communities and states—provided all that is bent unremittingly to the simple and supreme task, I think it would be reasonable to hope that the end of 1942 will see us quite definitely in a better position than we are now, and that the year 1943 will enable us to assume the initiative upon an ample scale.

The Senate Chamber, Washington, D.C., December 26, 1941.

Neck of England. When I warned them [the French Government] that Britain would fight on alone whatever they did, their generals told their Prime Minister and his divided Cabinet: "In three weeks England will have her neck wrung like a chicken." Some chicken! Some neck!

Canadian Parliament, Ottawa, December 30, 1941.

You Never Can Tell. There are times when so many things happen, and happen so quickly, and time seems to pass in such a way that you can neither say it is long or short, that it is easy to forget what you have said three months before. You may fail to connect it with what you are advocating at the particular moment. Throughout a long and variegated Parliamentary life this consideration has led me to try to keep a watchful eye on that danger myself. You never can tell. There are also people who talk and bear themselves as if they had prepared for this war with great armaments and long, careful preparation. But that is not true. In two and a half years of fighting we have only just managed to keep our head above water.

Commons, January 27, 1942.

St. Anthony. I can assure the House that I shall be ready to profit to the full from many constructive and helpful lines of thought which have been advanced, even when they come from the most hostile quarters. I shall not be like that saint to whom I have before referred in this House, but whose name I have unhappily forgotten, who refused to do right because the Devil prompted him. Neither shall I be deterred from doing what I am convinced is right by the fact that I have thought differently about it in some distant, or even in some recent past.

Commons, January 29, 1942.

Fall of Singapore. I speak to you all under the shadow of a heavy and far-reaching military defeat. It is a British and Imperial defeat. Singapore has fallen. All the Malay Peninsula has been overrun. Other dangers gather about us out there, and none of the dangers which we have hitherto successfully withstood at home and in the east are in any way diminished. This, therefore, is one of those moments when the British race and nation can show their quality and their genius. This is one of those moments when it can draw from the heart of misfortune the vital impulses of victory. Here is the moment to display that calm and poise combined with grim determination which not so long ago brought us out of the very jaws of death. Here is another occasion to show

—as so often in our long story—that we can meet reverses with dignity and with renewed accessions of strength. We must remember that we are no longer alone. We are in the midst of a great company. Three-quarters of the human race are now moving with us. The whole future of mankind may depend upon our action and upon our conduct. So far we have not failed. We shall not fail now. Let us move forward steadfastly together into the storm and through the storm.

London, February 15, 1942.

Critics. We are certainly aided by a great volume of criticism and advice from which it will always be our endeavour to profit in the highest degree. Naturally when one is burdened by the very hard labour of the task and its cares, sorrows and responsibilities, there may sometimes steal across the mind a feeling of impatience at the airy and jaunty detachment of some of those critics who feel so confident of their knowledge and feel so sure of their ability to put things right. If I should be forced—as I hope I shall not be—to yield to such a temptation, I hope you will remember how difficult it is to combine the attitude of proper meekness and humility towards assailants at home with those combative and pugnacious qualities, with the spirit of offensive and counter-attack, which we feel were never more needful than now against the common enemy.

Caxton Hall, London, March 26, 1942.

1942 Prospect. We have reached a period in the war when it would be premature to say that we have topped the ridge, but now we see the ridge ahead. We see that perseverance, unflinching, dogged, inexhaustible, tireless, valiant, will surely carry us and our allies, the great nations of the world, and the unfortunate nations who have been subjugated and enslaved, on to one of the most deep-founded movements of humanity, which have ever taken place in our history. We see that they will come to the top of the ridge, and then they will have a chance not only of beating down and subduing those evil forces which have withstood us so long, which have twice let ruin and havoc loose in the world, but they will have that further and grander prospect that beyond the smoke of battle and the confusion of the fight we shall have the chance to settle our countries and the whole world together, moving forward together on the high road. That is the prospect that lies before us if we do not fail. And we shall not fail.

Town Hall, Leeds, May 16, 1942.

One End. As in the last war, so in this, we are moving through many reverses and defeats to complete and final victory. We have only to endure and to persevere, to conquer. Now we are no longer unarmed; we are well armed. Now we are not alone; we have mighty allies, bound irrevocably by solemn faith and common interests to stand with us in the ranks of the United Nations. There can only be one end. When it will come, or how it will come, I cannot tell. But, when we survey the overwhelming resources which are at our disposal, once they are fully marshalled and developed —as they can be, as they will be—we may stride forward into the unknown with growing confidence. . . .

All the world, even our best friends, thought that our end had come. Accordingly, we prepared ourselves to conquer or perish. We were united in that solemn majestic hour; we were all equally resolved at least to go down fighting. We cast calculations to the winds; no wavering voice was heard; we hurled defiance at our foes; we faced our duty, and, by the mercy of God, we were preserved.

It fell to me in those days to express the sentiments and resolves of the British nation in that supreme crisis of its life. That was to me an honour far beyond any dreams or ambitions I had ever nursed, and it is one that cannot be taken away.   *London, May 10, 1942.*

Sea, Ocean, Land and Air. It is difficult to make the Russians comprehend all the problems of the sea and of the ocean. We are sea animals, and the United States is to a large extent ocean animals. The Russians are land animals. Happily, we are all three air animals. It is difficult to explain fully all the different characteristics of the war effort of various countries, but I am sure that we made their leaders feel confidence in our loyal and sincere resolve to come to their aid as quickly as possible and in the most effective manner, without regard to the losses or sacrifices involved so long as the contribution was towards victory.
Commons, September 8, 1942.

The End of the Beginning. The fight between the British and the Germans was intense and fierce in the extreme. It was a deadly grapple. The Germans have been outmatched and outfought with the very kind of weapons with which they have beaten down so many small peoples, and also large unprepared peoples. They have been beaten by the very technical apparatus on which they counted to gain them the domination of the world. Especially is this true of the air and of the tanks and of the artillery, which has come back into its own on the battlefield. The Germans have received back again that measure of fire and steel which they have so often meted out to others.

Now this is not the end. It is not even the beginning of the end. But it is, perhaps, the end of the beginning.

The Empire. Let me, however, make this clear, in case there should be any mistake about it in any quarter. We mean to hold our own. I have not become the King's First Minister in order to preside over the liquidation of the British Empire. For that task, if ever it were prescribed, someone else would have to be consulted.

Mansion House, London, November 10, 1942.

Victory at Alamein. Two Sundays ago all the bells rang out to celebrate the victory of our desert army at Alamein. Here was a martial episode in British history which deserved a special recognition. But the bells also carried with their clashing joyous peals our thanksgiving that, in spite of all our errors and shortcomings, we have been brought nearer to the frontiers of deliverance. We have not reached those frontiers yet, but we are becoming ever more entitled to be sure that the awful perils which might well have blotted out our life and all that we love and cherish will be surmounted, and that we shall be preserved for further service in the vanguard of mankind.

Blessings. We have to look back along the path we have trodden these last three years of toil and strife, to value properly all that we have escaped and all that we have achieved. No mood of boastfulness, of vain glory, of over-confidence must cloud our minds; but I think we have a right which history will endorse to feel that we had the honour to play a part in saving the freedom and the future of the world.

London, November 29, 1942.

Stamina. If by any chance unexpected good tidings came to us, that would be a matter which we could rejoice at, but we must not count upon. We count upon our strong right arms, upon our honest, hard-working hearts; we count upon our courage, which has not been found wanting either in domestic or foreign stresses during the whole course of the war. These are the simple virtues which our island race has cultured and nurtured during many generations, and these are the virtues which will bear us through all struggles and in which we must put our faith.

Just Cause. We are all of us defending something which is, I won't say dearer, but greater than a country, namely a cause. That cause is the cause of freedom and of justice; that cause is the cause of the weak against the strong; it is the cause of law against violence, of mercy and tolerance

against brutality and iron-bound tyranny. That is the cause we are fighting for. That is the cause which is moving slowly, painfully but surely, inevitably and inexorably to victory; and when the victory is gained you will find that you are—I will not say in a new world, but a better world; you are in a world which can be made more fair, more happy, if only all the peoples will join together to do their part, and if all classes and all parties stand together to reap the fruits of victory as they are standing together to bear, and to face, and to cast back the terrors and menaces of war.
Town Hall, Bradford, December 5, 1942.

Conference at Casablanca. The dominating aim which we set before ourselves at the Conference at Casablanca was to engage the enemy's forces on land, on sea and in the air on the largest possible scale and at the earliest possible moment. The importance of coming to ever closer grips with the enemy and intensifying the struggle outweighs a number of other considerations which ordinarily would be decisive in themselves. We have to make the enemy burn and bleed in every way that is physically and reasonably possible, in the same way as he is being made to burn and bleed along the vast Russian front from the White Sea to the Black Sea.
Commons, February 11, 1943.

Attrition. It is in the dragging-out of the war at enormous expense, until the democracies are tired or bored or split, that the main hopes of Germany and Japan must now reside. We must destroy this hope, as we have destroyed so many others, and for that purpose we must beware of every topic, however attractive, and every tendency, however natural, which turns our minds and energies from this supreme objective of the general victory of the United Nations. By singleness of purpose, by steadfastness of conduct, by tenacity and endurance such as we have so far displayed—by these and only by these, can we discharge our duty to the future of the world and to the destiny of man.
U. S. Congress, Washington, May 19, 1943.

Wishful Thinking. There is danger in wishful thinking that victory will come by internal collapse of the Axis. Victory depends on force of arms. I stand pat on a knockout, but any windfalls in the way of internal collapse will be gratefully accepted.
Washington, D.C., May 25, 1943.

Amphibious Operations. All large amphibious operations, especially if they require the co-operation of two or more countries, require long months of organization, with refinements and complexities hitherto unknown in war. Bold im-

pulses, impatient desires, and sudden flashes of military instinct cannot hasten the course of events.
Guildhall, London, June 30, 1943.

Great Causes. If we are together nothing is impossible. If we are divided all will fail. I therefore preach continually the doctrine of the fraternal association of our two peoples, not for any purpose of gaining material advantages for either of them, not for territorial aggrandizement or the vain pomp of earthly domination, but for the sake of service to mankind and for the honour that comes to those who faithfully serve great causes.
Harvard University, September 6, 1943.

Insurance against Blitz. At the beginning of the blitz I pressed upon him [Sir Kingsley Wood, Chancellor of the Exchequer] the vital need of doing something for the poor people whose houses were smashed up and whose businesses were destroyed, and he devised the elaborate insurance scheme, which has come into the fullest possible fruition. At one time, it looked as if the State were taking on a very heavy burden; but trees never grow up to the sky, and, as a matter of fact, not only have individuals been provided for and the loss inflicted by the enemy shared and spread over the shoulders of the whole community, but the scheme has ultimately turned out to be highly profitable to the Exchequer.
Commons, September 22, 1943.

Mysteries of the Future. I have no fear of the future. Let us go forward into its mysteries, let us tear aside the veils which hide it from our eyes, and let us move onward with confidence and courage. All the problems of the post-war world, some of which seem so baffling now, will be easier of solution once decisive victory has been gained, and once it is clear that victory won in arms has not been cast away by folly or by violence when the moment comes to lay the broad foundations of the future world order, and it is time to speak great words of peace and truth to all.
The Royal Albert Hall, London, September 29, 1943.

Youth. You young men here may be in the battle, in the fields or in the high air. Others will be the heirs to the victory your elders or your parents have gained, and it will be for you to ensure that what is achieved is not cast away, either by violence of passion or by sheer stupidity. But let keen vision, courage and humanity guide our steps, so that it can be said of us that not only did our country do its duty in the war, but afterwards in the years of peace it showed wisdom, poise and sincerity, which contributed in no small

degree to bind up the frightful wounds caused by the struggle.
        Harrow School, Harrow, November 5, 1943.

Climax of War. It is a reasonable assumption that, unless
we make some grave mistakes in strategy, the year 1944
will see the climax of the European war. Unless some happy
event occurs on which we have no right to count, and the
hand of Providence is stretched forth in some crowning
mercy, 1944 will see the greatest sacrifice of life by British
and American armies, and battles far larger and more costly
than Waterloo or Gettysburg will be fought. Sorrow will
come to many homes in the United Kingdom and throughout
the great Republic. British and American manhood—true
brothers in arms—will attack and grapple with the deadly
foe.   *Mansion House, London, November 9, 1943.*

Free Hand for Victors. The term "unconditional surrender"
does not mean that the German people will be enslaved or
destroyed. It means, however, that the allies will not be
bound to them at the moment of surrender by any pact or
obligation. There will be, for instance, no question of the
Atlantic Charter applying to Germany as a matter of right
and barring territorial transferences or adjustments in enemy
countries. No such arguments will be admitted by us as were
used by Germany after the last war, saying that they surrendered in consequence of President Wilson's fourteen points.
Unconditional surrender means that the victors have a free
hand. It does not mean that they are entitled to behave in
a barbarous manner, nor that they wish to blot out Germany
from among the nations of Europe. It we are bound, we
are bound by our own consciences to civilization. We are not
to be bound to the Germans as the result of a bargain struck.

Allied Command. The principle which should obviously be
followed between two allies working together as closely as
we and the United States is that the nationality of the com-
mander should generally follow the majority of the troops
in any theatre. In General Maitland Wilson and General
Alexander, we have at once the supreme commander in the
Mediterranean and the fighting head of the army in Italy.
We and our American Ally have full confidence in these
officers, under whom the United States General Devers and
General Clark, the most daring and gallant leader of the
Fifth Army, are the corresponding American chiefs. In Great
Britain, on the other hand, where forces are being assembled
for future operations of the greatest magnitude, General
Eisenhower, with whom we have worked for so long, so
happily and so successfully, has been placed at the summit

of the war direction, with Air Chief Marshal Tedder as his deputy and with his brilliant United States Chief of Staff, the trusty General Bedell Smith—these are the central figures of this command under whom many distinguished commanders, British and American, are serving, including General Montgomery; and these officers will, when the time comes and in accordance with the arrangements which have been made, lead our armies to the liberation of Europe.

Commons, February 22, 1944.

Invasion Plans. In April, 1943, General Morgan, of the British army, became head of the British and American Planning Staff, which surveyed the whole project by the decision of the Combined Chiefs of Staff Committee. They made a plan, which I took with me last year to Quebec, where it was submitted to the President and the Combined British and American Chiefs of Staff. This plan selected the beaches for the attack and presented the outlines of the scheme, together with a mass of detail to support it. It received, in principle, complete agreement. It is rather remarkable that a secret of this character, which had to be entrusted from the beginning to scores, very soon to hundreds and ultimately to thousands of people, never leaked out either in these Islands or the wide expanses of the United States.

Commons, August 2, 1944.

Army of Liberation. The speed with which the mighty British and American armies in France were built up is almost incredible. In the first 24 hours a quarter of a million men were landed, in the teeth of fortified and violent opposition. By the 20th day a million men were ashore. There are now between two and three million men in France. Certainly the progress in the power of moving troops and landing troops has vastly increased since the early days, when we had to plunge into the war with no previous experience. But the actual number of soldiers was only part of the problem of transportation. These armies were equipped with the most perfect modern weapons and every imaginable contrivance of modern war, and an immense artillery supported all the operations. Enormous masses of armour of the highest quality and character gave them extraordinary offensive power and mobility. Many hundreds of thousands of vehicles sustained their movements, many millions of tons of stores have already been landed—the great bulk of everything over open beaches or through the synthetic harbours which I described when last I spoke to the House.

Commons, September 28, 1944.

Enemy's Two Hopes. The enemy has two hopes. The first is that by lengthening the struggle he may wear down our resolution; the second, and more important hope, is that division will arise between the three great powers by whom he is assailed, and whose continued union spells his doom. His hope is that there will be some rift in this Alliance; that the Russians may go this way, the British and Americans that; that quarrels may arise about the Balkans or the Baltic, about Poland or Hungary, which he hopes will impair the union of our councils and, consequently, the symmetry and momentum of our converging advance. There is the enemy's great hope. It is to deprive that hope of all foundation and reality that our efforts must necessarily be bent.

Commons, October 27, 1944.

The Last Lap. This is just the moment not to slacken. All the races which the calendar holds, or nearly all of them, are won in the last lap; and it is then, when it is most hard, when one is most tired, when the sense of boredom seems to weigh upon one, when even the most glittering events, exciting, thrilling events, are, as it were, smothered by satiation, when headlines in the newspapers, though perfectly true, succeed one another in their growing emphasis, and yet the end seems to recede before us—like climbing a hill when there is another peak beyond—it is at that very moment that we in this Island have to give that extra sense of exertion, of boundless, inexhaustible, dynamic energy that we have shown, as the records now made public have emphasized in detail. Tirelessness is what we have to show now.

Commons, November 29, 1944.

National Exhaustion. We have sacrificed everything in this war. We shall emerge from it, for the time being, more stricken and impoverished than any other victorious country. The United Kingdom and the British Commonwealth are the only unbroken force which declared war on Germany of its own free will. We declared war not for any ambition or material advantage, but for the sake of our obligation to do our best for Poland against German aggression, in which aggression, there or elsewhere, it must also in fairness be stated, our own self-preservation was involved.

Cup of Success. Can we produce that complete unity and that impulse in time to achieve decisive military victory with the least possible prolongation of the world's misery, or must we fall into jabber, babel and discord while victory is still unattained? It seems to me to be the supreme question alike of the hour and the age. This is no new problem in the history of mankind. Very often have great combinations almost attained success and then, at the last moment, cast it away. Very often have the triumphs and sacrifices of armies come to naught at the conference table. Very often the eagles have been squalled down by the parrots. Very often, in particular, the people of this Island, indomitable in adversity, have tasted the hard-won cup of success only to cast it away.

Liberation of Europe. We have one principle about the liberated countries or the repentant satellite countries which we strive for according to the best of our ability and resources. Here is the principle. I will state it in the broadest and most familiar terms: Government of the people, by the people, for the people, set up on a basis of election by the free and universal suffrage, with secrecy of the ballot and no intimidation. That is and has always been the policy of this Government in all countries. That is our only aim, our only interest, and our only care. It is to that goal that we try to make our way across all the difficulties, obstacles and perils of the long road. Trust the people, make sure they have a fair chance to decide their destiny without being terrorized from either quarter or regimented. There is our policy for Italy, for Yugoslavia and for Greece. What other interests have we than that? For that we shall strive, and for that alone.

Commons, January 18, 1945.

Armistice. A quarter of a century ago . . . the House, when it heard . . . the armistice terms, did not feel inclined for debate or business, but desired to offer thanks to Almighty God, to the Great Power which seems to shape and design the fortunes of nations and the destiny of man; and I therefore . . . move "That the House do now attend at the church of St. Margaret, Westminster, to give humble and reverent thanks to Almighty God for our deliverance from the threat of German domination." This is the identical motion which was moved in former times.

Commons, May 8, 1945.

Hiroshima. There are voices which assert that the bomb should never have been used at all. I cannot associate myself with such ideas. Six years of total war have convinced most people that had the Germans or Japanese discovered this new weapon, they would have used it upon us to our complete destruction with the utmost alacrity. I am surprised that very worthy people, but people who in most cases had no intention of proceeding to the Japanese front themselves, should adopt the position that rather than throw this bomb, we should have sacrificed a million American and a quarter of a million British lives in the desperate battles and massacres of an invasion of

Japan. Future generations will judge these dire decisions, a
I believe that if they find themselves dwelling in a happi
world from which war has been banished, and where freed
reigns, they will not condemn those who struggled for the
benefit amid the horrors and miseries of this gruesome a
ferocious epoch. *Commons, August 16, 19*

Alive and Free. Upon Britain fell the proud but awf
responsibility of keeping the Flag of Freedom flying in t
Old World till the forces of the New World could arrive. B
now the tornado has passed away. The thunder of the canno
has ceased, the terror from the skies is over, the oppressors a
cast out and broken, and we find ourselves breathless but s
alive, exhausted but free. The future stands before us to ma
or mar. *Brussels, November 16, 19*

The Not So Bright New World

Reign of Law. The future towards which we are marchi
across bloody fields and frightful manifestations of destructi
must surely be based upon the broad and simple virtues a
upon the nobility of mankind. It must be based upon a rei
of law which upholds the principles of justice and fair pl
and protects the weak against the strong if the weak ha
justice on their side. There must be an end to predatory e
ploitation and nationalistic ambitions.
Commons, May 24, 19

A Great Age. We are living in a great age, of which it w
always be said that this present generation, in Britain a
in the United States, had cast upon them burdens and pr
lems without compare in the history of the world. Under t
severest stresses, and under the most hard and searching tri
they have shown themselves not unequal to those proble
On the contrary, they have triumphed over them, and th
cleared the way to the broad advance of mankind to lev
they have never yet attained, and to securities of which th
never will be deprived.
The Citadel, Quebec, September 16, 19

Unconditional Surrender. Peace, though based on unc
ditional surrender, will bring to Germany and Japan an i
mense, immediate amelioration of the suffering and ag
which now lie before them. We, the allies, are no monsters, t
faithful men trying to carry forward the light of the wo
trying to raise, from the bloody welter and confusion in wh

mankind is now plunged, a structure of peace, of freedom, of justice, and of law, which system shall be an abiding and lasting shelter for all.   *Commons, January 18, 1945.*

The Tragedy of Europe. The tragedy of Europe shocks mankind. It darkens the pages of human history. It will excite the amazement and horror of future generations. Here in these beautiful, fertile and temperate lands, where so many of the noblest races of mankind, the heirs of Roman civilization, the champions of Christian chivalry, have developed their character, their arts and their literature, we have twice in our own lifetime seen all rent asunder and torn to pieces in frightful convulsions which have left their mark in blackened devastation throughout many ancient states and famous cities.
                              Brussels, November 16, 1945.

Minority Government. When the Socialist Government, in their clumsy arrogance, imposed upon us wartime controls for five more long years, they had not got a majority of the electorate behind them. Together with the Liberals and Independents who voted, we represented a larger total of votes against the five years' restriction than those who voted for it. The Socialists have no majority in the nation; even with all the adventitious aid they got at the last election, they are a minority. They have a right to govern and administer the country but they have no right to ride rough-shod over the majority of their fellow countrymen.
                    Friends House, London, November 28, 1945.

Unity of Europe. The safety of the world requires a new unity in Europe, from which no nation should be permanently outcast. It is from the quarrels of the strong parent races in Europe that the world wars we have witnessed, or which occurred in former times, have sprung. . . .

If the dangers of war and tyranny are removed, there is no doubt that science and co-operation can bring in the next few years to the world, certainly in the next few decades newly taught in the sharpening school of war, an expansion of material well-being beyond anything that has yet occurred in human experience. Now, at this sad and breathless moment, we are plunged in the hunger and distress which are the aftermath of our stupendous struggle; but this will pass and may pass quickly, and there is no reason except human folly or sub-human crime which should deny to all the nations the inauguration and enjoyment of an age of plenty.
              Westminster College, Fulton, Missouri, March 5, 1946.

Message. In these last years of life there is a message of which I conceive myself to be a bearer. It is a very simple message which can be well understood by the people of both our countries. It is that we should stand together. We should stand together in malice to none, in greed for nothing, but in defence of those causes which we hold dear not only for our own benefit, but because we believe they mean the honour and the happiness of long generations of men.

The General Assembly of Virginia, Richmond,
March 8, 1946.

Aftermath of War. The problems of the aftermath, the moral and physical exhaustion of the victorious nations, the miserable fate of the conquered, the vast confusion of Europe and Asia, combine to make a sum total of difficulty, which even if the Allies had preserved their wartime comradeship, would have taxed their resources to the full. Even if we in this Island had remained united, as we were in the years of peril, we should have found much to baffle our judgment, and many tasks that were beyond our strength. . . .

So far as it remains in the power of this Island people to influence the course of events, we must strive over a period of years to redeem and to reincorporate the German and the Japanese peoples in a world system of free and civilized democracy. The idea of keeping scores of millions of people hanging about in a sub-human state between earth and hell, until they are worn down to a slave condition or embrace Communism, or die off from hunger, will only, if it is pursued, breed at least a moral pestilence and probably an actual war.

Commons, June 5, 1946.

Standard Bearer. I have naturally considered very carefully what is my own duty in these times. It would be easy for me to retire gracefully in an odour of civic freedoms, and this plan crossed my mind frequently some months ago. I feel now, however, that the situation is so serious and what may have to come so grave, that I am resolved to go forward carrying the flag as long as I have the necessary strength and energy, and have your confidence. It is of the highest importance to our name and endurance as a great power, and to the cohesion of our national and imperial life, that there should be re-established at the earliest moment some poise and balance between the political forces in our Island, and that those who were so unexpectedly clad with overwhelming Parliamentary power should be made to realize that they are the servants, and not the masters, of the British nation.

Blackpool, October 5, 1946.

The Kremlin. We are in the presence of the collective mind, whose springs of action we cannot define. There are thirteen or fourteen very able men in the Kremlin who hold all Russia and more than a third of Europe in their control. Many stresses and pressures, internal as well as external, are working upon them, as upon all human beings. I cannot presume to forecast what decisions they will take, or to observe what decisions they may have already taken; still less can I attempt to foresee the time factor in their affairs.

Commons, October 23, 1946.

Nuremberg Trials. The Nuremberg trials are over, and the guilty leaders of the Nazi regime have been hanged by the conquerors. We are told that thousands yet remain to be tried, and that vast categories of Germans are classed as potentially guilty because of their association with the Nazi regime. After all, in a country which is handled as Germany was, the ordinary people have very little choice about what to do. I think some consideration should always be given to ordinary people. Everyone is not a Pastor Niemoller or a martyr, and when ordinary people are hurled this way and that, when the cruel hands of tyrants are laid upon them and vile systems of regimentation are imposed and enforced by espionage and other forms of cruelty, there are great numbers of people who will succumb.

Commons, November 12, 1946.

Two Convictions. I have two convictions in my heart. One is that, somehow or other, we shall survive, though for a time at a lower level than hitherto. The late Lord Fisher used to say "Britain never succumbs." The second is that things are going to get worse before they are better.

Commons, March 12, 1947.

Feuds in Europe. What is Europe now? It is a rubble heap, a charnel-house, a breeding-ground of pestilence and hate. Ancient nationalistic feuds and modern ideological factions distract and infuriate the unhappy, hungry populations. Evil teachers urge the paying-off old scores with mathematical precision, and false guides point to unsparing retribution as the pathway to prosperity. . . .

In our task of reviving the glories and happiness of Europe, and her prosperity, it can certainly be said that we start at the bottom of her fortunes. Here is the fairest, most temperate, most fertile area of the globe. The influence and the power of Europe and of Christendom have for centuries shaped and dominated the course of history. The sons and daughters of Europe have gone forth and carried their message to every part of the world. Religion, law, learning, art, science, industry, throughout the world all bear, in so many lands, under every sky and in every clime, the stamp of European origin, or the trace of European influence.

The Royal Albert Hall, London, May 14, 1947.

Social Justice. The scheme of society for which we stand is the establishment and maintenance of a basic minimum standard of life and labour below which a man or woman of goodwill, however old and weak, will not be allowed to fall. The food they receive, the prices they have to pay for basic necessities, the homes they live in, must be the first care of the State, and must have priority over all other peace-time requirements. Once that standard is being faithfully and even rigorously worked for by all concerned and without prejudice to it, we propose (if and when we have the power) to set the people free as quickly as possible from the controls and restrictions which now beset their daily life. We propose to sweep away with sturdy strokes the vast encumbrance of regulations and penalties which are to-day preventing our people from making a good living in their island home. Once the basic standard has been established we shall liberate the energies, the genius, the contrivance of the British nation from the paralyzing and humiliating thralldom in which they are now plunged. Above the minimum basic standard there will be free competition. Everyone will be free to make the best of himself without jealousy or spite by all the means that honour, and the long-respected laws and customs of our country allow.

Brighton, October 4, 1947.

Invisible Economics. The difference between what is seen and what is not seen was often noticed by the old economists. What is not seen in the infinite variety of individual transactions and decisions which, in a civilized society, within the framework of just and well-known laws, insure the advantage not only of the individual concerned, but of the community, and provide that general body of well-being constituting the wealth of nations. All this is blotted out by an over-riding State control, however imposing some of its manifestations may be. It is the vital creative impulse that I deeply fear the doctrines and policy of the Socialist Government have destroyed, or are rapidly destroying, in our national life. Nothing that they can plan and order and rush around enforcing will take its place. They have broken the mainspring, and until we get a new one the watch will not go.

Commons, October 28, 1947.

Dictatorship in Britain. As a free-born Englishman, what I hate is the sense of being at anybody's mercy or in anybody's power, be it Hitler or Attlee. We are approaching very near to dictatorship in this country, dictatorship that is to say—I will be quite candid with the House—without either its criminality or its efficiency. *Commons, November 11, 1947.*

Helpless Millions. But now all these millions of humble humans are hustled and harried this way and that, first by nationalistic or imperialistic ambitions or appetites, now by ideological doctrines and hatreds, and all their small lives may be shattered and convulsed, millions at a time, and they may be only regimented up to suffering wounds and unrewarded toil. We, their representatives in this world-famous assembly, have a great responsibility, and we cannot always discharge it by treading easy paths and saying smooth things.
Commons, January 23, 1948.

Consuming the Substance. How are we keeping going from day to day? Let me tell you. We are living on the last remaining assets and overseas investments accumulated under the capitalistic system—that is what we are living on: we are living on them in the hope that we may bridge the gap before the new American grant-in-aid under the Marshall Plan comes in. Our last reserves will then be nearly gone, and even with the American help there will be a heavy deficit to be met each year on all our overseas purchases.
London, February 14, 1948.

Unity of Europe. There can be no hope for the world unless the peoples of Europe unite together to preserve their freedom, their culture and their civilization founded upon Christian ethics.
The Royal Albert Hall, London, April 21, 1948.

Inheritance of Europe. It is time indeed that that voice [of Europe] should be raised upon the scene of chaos and prostration, caused by the wrongs and hatreds of the past, and amid the dangers which lie about us in the present and cloud the future. We shall only save ourselves from the perils which draw near by forgetting the hatreds of the past, by letting national rancours and revenges die, by progressively effacing frontiers and barriers which aggravate and congeal our divisions, and by rejoicing together in that glorious treasure of literature, of romance, of ethics, of thought and toleration belonging to all, which is the true inheritance of Europe, the expression of its genius and honour, but which by our quarrels, our follies, by our fearful wars and the cruel and awful deeds that spring from war and tyrants, we have almost cast away.

Unification of Europe. Europe can only be united by the heartfelt wish and vehement expression of the great majority of all the peoples in all the Parties in all the freedom-loving countries, no matter where they dwell or how they vote.

Longing of the Masses. I have the feeling that after the second Thirty Years' War, for that is what it is, through which we have just passed, mankind needs and seeks a period of rest. After all, how little it is that the millions of homes in Europe represented here to-day are asking. What is it that all these wage-earners, skilled artisans, soldiers and tillers of the soil require, deserve, and may be led to demand? Is it not a fair chance to make a home, to reap the fruits of their toil, to cherish their wives, to bring up their children in a decent manner and to dwell in peace and safety, without fear of bullying or monstrous burdens or exploitations, however this may be imposed upon them? That is their hearts' desire. That is what we mean to win for them.

The Hague, May 7, 1948.

Socialism. The old Radical campaign against exploitation, monopolies, unfair rake-offs and the like, in which I took a part in my young days, was a healthy and necessary corrective to the system of free enterprise. But this grotesque idea of managing vast enterprises by centralized direction from London can only lead to bankruptcy and ruin.

Perth, May 28, 1948.

Sharing of Miseries. I do not wonder that British youth is in revolt against the morbid doctrine that nothing matters but the equal sharing of miseries: that what used to be called the submerged tenth can only be rescued by bringing the other nine-tenths down to their level; against the folly that it is better that everyone should have half rations rather than that any by their exertions, or ability, should earn a second helping.

London, June 22, 1948.

Overbalance of Power. As I look upon the future of our country in the changing scene of human destiny I feel the existence of three great circles among the free nations and democracies. I almost wish I had a blackboard. I would make a picture for you. I don't suppose it would get hung in the Royal Academy, but it would illustrate the point I am anxious for you to hold in your minds. The first circle for us is naturally the British Commonwealth and Empire, with all that that comprises. Then there is also the English-speaking world in which we, Canada and the other British Dominions and the United States play so important a part. And finally there is United Europe. These three majestic circles are co-existent and if they are linked together there is no force or combination which could overthrow them or even challenge them.

Llandudno, October 9, 1948.

The New Century. The advantages of the nineteenth century, the literary age, have been largely put away by this terrible twentieth century with all its confusion and exhaustion of mankind.   *University of London, November 18, 1948.*

Century of the Common Man. Little did we guess that what has been called "The Century of the Common Man" would witness as its outstanding feature more common men killing each other with greater facilities than any other five centuries put together in the history of the world.
Boston, Mass., March 31, 1949.

Expansion in Numbers. The outstanding feature of the twentieth century has been the enormous expansion in the numbers who are given the opportunity to share in the larger and more varied life which in previous periods was reserved for the few and for the very few. This process must continue at an increasing rate. If we are to bring the broad masses of the people in every land to the table of abundance, it can only be by the tireless improvement of all our means of technical production, and by the diffusion in every form of education of an improved quality to scores of millions of men and women.
*Massachusetts Institute of Technology, Boston,
March 31, 1949.*

Socialism. A young nation, like Australia, dwelling in a continent growing ample food for itself and for export, may try experiments in Socialism without the risk of fatal injury, but the 50,000,000 gathered together in this small Island are in a very different position. . . .

The whole enterprise, contrivance and genius of the British nation is being increasingly paralysed by the war-time restrictions from which all other free nations have shaken themselves clear, but these are still imposed upon our people here in the name of a mistaken political philosophy and a largely obsolete mode of thought.   *B.B.C., London, January 21, 1950.*

Individual and State. The British nation now has to make one of the most momentous choices in its history. That choice is between two ways of life: between individual liberty and State domination: between concentration of ownership in the hands of the State and the extension of a property-owning democracy; between a policy of increasing restraint and a policy of liberating energy and ingenuity: between a policy of levelling down and a policy of finding opportunities for all to rise upwards from a basic standard.
Woodford, January 28, 1950.

Centralization. The Conservative Party of our day is the heir and apostle of those great traditions and principles of Tory democracy enunciated by Benjamin Disraeli and after him by my father, Lord Randolph Churchill. One of those principles, whose truth is borne out again and again upon the pages of history, is Disraeli's oft-cited maxim, "Centralization is the death-blow of public freedom." The truth of these words was never more apparent than it is to-day, nor more relevant to the thought and resolve of those who would have men not only live, but live freely.

Autarchy. If the French woke up to-morrow morning and found that all the rest of the world had sunk under the sea, and that they were alone, they could make a pretty good living for themselves from their fertile soil. But if Britain woke up to-morrow morning and found nothing but salt water on the rest of the globe, about one-third of our people would disappear. *Town Hall, Leeds, February 4, 1950*.

Rationing. In war-time rationing is the alternative to famine. In peace it may well become the alternative to abundance. *Devonport, February 9, 1950*.

Conquest of Nature. Man in this moment of his history has emerged in greater supremacy over the forces of nature than has ever been dreamed of before. He has it in his power to solve quite easily the problems of material existence. He has conquered the wild beasts, and he has even conquered the insects and the microbes. There lies before him, as he wishes, a golden age of peace and progress. All is in his hand. He has only to conquer his last and worst enemy—himself. With vision, faith and courage, it may be within our power to win a crowning victory for all. *Commons, March 28, 1950*.

Fifty Millions. Never forget that fifty millions have come into being in Great Britain under the impact and inspiration of former generations and now if our native genius is cribbed, cabined and confined, these fifty millions will be left physically stranded and gasping, like whales which swum upon the high tide into a bay from which the waters have receded. *Woodford, July 21, 1951*.

Frenzy. The human race is going through tormenting convulsions and there is a profound longing for some breathing space, for some pause in the frenzy. *London, October 8, 1951*.

The Last Prize. If I remain in public life at this juncture it is because, rightly or wrongly, but sincerely, I believe that I may be able to make an important contribution to the prevention of a third world war and to bringing nearer that lasting peace settlement which the masses of the people of every race and in every land fervently desire. I pray indeed that I may have this opportunity. It is the last prize I seek to win. I have been blessed with so much good fortune throughout my long life, and I am treated with so much kindness by my fellow countrymen far outside the ranks of Party, and indeed also in the United States and in Europe, that all the daydreams of my youth have been surpassed.

Plymouth October 23, 1951.

Nuclear Weapons. Moralists may find it a melancholy thought that peace can find no nobler foundations than mutual terror.   *Commons, March 5, 1952.*

Healthy Growth. The British oak on which for centuries our navy depended, grows slowly and noiselessly without headlines or sensation, and no one should ever cut one down without planting another. It is very much easier and quicker to cut down trees than to grow them. In cases where bad, oppressive laws warp the free development of human society, much cutting down may be needed, and sometimes the forest itself has to be cleared. Great work was done by the Liberal and Conservative Parties in the nineteenth century, but the twentieth century with its terrible events has brought us problems of a different order, not many of which can be solved merely by passing Acts of Parliament.

Woodford, September 6, 1952.

The Principal Foe. The British and Americans do not war with races or governments as such. Tyranny, external or internal, is our foe whatever trappings and disguises it wears, whatever language it speaks, or perverts.

Dorchester Hotel, London, July 4, 1953.

A Sure and Lasting Peace. If I stay on for the time being, bearing the burden of my age, it is not because of love for power or office. I have had an ample feast of both. If I stay, it is because I have the feeling that I may, through things that have happened, have an influence on what I care about above all else—the building of a sure and lasting peace.

Margate, October 10, 1953.

Price of Peace. Patience and perseverance must never be grudged when the peace of the world is at stake.

Commons, February 25, 1954.

The Armageddon of Atomic War

Atomic Power. This revelation of the secrets of nature, long mercifully withheld from man, should arouse the most solemn reflections in the mind and conscience of every human being capable of comprehension. We must indeed pray that these awful agencies will be made to conduce to peace among the nations, and that instead of wreaking measureless havoc upon the entire globe, may become a perennial fountain of world prosperity.

London, August 6, 1945.

First Atomic Explosion. On July 17th there came to us at Potsdam the eagerly-awaited news of the trial of the atomic bomb in the Mexican desert. Success beyond all dreams crowded this sombre, magnificent venture of our American allies. The detailed reports of the Mexican desert experiment, which were brought to us a few days later by air, could leave no doubt in the minds of the very few who were informed, that we were in the presence of a new factor in human affairs, and possessed of powers which were irresistible. . . .

The decision to use the atomic bomb was taken by President Truman and myself at Potsdam, and we approved the military plans to unchain the dread, pent-up forces. . . .

The bomb brought peace, but men alone can keep that peace, and henceforward they will keep it under penalties which threaten the survival, not only of civilization but of humanity itself. I may say that I am in entire agreement with the President that the secrets of the atomic bomb should so far as possible not be imparted at the present time to any other country in the world. This is in no design or wish for arbitrary power, but for the common safety of the world. Nothing can stop the progress of research and experiment in every country, but although research will no doubt proceed in many places, the construction of the immense plants necessary to transform theory into action cannot be improvised in any country.

Commons, August 16, 1945.

Atomic Weapons. The dark ages may return—the Stone Age may return on the gleaming wings of science; and what might now shower immeasurable material blessings upon mankind may even bring about its total destruction. Beware I say! Time may be short. . . .

It would nevertheless be wrong and imprudent to entrust the secret knowledge or experience of the atomic bomb, which the United States, Great Britain and Canada now share, to the world organization, while it is still in its infancy. It would be criminal madness to cast it adrift in this still agitated and non-united world. No one in any country has slept less well in their beds because this knowledge and the method and the raw materials to apply it are at present largely retained in American hands. I do not believe we should all have slept so soundly had the position been reversed and if some Communist or Neo-Fascist State monopolized for the time being these dread agencies. The fear of them alone might easily have been used to enforce totalitarian systems upon the free democratic world, with consequences appalling to human imagination.   *Fulton, Missouri, March 5, 1946.*

Atomic Bomb as Shield. In these present days we dwell strangely and precariously under the shield and protection of the atomic bomb. The atomic bomb is still only in the hands of a State and nation which we know will never use it except in the cause of right and freedom. But it may well be that in a few years this awful agency of destruction will be widespread and the catastrophe following from its use by several warring nations will not only bring to an end all that we call civilization, but may possibly disintegrate the globe itself.   *Zürich University, September 19, 1946.*

March of Science. It is arguable whether the human race have been gainers by the march of science beyond the steam engine. Electricity opens a field of infinite conveniences to ever greater numbers, but they may well have to pay dearly for them. But anyhow in my thought I stop short of the internal combustion engine which has made the world so much smaller. Still more must we fear the consequences of entrusting to a human race so little different from their predecessors of the so-called barbarous ages such awful agencies as the atomic bomb. Give me the horse.
Royal College of Physicians, July 10, 1951.

Modern War. The penalties have grown to an extent undreamed of; and at the same time, many of the old incentives which were the cause of the beginning of so many wars, or features in their beginning, have lost their significance. The desire for glory, booty, territory, dynastic or national aggrandizement; hopes of a speedy and splendid victory with all its excitement—and they are all temptations from which even those who only fight for righteous causes are not always exempt—are now superseded by a preliminary stage of measureless agony from which neither side could at present protect itself.   *Commons, March 5, 1952.*

Hydrogen Bomb. The hydrogen bomb carries us into dimensions which have never confronted practical human thought and have been confined to the realms of fancy and imagination. *Commons, April 4, 1954.*

Division of the World. We live in a period, happily unique in human history, when the whole world is divided intellectually and to a large extent geographically between the creeds of Communist discipline and individual freedom, and when at the same time, this mental and psychological division is accompanied by the possession by both sides of the obliterating weapons of the nuclear age. . . .

Swift Retaliation. Major war of the future will differ, therefore, from anything we have known in the past in this one significant respect, that each side, at the outset, will suffer what it dreads the most, the loss of everything that it has ever known of. The deterrents will grow continually in value. In the past, an aggressor has been tempted by the hope of snatching an early advantage. In future, he may be deterred by the knowledge that the other side has the certain power to inflict swift, inescapable and crushing retaliation. . . .

Child of Terror. It may well be that we shall by a process of sublime irony have reached a stage in this story where safety will be the sturdy child of terror, and survival the twin brother of annihilation. *Commons, March 1, 1955.*

CHRONOLOGY

of the more important events in the life of Sir Winston Churchill

1874: Winston Leonard Spencer Churchill, son of Lord and Lady Randolph Churchill, is born prematurely at Blenheim Palace (November 30th).

1888: Enters Harrow in the bottom form (April).

1892: Leaves Harrow (December) and is seriously injured in an accident.

1893: Enters the Royal Military College, Sandhurst, as a cavalry cadet (June 28th).

1894: Prepared, but not required, to make a speech on behalf of the Entertainment Protection League.
Passes out of Sandhurst (December).

1895: His father dies (January 24th).
Gazetted to the 4th Hussars (April 1st).
Visits Cuba to study the fighting there (November).
He writes his first article, a descriptive letter to the *Daily Graphic* (published December 6th).

1896: Leaves for India with the 4th Hussars, takes up polo and discovers Gibbon and Macaulay.

1897: During leave, accompanies the Malakand Field Force against the Pathans as a war correspondent.

1898: Takes part in the Battle of Omdurman, at his own expense (September 2nd).
Sails to India to rejoin his regiment (December 1st).
Published: *The Malakand Field Force.*

1899: Leaves the Army.
Fights his first by-election, unsuccessfully, at Oldham (July).
Sent to South Africa as a war correspondent by the *Morning Post* (October).
Captured by the Boers (November 15th) but escapes (December 13th). A reward of £25 is offered for his recapture.
Published: *The River War.*

1900: Accepts a commission in the South African Light Horse.

One of the first to enter captured Pretoria (June 5th).
Returns to England (July).
Elected Conservative Member of Parliament for Oldham in a General Election (October 1st).
Gives the first lecture of an American tour in New York, with Mark Twain in the chair (December 16th).
Published: *Savrola, London to Ladysmith via Pretoria, Ian Hamilton's March*.

1901: Takes his seat in Parliament (January).
Makes his maiden speech (February).
Attacks the Estimates (May 13th).

1903: Attacks Joseph Chamberlain's policy of Protection (May 28th).
Published: *Mr. Brodrick's Army*.

1904: A large number of Unionists leaves the chamber of the House when he rises to speak (March 21st).
Forced to abandon his speech on the Trades Disputes Bill when his memory fails (April 22nd).
Crosses the floor of the House to sit with the Liberal Party (May 31st).

1906: Is elected Liberal Member of Parliament for North-West Manchester in General Election.
Joins the Government as Under-Secretary for the Colonies.
Published: *Lord Randolph Churchill*.

1907: Made a Privy Councillor.

1908: Appointed President of the Board of Trade with a seat in the Cabinet and therefore has to seek re-election. He is defeated at Manchester (April 24th) but elected to represent Dundee (May 23rd).
Marries Miss Clementine Hozier at St. Margaret's Church, Westminster (September 12th).
Published: *My African Journey*.

1909: Instrumental in the setting up of Labour Exchanges.
His daughter Diana is born.

1910: Becomes Home Secretary and introduces the Mines Accidents Act.
Attends manoeuvres of the German Army near Wurzburg.

1911: Present at the "siege of Sidney Street" (January 3rd).
Calls out the military on the occasion of a railway strike (August).
Becomes a member of the Committee of Imperial De-

fence and circulates to the Cabinet (August 13th) a memorandum on "Military Aspects of the Continental Problem."

Becomes First Lord of the Admiralty (October 25th) and appoints a new Admiralty Board (November 28th).

His son Randolph is born (May 28th).

1912: Raises the rate of battleship construction from two to four a year, although urging Germany to agree to a "shipbuilding holiday."

1913: Becomes an Elder Brother of Trinity House.

1914: Secures Parliamentary approval of a plan for buying control of a Persian oilfield to secure supplies for naval ships newly converted to oil burning (June 17th).

Orders a mobilization exercise for the fleet, which does not disperse when the exercise ends (July).

Orders full naval mobilization (August 2nd).

Organizes the defence of Antwerp during the Battle of Ypres (October 2nd).

His daughter Sarah is born (October).

Elected Lord Rector of Aberdeen University.

1915: Proposes a joint naval and military attack on the Dardanelles at a meeting of the War Council (January 3rd).

Removed from the Admiralty in the new Coalition Government and appointed Chancellor of the Duchy of Lancaster (May 28th).

Experiments with his children's paintboxes and takes up oil painting as a hobby.

Resigns from the Cabinet, returns to the Army and leaves for France (November 19th) with the 6th Royal Scots Fusiliers.

1916: Returns to political life in London (May).

1917: Becomes Minister of Munitions in Lloyd George's Government (July 16th).

1918: Visits France to survey the position for Lloyd George (March).

Becomes Secretary of State for War and Minister for Air (December).

1921: Succeeds Lord Milner as Colonial Secretary and attends a Middle Eastern Conference at Cairo (March).

Assists Lloyd George in negotiations with Sinn Fein leaders.

Appeals to the Dominions for support against the threatened Turkish invasion of Thrace.

His mother dies.

1922: Resigns the post of Colonial Secretary after his defeat at Dundee in the General Election: during his campaign his appendix is removed.
Becomes a Companion of Honour.

1923: Stands at an election for West Leicester as a Liberal Free Trader and is defeated.
Published: *World Crisis* (Six volumes, 1923-31).

1924: Breaks with the Liberal Party (February) and stands as a Constitutionalist for the Abbey Division of Westminster in a by-election, but is defeated (March 20th).
Wins a libel case against Lord Alfred Douglas.
In a General Election is elected Member of Parliament for Epping as a Constitutionalist and Anti-Socialist, with Conservative support.
Becomes Chancellor of the Exchequer in Stanley Baldwin's Government (November).

1925: Introduces his first Budget and announces the decision to return to the Gold Standard (April 28th).
Receives the honorary degree of D.C.L. from Oxford University.

1926: Organizes and edits *The British Gazette* during the General Strike (May).

1928: Takes up brick-laying as a hobby and joins the Amalgamated Union of Building Workers.

1929: Loses office when Baldwin resigns after his Party's defeat in the General Election (May).
Elected Lord Rector of Edinburgh University.

1930: Resigns from the Conservative "Shadow Cabinet" after a disagreement with Baldwin on policy in India (January).
Becomes Chancellor of Bristol University (January).
Resigns from the chairmanship of the Conservative Finance Committee (April).
At Oxford, delivers the Romanes lecture, on Party Government and the Economic Problem.
Published: *My Early Life*.

1931: Is a member of the Conservative majority supporting the Government, but without office (August).
Published: *India*.

1932: Published: *Thoughts and Adventures*.

1933: Published: *Marlborough*, Volume I.

1934: Published: *Marlborough*, Volume II.

1936: Attempts, unsuccessfully, to prevent the abdication of King Edward VIII.
Published: *Marlborough*, Volume III.

1937: Exclusion from office is continued when Neville Chamberlain succeeds Baldwin.
Published: *Great Contemporaries*.

1938: Protests against Chamberlain's policy of "buying a few years of peace" (April).
Attacks the Munich agreement as "a total and unmitigated defeat" (September).
Published: *Marlborough*, Volume IV.

1939: Joins Chamberlain's Cabinet as First Lord of the Admiralty (September) and sets the convoy system in operation.
Urges the creation of an all-party Government.
Published: *Step by Step*.

1940: Gives direct orders for the boarding of the *Altmark* and rescue of British prisoners (February 16th).
Appointed head of the Committee of Service Ministers (April).
Makes a statement on naval operations after the first battle of Narvik (April 11).
Succeeds Chamberlain as Prime Minister, forming a Coalition Government to include the Labour and Liberal Parties (May 10th).
In his first speech as Prime Minister he offers the House of Commons nothing but "blood, toil, tears and sweat" (May 13th).
In his first broadcast as Prime Minister he warns the nation of the coming "battle for our Island" (May 19th).
Reports to the House of Commons the news of Dunkirk and determination not to surrender (June 4th).
Invites France to join Great Britain in a Federal Union (June 16th).
Makes a statement on the possibilities of invasion (June 18th).
Makes a statement on Oran where a British fleet has caused great damage to French ships which refused either to join the British or to allow themselves to be interned (July 4th).
In the House of Commons he pays tribute to the gallantry of fighter pilots (August 20th).
Makes a statement on German invasion preparations to the House of Commons (September 17th).

Elected leader of the Conservative Party (October 9th).
Attends the christening of his grandson, Winston (December 1st).

1941: Becomes Lord Warden of the Cinque Ports.
Answers critics of the Crete campaign in the House of Commons (June 10th).
When Russia is invaded, he broadcasts an assurance of help (June 22nd).
At sea, he signs the Atlantic Charter with President Roosevelt (August 9th).
Visits Iceland (August 17th).
Concludes the Anglo-American Agreement (September).
Introduces a new National Service Bill, which includes provisions for the conscription of women (December 2nd).
Addresses a joint meeting of both Houses of Congress in Washington (December 26th).
Addresses the Canadian Legislature at Ottawa (December 30th).

1942: Broadcasts on the occasion of the fall of Singapore (February 15th).
Announces the mission of Sir Stafford Cripps to India offering Dominion status (March 11).
Flies to the United States to discuss the proposed invasion of North Africa with President Roosevelt (June 18th).
After visiting Cairo, El Alamein and Teheran, arrives in Moscow (August 12th).

1943: Attends the Allied Conference at Casablanca, agreeing that peace must come only by the unconditional surrender of the Axis Powers (January 14th).
Holds discussions with the President of Turkey at Adana (January 30th).
Elected an Honorary Academician Extraordinary of the Royal Academy.
Addresses U.S. Congress (May 19th).
Visits North Africa to consult with Generals de Gaulle and Giraud (May 30th).
In a speech at the Guildhall, he gives a pledge to crush Japan after Germany (June 30th).
Arrives in Canada for further conferences with President Roosevelt (August 10th).
In a speech at Harvard, he advocates the world teaching of Basic English (September).

Attends a conference of the Allied leaders in Cairo, followed by another in Teheran where he and President Roosevelt are joined by Marshal Stalin. Returns to Cairo for discussions with the President of Turkey (November).

Falls ill with pneumonia but is saved by a new drug, M and B 693. He goes to Marrakesh for his convalescence (December).

1944: Arrives back in London (January).

Opens the conference of Commonwealth Prime Ministers in London (May 1st).

Six days after D-Day he tours the battle-front in France (June 12th).

Arrives in Italy to meet the Pope and Yugoslav representatives (August 11th).

Confers with President Roosevelt in Quebec (September 10th).

Confers with Marshal Stalin in Moscow (October 9th).

At the time of the invitation to France to become a member of the European Advisory Commission, he visits Paris (November 10th).

Arrives for a conference with Greek political representatives in Athens (December 25th).

1945: Meets President Roosevelt at Malta (February 2nd). He and President Roosevelt join Marshal Stalin at Yalta (February 4th).

Confers with rulers of Middle Eastern states in Cairo (February 16th).

Broadcasts the news of the unconditional surrender of all German fighting forces (May 8th).

Resigns the Premiership and is invited to form a new administration (May 23rd).

Attends a Three-Power Conference at Potsdam (July 17th).

Resigns the Premiership when the Conservative Party is defeated in a General Election (July 26th).

1946: Awarded the Order of Merit (January 8th).

Delivers a speech in Fulton, Missouri, coining the phrase "the iron curtain" and advocating "fraternal association of the English-speaking peoples" (March 5th).

Published: *Victory*.

1947: Advocates the European Movement in a speech at the Royal Albert Hall, London (May 14th).

Exhibits at the Royal Academy.

1948: Addresses the Congress of Europe at The Hague (May).
Published: *Painting as a Pastime, The Gathering Storm.*

1949: Awarded the Grotius Medal (February 3rd).
Addresses Massachusetts Institute of Technology (March 31st).
Addresses, discouragingly, the first meeting of the Council of Europe at Strasbourg (August 9th).
Published: *Their Finest Hour.*

1950: At a meeting of the Council of Europe he advocates a European Army (August).
Visits Denmark and receives a prize from the Sonning Foundation (October 9th).
Published: *The Grand Alliance.*

1951: Following a Conservative victory in a General Election, he becomes Prime Minister again (October 26th).
Published: *The Hinge of Fate.*

1952: The *Daily Mirror* publishes a full apology for the story headlined "Whose finger on the trigger?" (May 24th).
Published: *Closing the Ring.*

1953: Made a Knight of the Garter (April 24th).
Awarded the Nobel Prize for Literature (October 15th).
Attends a conference at Bermuda with the President of the United States and the Prime Minister of France (December).

1954: Visits Washington for discussions with President Eisenhower (June).
Supports the Nine-Power Conference in London (September).
In a speech at his constituency of Woodford, he starts a controversy with the mention of a telegram sent to Field-Marshal Montgomery on the subject of German arms (November 23rd).
To celebrate his 80th birthday, he is presented by both Houses of Parliament with his portrait painted by Graham Sutherland (November 30th).
Published: *Triumph and Tragedy.*

1955: Resigns the Premiership and Leadership of the Conservative Party (April 5th).
Accepts the Freedom Award (October 9th) and the Williamsburg Award (October 16th).

1956: Receives the Benjamin Franklin Medal (January 11th).
Published: *History of the English-Speaking Peoples,* Vol. I.

Index